THE PROVERBS OF MIDDLE-EARTH

DAVID ROWE

FOREWORD BY PETER KREEFT

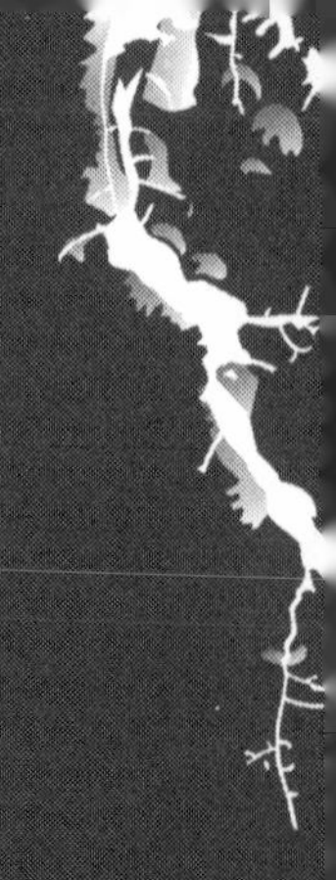

Second Edition
ISBN-10: 0999591401
ISBN-13: 978-0-9995914-0-6

Printed in U.S.A.

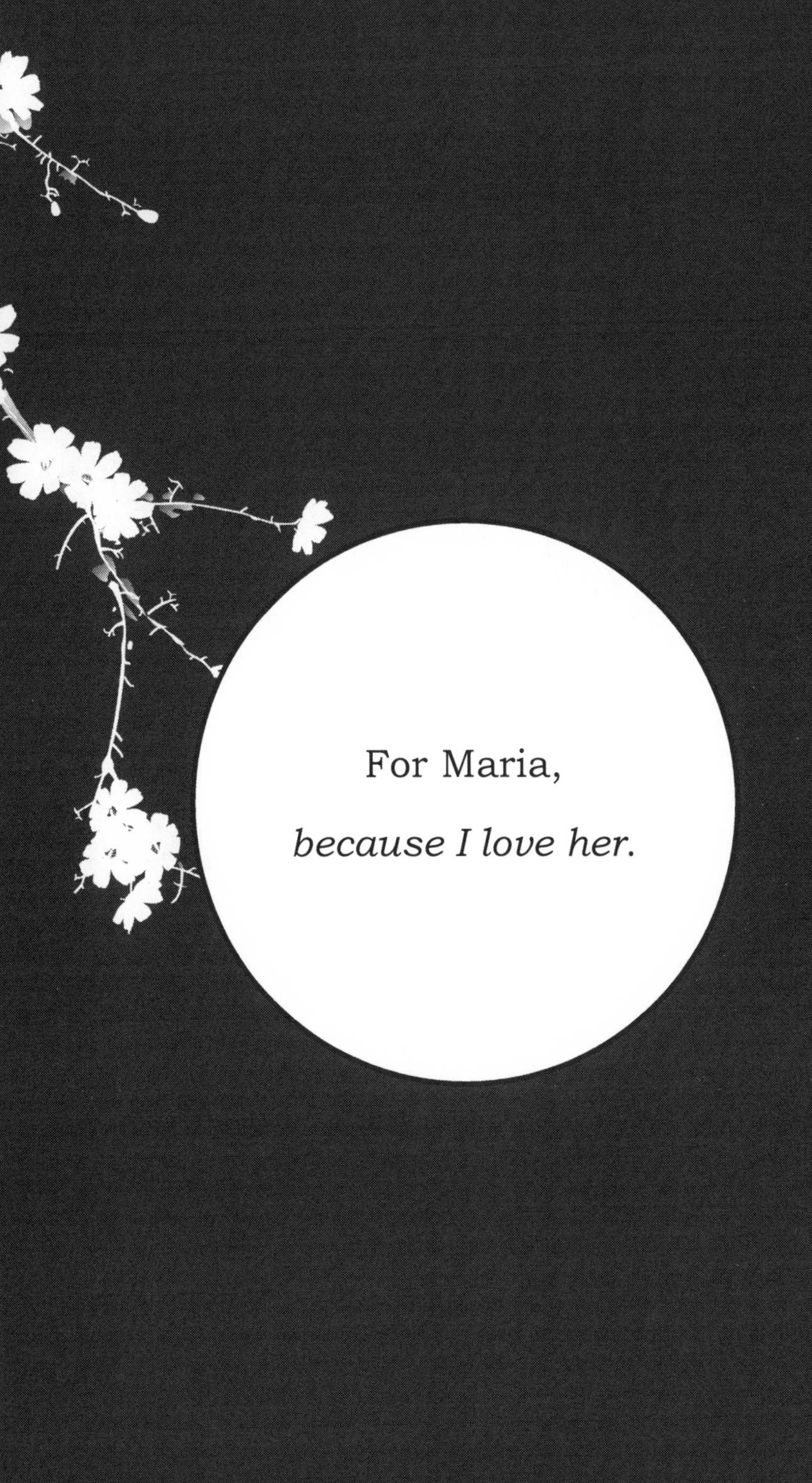

For Maria,

because I love her.

Contents

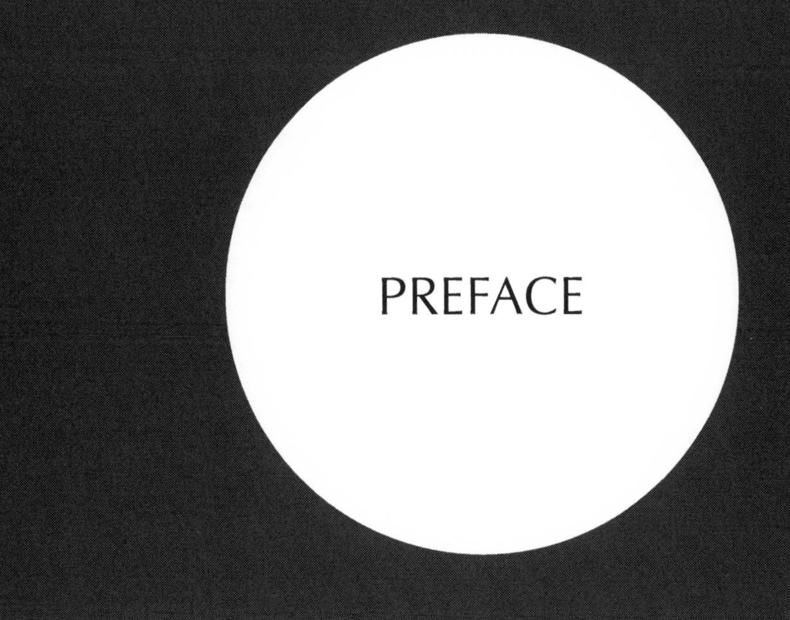

PREFACE

I propose to talk about proverbs, though I am aware that this is a rash adventure. After all, these sayings, this wisdom, these oral traditions belong to a world that is little more than lies breathed through silver. It's a story, a fiction, a sham. IT'S NOT REAL. And yet these imaginary people and their words contain more truth than most of us ever stumble across in our humdrum, run of the mill, non-fictional lives.

Why do I think it worth delving into the invented proverbial heritage of a fictional world? I have many motives, but chief among them is a reason of which, I believe, JRR Tolkien would heartily approve: I enjoy it. I love Middle-earth deeply and dearly, with a passion undimmed by the passing of time—in fact strengthened by it.

Having first stepped into the Road aged about six,[1] I failed to keep my feet. I was swept away. *It is a dangerous business, stepping out of your door,* and I had no idea where I would be swept off to. Peter Kreeft says that 'No one reads *The Lord of the Rings* once,'[2] and that is certainly true for me. I have dipped in and out constantly, passage by passage, for over a quarter of a century; one foot in Tolkien's world and the other in my own. I love it. And that is why this book exists.

---

1 Initially via Nicol Williamson's exquisite reading of *The Hobbit* for Argo Records, and Brian Sibley's majestic audio dramatisation of *The Lord Of The Rings* for the BBC.

2 Peter Kreeft, *The Philosophy of Tolkien* (Ignatius Press, 2005), p. 9.

It is also, almost certainly, why you are reading it. If not—if this volume has been foisted on you by some well-meaning person—then shortly you will probably feel as if you have been dragged to church by a wide-eyed believer and expected to join in. Forgive them: they know not what they do. Though perhaps this is your chance to be swept away too.

And for those, like me, who know that the longer you get to spend in Middle-earth, the better, I hope that this book and its insights scratch a hitherto-unseen itch, and that your future experience of Middle-earth is enriched as a result.

David Rowe

Charleston, South Carolina
September 2016

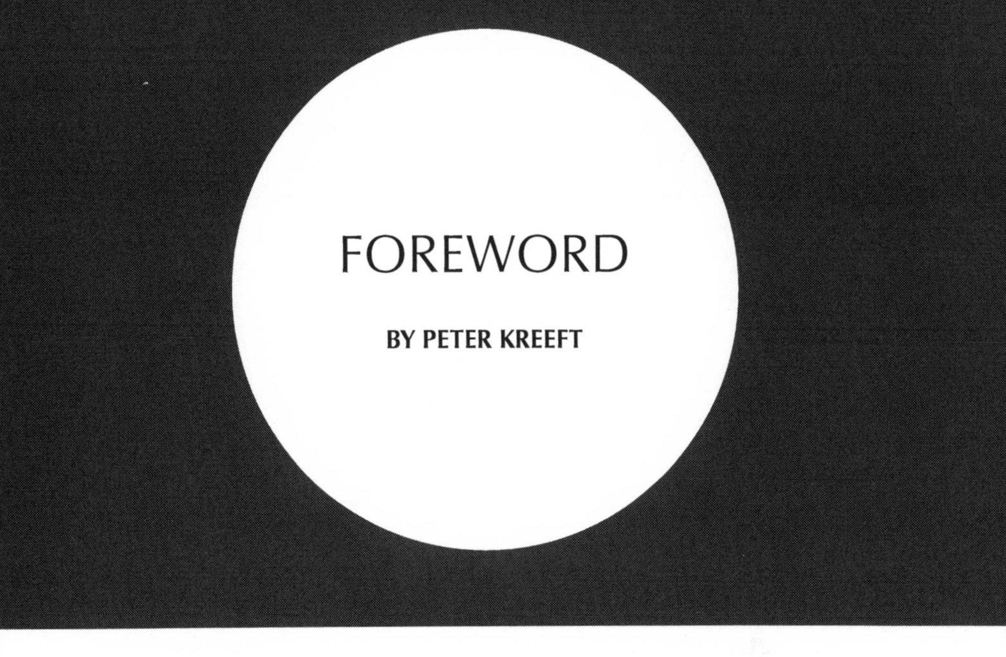

FOREWORD

BY PETER KREEFT

A foreword to a book has two purposes: to tell the prospective reader what the book is about, and to persuade him or her to read it.

But let me tell you a secret. Most authors who write forewords to other writers' books don't usually read the whole book, only enough of it to know what it's about and why it's good enough for them to put their name to.

I've now been asked to write a foreword or introduction to about 50 books, but have done it for only 5 or 6, because I will do it only out of love, not duty—duty is a desperate fallback when love fails. (This is why the Judaeo-Christian ethic of love is better and stronger than the Kantian ethic of duty, by the way.) If I don't love the book enough to read the whole thing through for myself, for pleasure, then I won't try to persuade other people to read it either.

The Proverbs of Middle-earth is worth reading, for fun as well as for (mental) profit. Those two are the twin purposes of books: literary critics used to say that a book should 'please and instruct,' while an old Arabic proverb says the same thing: 'Before you shoot the arrow of truth, dip it in honey.' This book is both a quiver-full of well-pointed arrows, and a large jar of honey. It is a romp, as well as a thorough and deeply penetrating exploration of its subject.

Its subject is not only the *proverbs* of the numerous species and civilizations in Tolkien's Middle-earth (as its title advertises), but also of the cultures these proverbs express. The short and simple proverbs are the humble little gates into the big, wide, and complex cities of these various cultures.

So this book is really an act of anthropology. And while we may think of Tolkien's inventions as fantastical, this is not fantasy but realism. The cultures Tolkien invented are real—even the non-human species are real. In reading about elves and ents, Gondor and Gimli, we are reading about ourselves.

An author of fiction can't create characters interesting enough for the reader to care about and identify with if the author does not find models for all his characters in his own experience, and ultimately in his own self. For the reader to identify with these characters, the author must do so first, and for the author to identify with his characters, he must first identify *himself* with them.

This is true even of villains. Unless you can honestly say, 'There, but for the grace of God, go I,' you can't persuade readers to do it either. Unless the author can see what Max Picard, in his shattering title, called the "Hitler in Ourselves," any story about Hitler that you write, whether factual or fictional, will be only a trip to the zoo to laugh at, or pity, or dissect the animal in the cage. But not to understand it—ie. to stand under it and let it fall on you with its own force and identity intact. Tolkien did this, and in taking care to make his fantasy real, he made it possible for us to see ourselves in his characters and cultures.

So read this book (1) for pleasure. But the pleasure comes from (2) opening up to these proverbs, to their riches and their wisdom. But this is only the door to (3) exploring eleven cultures and worldviews, recognizing what they love and value, which in turn is a way to (4) explore the many rooms in the cellar of Tolkien's incredible creative mind, and by doing that (5) to find all of these rooms, all of these characters, in yourself and in the real people with whom we share our world.

That is the highest function of fantasy: truth, insight, understanding. Those who dislike Tolkien always dislike the genre itself, scorning its 'escapism.' They forget that Fantasy does not only help us escape from circumstances, but also from falsehoods, self-deceptions, and narrowness of vision; from the familiarity that breeds not only contempt but also boredom with ourselves and each other. It helps us to escape into wisdom.

I'm a philosopher, and I admire Socrates more than any other thinker. This book is Socratic. It is an indirect exercise in 'Know thyself!' through getting to know the characters and cultures in Middle-earth (which, after all, is only another name for our Earth, the third rock from the Sun). Through unpacking the wisdom in the proverbs of those different species, we see that they all speak to something deep within our species.

I'm as pleased as a pickle that I was sent this wonderfully Socratic book. If you want pleasure and profit, arrows of truth dipped in honey, read on and 'Know thyself!'

Dr. Peter Kreeft

Boston College, MA
Author of The Philosophy of Tolkien (Ignatius Press, 2005)

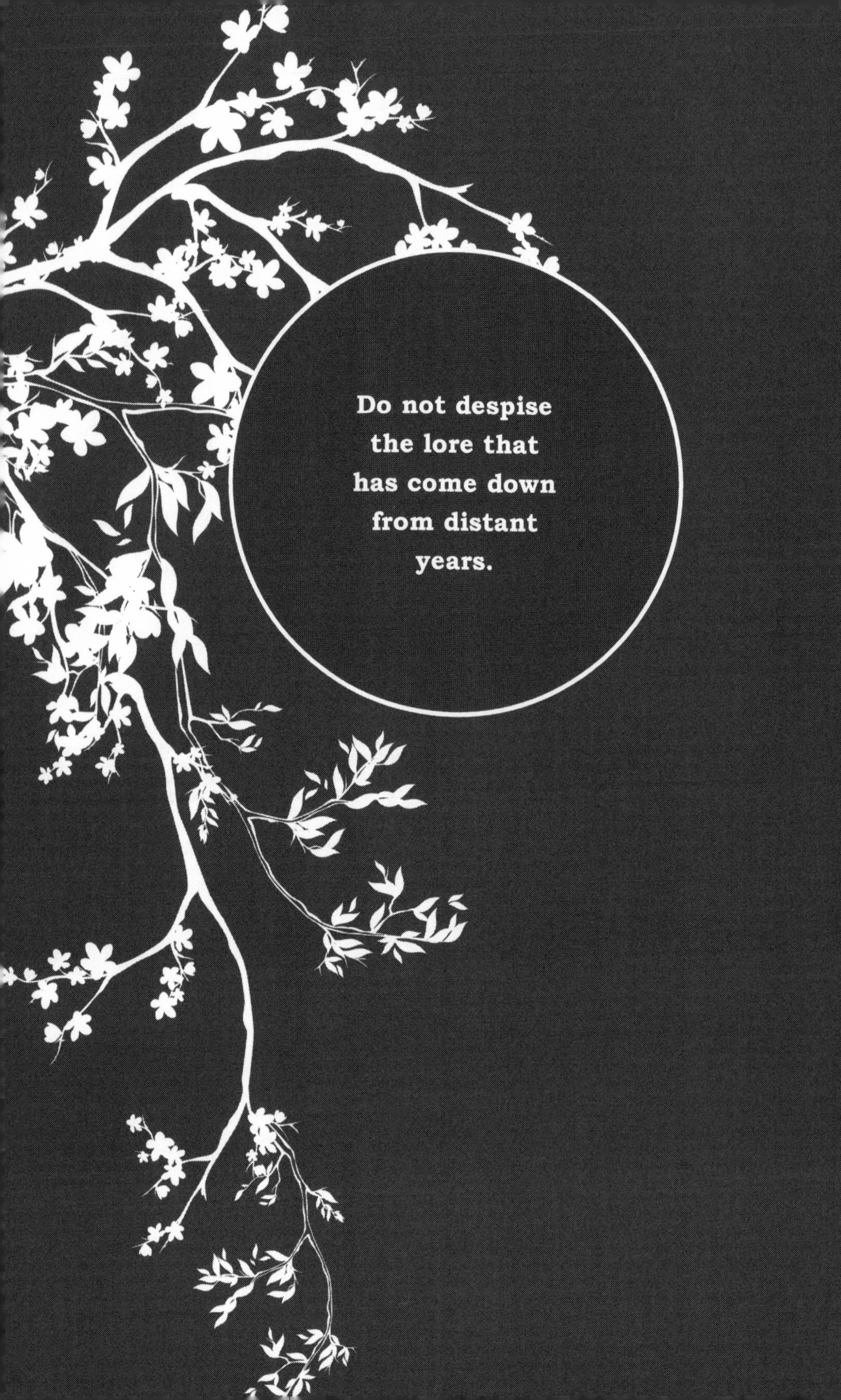
Do not despise
the lore that
has come down
from distant
years.

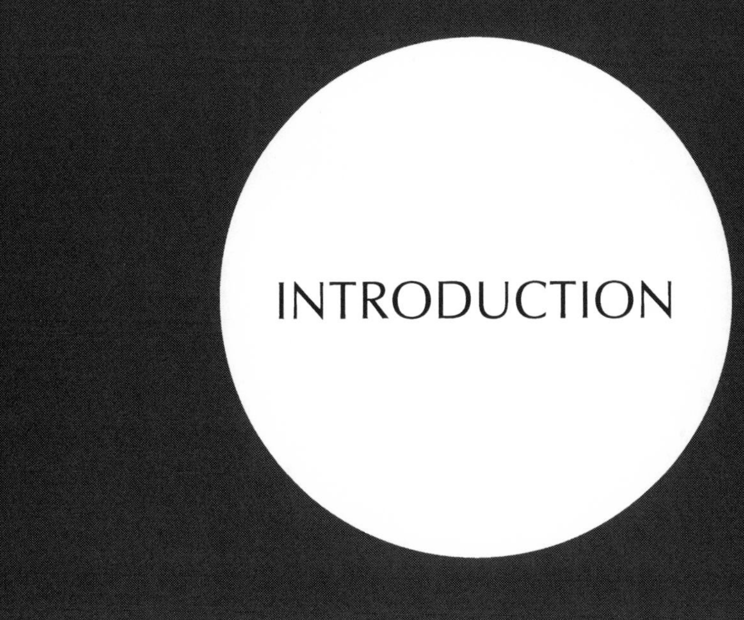

INTRODUCTION

Concerning Arda

'It had begun with a leaf caught in the wind...'[3]

In *Leaf by Niggle*, JRR Tolkien wrote of a painter whose great unfinishable artwork, a magnificent tree with innumerable branches and fantastical roots, dominated his thoughts and his life. Niggle wasn't a perfect painter; he was of the sort who can paint leaves better than trees, and as a result his Great Tree was never quite as magnificent as the one in his imagination, though the details were good. Niggle would 'spend a long time on a single leaf,' obsessing over the finer points, but gradually glimpsing, through the gaps in the leaves and boughs, a wider country opening out behind the tree, a country of marching forests and mountains tipped with snow. The whole thing, Niggle reflected, was 'wholly unsatisfactory, and yet very lovely, the only really beautiful picture in the world.'[4]

Arda, the world of which Middle-earth is but a part and *The Lord Of The Rings* only a chapter, is Tolkien's Tree, discovered almost by accident as he was busy painting leaves. The whole marvellous artwork remains as unfinished as Niggle's picture,[5] but its details—the leaves—are exqui-

3 JRR Tolkien, *Tales From The Perilous Realm* (Harper Collins, 2002), p. 122.

4 Tolkien, *Tales From The Perilous Realm*, p. 123.

5 Tolkien never completed his legendarium, and was still revising aspects of *The Silmarillion* when he died. Humphrey Carpenter records that 'Tolkien... though he wrote fast, took endless pains over revision and regarded it as a continuing process that

site, reflecting the near-obsessive priorities of their creator. In investigating one small aspect of the whole, this book is an exercise in leaf-love, in delighting in the details over which Tolkien niggled.

'Man, Sub-creator, the Refracted Light'[6]

Tolkien's original hope, to provide a mythology for his beloved but generally legend-free England, was far more than a quest for exciting stories. He believed that the creative process of myth-making is nothing short of a sacred task; that humans have a special responsibility to reflect their Creator by becoming sub-creators. As a result, Tolkien sought to bring into being an internally cohesive sub-creation, credible in every way; having the air of being well-worn and lived in, not fresh from the oven.

When sub-creation is successful, the inner consistency of wholly fictional environments is so convincing, so real, that the imagination is enchanted and the reader under the storyteller's spell.[7] But this ambition (in Tolkien's estimation, at least) could only be fully realised by the handcrafting of an entire world—from the minutiae of geology and regional flora to the dealings of characters and cultures over the course of millennia. Each intricately detailed leaf on Tolkien's Tree demonstrates this tireless pursuit of depth and a convincing 'inner reality.'

The Council of Elrond, for example, begins with an extended history lesson before showcasing a range of cross-cultural disagreements, all packed with authentic-feeling historical and anthropological detail (and not a few proverbs). Likewise, when Pippin corrects King Théoden's *Holbytlan* to *Hobbits* the narrative is not advanced, but the exchange has an underlying etymological integrity that serves to provide (what Tom Shippey calls) the 'illusion of historical truth.'[8]

There are no short cuts to an authentic-feeling secondary world. It took Tolkien a lifetime of niggling, an approach that allowed the proliferation of so many thoroughly thought-through ingredients that Middle-earth feels earthy, authentic, and true. The result is a sub-creation in which

---

was not necessarily complete when the book was published.' (Humphrey Carpenter, *The Inklings* (Harper Collins, 1997), pp. 47-8).

6 From Tolkien's poem *Mythopoeia* (as quoted in Carpenter, *The Inklings*, p. 63).

7 Tolkien was well-aware that the Old English word *spell*—most notably preserved in Modern English as *gospel*—means 'story,' etymologically linking the craft of tale-telling with its enchanting effect.

8 Tom Shippey, *The Road to Middle-earth* (Houghton Mifflin, 2003), p. 76.

every single facet, no matter how minor, is *intentional*, which in turn means that deeper study is always rewarded. As Shippey says, it is 'a world where you can ask a question... and you'll get an answer; and if you ask a question about the question, or a question about the answer, then you'll get more answers.'[9]

The proverbs of Middle-earth are some of the loveliest leaves on Tolkien's Tree: beautiful and intricate, if rarely necessary as far as the plot is concerned. They also constitute one of the most widely-occurring streams of credibility-building detail in Tolkien's work, meaning that studying them is one of the best ways in which questions-about-questions can be answered, and Tolkien's convincing, satisfying world enjoyed.

Concerning Proverbs

'Too many cooks spoil the broth'

Virtually anywhere in the English-speaking world, the first three words of the above sentence are enough. Say 'Too many cooks' and not only will hearers be able to complete the saying, but they will also be familiar with both its message and its traditional counterpoint: Many hands make light work. It is hard to believe that at some point in history these sayings were invented—that on one particular day, those particular words were first put in that particular order—especially since we have as little idea of the source[10] as we do of the person from whom we as individuals first learned it. But we have learned it. 'Too many cooks...' has passed into our personal consciousness, because it first passed into the collective consciousness by becoming a proverb.

Proverbs are vessels of transmission, the ships in which wisdom sails. They come into being because of the tremendous value of hard-won wisdom, and the consequent need to pass it on. In the words of Sophocles, wisdom 'outweighs any wealth,' and in order to share that wealth—to avoid the need for every individual in every generation to relearn the same lessons from scratch—a method or means to preserve and com-

9 Interviewed in 'JRR Tolkien: 1892-1873—A Study of the Maker of Middle-earth,' https://www.youtube.com/watch?v=HkmNHP58OhU retrieved on May 24, 2014.

10 The first known citing in print is from 1662, in Sir Balthazar Gerbier's *Three Chief Principles Of Magnificent Building,* where it already presumed to be ancient and generally known.

municate is required. Today, we simply write things down, but such an option is not always available.

In our digital world, six centuries on from Gutenburg's printing press, transmission of data is so flawlessly slick and quick that we rarely give it a thought. But long before societies had even developed the scripts and methods by which to write and make records, the communication of learning and law from one generation to the next was central to society. In those contexts, all information was communicated by word-of-mouth rather than word-on-page, making oral tradition the great educator.

All such oral societies, ancient and contemporary, have a corporate repository of folk wisdom; a body of inherited material passed from person to person and therefore from generation to generation. Proverbs and poems, songs and stories, riddles and rhymes of lore—these are the constituent parts of oral tradition, weapons in the perennial war against ignorance and foolishness. They teach, they scold, they warn, and they encourage. And they all appear in Middle-earth. And while proverbs are not the sole element of oral tradition, they are the portion that deals specifically with wisdom. Ethical principals, rules of conduct, and a range of sage perspectives on the nature of reality are all communicated by means of traditional sayings.

While some proverbs come into the collective consciousness via the work of an individual—John Donne's *No man is an island*, for example, or Teddy Roosevelt's *Speak softly, and carry a big stick*—the most common source of sayings is simply 'tradition,' that is to say, a combination of anonymous and multiple authors. Reference to oral tradition is therefore akin to quoting a favourite poet or orator, except that it is not an individual whose wisdom is being cited, but an entire culture. 'As my old Gaffer used to say…' is not Sam Gamgee crediting his father as the inventor of an insight, but recognising the person from whom one aspect of Hobbit-sense was most often, or most memorably, received.

Since a society, or a Gaffer, will only honour those insights which have stood both the test of time and the present need, each transmitter of a proverb acts as a sieve, weeding out and throwing away the unnecessary or obsolete, and allowing the tried and true to be passed on. This refining process also serves to make proverbs more ear-catching and easily-remembered, by employing the devices commonly associated with poetry: meter and metaphor, assonance and alliteration.

What Makes a Proverb a Proverb?

In order to find the proverbs of Middle-earth, we need to know how to identify them. What is a proverb? It's an awkward question. In spite of having a stream of academic study—paremiology—entirely devoted to them, it seems that proverbs are easier to discern than to define. Professor Wolfgang Mieder of the University of Vermont, long considered the world's pre-eminent paremiologist, says that 'A proverb is a concise statement of an apparent truth that has had, has, or will have currency among the people.'[11] Problematically, this definition implies that virtually any phrase can be a proverb, if it gains 'currency among the people' as a conscious reference to received wisdom. No parameters of style or content are defined.

This boundary-free definition is frustrating, but it is accurate. While proverbs are often thought of as poetic expressions—and many do make use of imagery, alliteration, or rhyme—some of the most common (*Absence makes the heart grow fonder*, for example, or *There's no such thing as a free lunch*) have no poetic features at all; some simply assert a bare fact and no more. And yet, somehow, we still recognise a proverb when we hear one.

If, in conversation, proverbs are relatively easy to discern, they are less so in print. Most of the phrases that have been identified as proverbs in this volume could be nothing else, or at least have the balance of probability comfortably on their side, but others are arguable. Since any phrase might potentially gain 'currency among the people' and be used as a proverb, how can the proverbs of *The Lord Of The Rings* or *The Hobbit* be detected?

Tom Shippey, discussing the same question, makes it clear that when on this search 'you cannot always tell what is a proverb and what is not.'[12] Yet sometimes it is straightforward. For a start, some are explicitly described as such. *Never laugh at live dragons,* says Bilbo to himself, 'and it became a favourite saying of his, and passed into a proverb.'[13] Others are recognisable for the simple fact that they are not Tolkien's inventions at all: Gollum's *More haste, less speed*; Merry's *Mind your Ps*

---

11 Wolfgang Mieder, quoting Stuart Gallacher (www.forbes.com/2009/08/12/wolfgang-mieder-proverbs-opinions-mieder.html accessed on May 31, 2014).

12 Tom Shippey, *Roots and Branches* (Walking Tree, 2007), p. 307.

13 JRR Tolkien, *The Hobbit* (Harper Collins, 2006), p. 263.

and Qs; and Farmer Maggot's *All's well as ends well,* are all in contemporary use and therefore recognisably proverbial.

Further help in identifying proverbs in the text is found when phrases are credited to tradition by their speakers, as when Butterbur qualifies *There's no accounting for East and West,* with 'as we say in Bree,'[14] or when Gildor prefixes *Do not meddle in the affairs of Wizards, for they are subtle and quick to anger,* with 'it is said.'[15] While these signpost-phrases helpfully clarify that we are reading a citation and not a normal part of speech, they are a formality mainly used when strangers of different origins meet.[16] In normal conversation, particularly between close friends, signposting of proverbs is rare.[17]

Standalone sentences, especially those with poetic features like Boromir's rhyming couplet *The wolf that one hears is worse than the orc that one fears* (and Aragorn's reply-in-kind, *Where the warg howls, there also the orc prowls*), sometimes declare themselves as proverbs, while others have what Michael Stanton describes as 'a definite air of sayings that are being repeated, not originated.'[18] Beyond that point, however, the waters become murky and discerning what is or isn't a proverb starts to become a matter of taste and opinion. Do *Never travel far without a rope* and *Do not speak before your master* have currency among the people as oral encapsulations of tradition wisdom, or are they merely sensible advice spontaneously spoken? We cannot know. Likewise, while some proverbs may be recognised due to their poetic properties, the heightened language in which many of Middle-earth's more cultured peoples speak confuses the matter. For example, the phrase *Seeing is both good and perilous* may sound proverbial due to its lyrical elegance and grace, but so also does everything else Galadriel says.

Deciding which of Middle-earth's phrases can be identified proverbs is, to a degree, a matter of personal preference and shrouded in subjectivity. But what is undeniable is that Middle-earth has hundreds of proverbs.

---

14 JRR Tolkien, *The Lord of the Rings* (Harper Collins, 1991), p. 153.

15 Many such proverbs are additionally italicised in the text, though not all.

16 Other examples include the Hobbits' *Handsome is as handsome does* to Strider in Bree, Faramir's *Night oft brings news to near kindred* to Frodo and Sam in Ithilien, and Beregond's *At the table small men may do the greater deeds* soon after meeting Pippin.

17 The exception being Sam Gamgee, who rarely uses a saying without signalling its provenance. Whether this is a matter of deference (to those he considers his superiors) or bashfulness is not clear, though if so either would be characteristic.

18 Michael Stanton, '"Advice Is A Dangerous Gift," (Pseudo)Proverbs In The Lord Of The Rings,' *Proverbium 13*, (University of Vermont, 1996), p. 335.

Scattered throughout the Tolkien corpus we hear proverbial-sounding sayings in the mouths of every culture and people. While the proverbs identified in this volume are limited to those from books published in Tolkien's lifetime—*The Hobbit* and *The Lord Of The Rings*—this does not reflect the full range of Arda's proverbial depth. *The Silmarillion*, *Unfinished Tales*, and *The Children Of Húrin* each contain a further treasure trove of proverbial material, demonstrating that Tolkien's commitment to convincing inner reality was not a late addition, tacked on to the texts at the last minute to add a sheen of realism, but was entwined within the creative process itself. The Tree grew from its leaves, not the other way around.

The Purpose of this Investigation

This volume could simply be a list of sayings, with comments attached. Instead, it uses the proverbs of Middle-earth as a lens through which to carry out an investigation of Middle-earth's cultures. By doing so, we are able to appreciate not only the insight and poetic quality of particular sayings, but also the fact that they form a coherent part of their speakers' philosophical worldview: Elven proverbs are distinctly Elvish, the Ents' proverbs are distinctly Entish, and so on.

What we quickly discover is that Tolkien did not merely create hundreds of erudite, apposite, and funny sayings—however great an artistic achievement that is—he also invented entire wisdom traditions in which these sayings belong. Just as different contemporary nations often have contrasting perspectives, so each civilisation of Middle-earth has a distinct worldview or philosophical culture. Each of these becomes apparent when we look through the lens of their proverbs: the national character and philosophy of each of Tolkien's cultures—from the small-minded pragmatism of rustic Hobbits to the disciplined dignity of Gondor—has been written into their wisdom traditions. Tolkien's legendarium is founded on details such as these; its world created from the bottom-up, and therefore richly rewarding to those who take the time to dive in and investigate its depths.

The proverbs of Middle-earth tell us the perspectives of Middle-earth, but not only national perspectives. Whenever the available number of proverbs from a single culture is large, we are able to discern more than the prevailing national wisdom: we can also see when an individual's philosophy is at odds with that of his or her people.[19] As one looks into these minutiae—asking questions about questions, as it were—the depth of detail in Tolkien's Tree is showcased. We can see that the philosophical DNA of each people is rooted in their historical narrative,[20] and that individual characters' perspectives reflect both national and personal narrative.[21] This book will explore these perspectives, where—just like Niggle's immaculately detailed leaves—Tolkien's astonishing attention to detail is affirmed.

> *'Do not despise the lore that has come down from distant years; for oft it may chance that old wives keep in memory word of things that once were needful for the wise to know.'*[22]

Tolkien's Great Tree is both impressive in its vast grandeur and delightful in its multitude of exquisitely-detailed leaves, any one of which may be poured over till heart's content. In focusing on one such class of leaf, this volume has no intent to raise it above the other facets of Tolkien's epic artwork, only to heed Celeborn's advice: not to despise 'lore' but to draw attention to and recognise the particular beauty and value that it has contributed to the whole.

---

19 Examples being Éowyn's dismissal of the Rohirrim's standard ethic of duty, Bilbo and Frodo's rejection of the parochialism of the Shire, and Gimli's outgrowing of the Dwarves' distrust of other peoples.

20 For example, Elrond's scepticism about oaths and the Rohirrim's veneration of them reflect the effect of oaths made by their forefathers: Fëanor and Eorl respectively.

21 Such as Bilbo using proverbs learned on his travels, and teaching them to Frodo and other hobbits.

22 Tolkien, *The Lord of the Rings*, p. 365.

CHAPTER ONE

THE HOBBITS

'Hobbits really are amazing creatures. You can learn all there is know about their ways in a month, and yet after a hundred years they can still surprise you.'[23]

A writer's role is usually limited to telling gripping, gratifying tales, but Tolkien went beyond that, also creating original creatures, cultures, and landscapes of eye-watering depth and invigorating beauty. Not surprisingly, he was often asked to identify his sources of inspiration. In response, Tolkien wrote that 'such a story... grows like a seed in the dark out of the leaf-mould of the mind... what one throws on one's personal compost-heap.'[24]

The leaf-mould of Tolkien's mind was extraordinarily rich. Like Niggle's Tree, which started simply only to outgrow even its creator's capacity to complete it, Arda's vast tapestry had a long germination process and took on a life of its own, fed by nutrients of many sorts and origins, some identifiable and others less so.

Humphrey Carpenter suggests of Tolkien that 'by the time he reached middle age, his imagination no longer needed to be stimulated... it was almost exclusively upon early experience, sufficiently broken down by

23 Tolkien, *The Lord of the Rings*, p. 61.

24 Humphrey Carpenter, *Tolkien: A Biography* (Houghton Mifflin, 1977), p. 126.

time, that he nourished the seeds of his imagination.'[25] Any analysis of Tolkien's early life leads us to Hobbits, and to their land, the Shire.

Tolkien is well known for declaring himself to be a hobbit (in all but size). His idyllic early childhood, between the ages of four and eight, was spent in Sarehole, at that time a tiny hamlet in rural Warwickshire; and it was from the leaf-mould of these years that the Shire grew. The hamlet itself re-emerged as Hobbiton; the little river with its mill became the Water; the neighbours, an ill-favoured miller and his boy, returned as Sandyman and his son Ted; and even the terrifying farmer who caught Tolkien picking mushrooms found his place as Maggot.[26] Such early experiences also provided noteworthy names, such as 'Bag End' (a nick-name for the house of his Aunt Jane Neave[27]), 'Gamgee' (a local name for cotton wool), and even 'Baggins' (a between-meals snack[28]). Each endured in Tolkien's mind, seeds ready to grow. And in time, from a hole in the ground, the first hobbits emerged.

'Hobbits are just, well, rustic English people'[29]

Like Tolkien's childhood neighbours in Sarehole, Hobbits are not learned, highly-lettered, nor widely-informed about the world. They have neither a technological nor a particularly artistic culture, and generally distrust the complex and the unfamiliar. But they do 'have a fund of wisdom and wise sayings that men have mostly never heard or have forgotten long ago.'[30] It is this oral heritage that makes the Holbytlan so deeply sensible: the received wisdom of far-off years is employed and engaged with on an ongoing basis.

Hobbits may be simple but they are not stupid. They may be ignorant of the Wide World but they know their own land as well as their own hands and toes.[31] Diminutive, quiet, and unwarlike, there is still 'a seed of courage hidden (often deeply, it is true) inside the fattest and most timid hobbit, waiting for some final and desperate danger to make it grow.'[32] *Valour cannot be computed by stature,* as Gandalf puts it.

---

25 *Ibid.*

26 Carpenter, *Biography,* p. 20-21.

27 Carpenter, *Biography,* p. 106.

28 Shippey, *The Road to Middle-earth,* p. 71-72.

29 Interview with BBC Radio, 1971.

30 Tolkien, *The Hobbit,* p. 83.

31 Tolkien, *The Hobbit,* p. 346.

32 Tolkien, *The Lord of the Rings,* p. 137.

In spite of the assumptions often made about simple, rustic peoples (usually by less happy but technologically-superior societies), the Shire-folk are resplendent with wisdom, in spite of their illiteracy, lack of knowledge, and unwillingness to bother with 'the business of their betters.' Perhaps because of it.

Development of Hobbit-Sense

While at different points in their history the *Holbytlan* (or *Periannath*) had been three semi-estranged tribes—the Harfoots, Fallowhides, and Stoors—by the time of the War of the Ring these ethnic groups (and the experiences and traditions specific to each) had more-or-less coalesced to a single society, based in the land the King had given them: the Shire. Having settled at various times in Wilderland, Dunland, the Angle, Bree, and elsewhere, enduring hardship, conflict, and an assortment of the Big People and their troubles, they (presumably) had seen enough to convince themselves that the Shire was perfection. They 'fell in love with their new land,'[33] planted themselves in it, and got on with life in their simple-but-shrewd well-ordered way.

The Shire provided a sheltered, fertile oasis amid the wide, desolate leagues of Eriador: safe (on the whole) from the rigours of war, famine, and plague; and self-sufficient enough to minimise contact with the Outside. With their wandering past behind them, the three tribes amalgamated into a united (though not uniform) society. The water-loving Stoors tended to settle in the Marish and near the Brandywine River, and the Harfoots predominated everywhere else, while the Fallowhides generally became the leaders or chieftains of the fledgling land.

It was during this colonisation period that the Hobbits' own records began, including the Shire Reckoning and such books as they had; primarily genealogies and other volumes 'filled with things they already knew.'[34] The long years before the settlement of the Shire were only remembered orally, although many of the traditions that endured were subsequently recorded in the spate of new writing that was undertaken in the years following the return of the King. Such works as the *Red Book of Westmarch* (which included the writings of Bilbo and Frodo Baggins), *Old Words and Names in the Shire*, the *Reckoning of Years*, and *Herblore*

33 Tolkien, *The Lord of the Rings*, p. 4.

34 Tolkien, *The Lord of the Rings*, p. 7.

of the Shire (all compiled or written by Merry Brandybuck) all came into existence at this time.

These books, however, were the clear exception to the general rule, which was that most hobbits, being illiterate, received their learning informally and orally. Proverbs—short, memorable encapsulations of thought, readily used and easily remembered—would have had had a central role in the average hobbit's education, and therefore played a key part in the development and passing on of Hobbit-sense.

Michael Stanton observes that due to the straightforward matter-of-factness of their culture, 'Hobbits… seem favourably disposed to the clarity and pointedness of proverbial language.'[35] In other words, the characteristic features of proverbs—that they are 'trite, obvious, known to everyone, general not particular, show no interest in the *mot juste*…'[36] etc.—are distinctive of the Halflings themselves. Hobbits and proverbs suit one another.

Hobbit-proverbs are usually used in an obvious, explicit way: quoted formally rather than finding their way surreptitiously into speech. Bilbo's 'as my father used to say,'[37] Sam's 'as my Gaffer used to say'[38] and Pippin's 'as we say in the Shire'[39] point to an underlying assumption that inherited tradition carries special weight and authority. This habit of signposting proverbs also expresses an unwillingness on the part of individuals to claim personal credit for their insights. Hobbit-sense is a very much a communal phenomenon, and there are no professional lore-masters in the Shire. Tradition is their teacher.

The basic argument for trusting tradition is simply that its wisdom is not theoretical, but has proven its worth again and again. Truths once learned will not suddenly cease to be true, so they are trusted and passed on—usually by means of 'a proverb or riddle or poem'[40]—each generation learning the cumulative lessons of its predecessors. Hobbits consider learning from and submitting to the insight of forebears both shrewd and proper.

35 Stanton, *Op. Cit.*, p. 334.

36 Shippey, *Roots and Branches*, p. 305.

37 Tolkien, *The Hobbit,* p. 256.

38 Tolkien, *The Lord of the Rings*, p. 685.

39 Tolkien, *The Lord of the Rings*, p. 167.

40 Kreeft, *Op. Cit.*, p. 135.

Unlike the other peoples of Middle-earth, Hobbits rarely refer to their wisdom tradition in mixed company—i.e. in the presence of Big People. When conferring together (debating the route to Bucklebury, or deciding whether to trust the mysterious Strider) Hobbits will recite proverbs as a matter of course, but when under the leadership of others (at the Council of Elrond, for example, or as part of the Fellowship) no such contributions are made. This silence is almost certainly a self-effacing one: while Hobbits see their plain wisdom as all well and good in the Shire, they believe it falls short elsewhere. But Elrond quashes this thought emphatically:

> *This is the hour of the Shire-folk, when they arise from their quiet fields to shake the towers and counsels of the Great.*[41]

Nevertheless, the Little People remain restrained. Put Hobbits in counsels of war, discerning the devices of evil, and they will fall silent. But get them discussing ale (*Proper fourteen-twenty!*) or bath-times (*A loon is he that will not sing*), rivers (*Boats are quite tricky enough for those that sit still*) or baby-names (*Make it short, then you won't have to cut it short*), and a wealth of tried-and-tested sayings leap forth.

The Strata of the Shire

In the same way that the *Holbytlan* have an ethnic heritage that is threefold and yet overlapping, three different intermingling streams can be identified within the wisdom culture of the Shire-folk. Each source produces characteristic proverbs grown from the leaf-mould of their sphere's own experience.

First are the **Rustics**, the salt-of-the-earth Hobbits who make up the majority of the population. Farmer Maggot, Ted Sandyman, and Tom Cotton are examples of this rural working class of farmers, tradesmen (such as ropers, millers, and smiths), and others whose skill is primarily in their hands. Gaffer Gamgee is the pre-eminent fount of this stream of wisdom: a hobbit who has never travelled nor been trained for any task more far-reaching than gardening, yet is emblematic of good solid Hobbit-sense. The majority of Hobbit-proverbs are apparently Rustic in origin.

Second come the **Educated** or **Gentlehobbits**, those of the great or wealthy families who make up an informal Hobbit aristocracy. Their

41 Tolkien, *The Lord of the Rings*, p. 264.

status as landowners (but not land-workers) lends a civic authority, though one that is expressed mildly: in the administration of the Shire, rather than the wielding of power. The families of such figures as the Thain, the Master of Buckland, and the Mayor would have belonged to this group, as well as plantation-owners like the Sackville-Bagginses and Hornblowers. Gentlehobbits have their own sayings, but also use proverbs learned from their Rustic neighbours (though it is rare for the exchange to go the other way).

The third stream of Hobbit wisdom is that of the **Travellers**, those exceptional few who at some point leave the protected comfort of the Shire, widening their experience and adding proverbs and perspectives from non-Hobbit origins to their native wisdom. These include Gentlehobbits like Bilbo and Frodo, as well as the Rustic Sam. All are transformed by their engagement with the Outside, increasing their understanding, insight, and knowledge, but also making themselves the objects of suspicion or ridicule at home.

These three streams correspond with the three classes of Shire society, which (as Kreeft observes) is a society made up of 'fixed roles, and hierarchy.'[42] Different hobbits each have their own part to play in the well-functioning whole, with no great envy or competition evident,[43] reflecting Tolkien's own pre-modern competition-free attitude to class.[44]

In the Shire, as Tom Shippey observes, 'there is a class-system: but the system has gaps. There is no-one at the top of it.'[45] Originally, as part of Arthedain, it had been under the authority of the King, but there had been no King for a thousand years. In the absence of a monarch, the Shire had become a quirk: a half republic, half aristocracy, in which ultimate power is not exercised and—most importantly—is not sought.

42 Kreeft, *Op. Cit.*, p. 214.

43 Likewise, Ralph C. Wood observes that 'the universe as Tolkien conceives it is hierarchical,' with no competition between Ilúvatar, the Valar, and the Children of God (Ralph C. Wood, *The Gospel According to Tolkien* (Westminster John Knox Press, 2003), p. 11). The greatest discord happens when Melkor challenges that hierarchy, desiring a role greater than the one to which he has been appointed.

44 Carpenter writes of Tolkien that 'His own view of the world, in which each man belonged or ought to belong to a specific 'estate,' whether high or low… made him highly sympathetic to his fellow-men, for it is those who are unsure of their status in the world, who feel they have to prove themselves and if necessary put down other men to do so, who are the truly ruthless.' (Carpenter, *Biography*, p. 127-128.)

45 Shippey, *Roots and Branches*, p. 287.

With no one sitting on top of the pile, no tyranny and no coercion, the Shire embodies a philosophy that stands as the antithesis to Friedrich Nietzsche's theory of 'will to power.'[46] It was Nietzsche's belief that the world is driven and motivated by the desire to advance the self by overcoming others, striving 'to grow, to gain ground, attract... and acquire ascendency.'[47] But Shire-hobbits do not reflect this in the least. They—the occasional, immediately-derided Sackville-Baggins aside—have no will to power, and no desire or temptation to dominate. The lack of jealousy or discord between Rustics, Gentlehobbits, and Travellers is striking. Hobbits appear free from ambition or greed of wealth, and are proven wise for it.

The Rustics

> *'There's earth under his old feet, and clay on his fingers; wisdom in his bones, and both his eyes are open.'*[48]

It is Farmer Maggot about whom these words of Tom Bombadil are spoken, but they could just as easily stand for most of the common Hobbits of the Shire: plain and earthy, uncluttered and unadorned; but prudent, observant, and shrewd.

Proverbs, due to their oral nature, are often the special preserve of the unschooled and illiterate: people who cannot run to a library or a professor for specialist information, but instead look to sayings, stories, and songs. Rustic hobbits are such as these. They live in a small world, physically and philosophically, centred on twin focuses of growing food and eating it. This leaves them unaffected by pretention or ostentation, and uninterested in raising their sights beyond day-to-day living.

The proverbs used by the Rustics are terse, often humorous, and defiantly pragmatic; primarily concerned with passing on plain Hobbit-sense rather than engaging in complex issues of ethics or propriety. Such sayings grow out of the objects and tasks of every-day life, hence Farmer Cotton's idiomatic assertion that *You've got to have grist before you can grind*, the Gaffer's *It's the job that's never started as takes longest to finish,* and Sam's *If you're short of sleep cold water on the neck's like rain*

46 A phrase coined in 1883 in *Thus Spake Zarathustra*.

47 Friedrich Nietzsche, *Beyond Good and Evil*, translated by Helen Zimmern (MacMillan: New York, 1907). p. 226.

48 Tolkien, *The Lord of the Rings*, p. 130.

on a wilted lettuce. There is no high philosophy here, just the simple lessons of the simple life.

The Rustics believe in keeping one's head down and getting on with the task at hand in as straightforward a manner as possible, not surprisingly since they have survived and flourished by sticking to what they know and looking askance at everything else. In this light, a saying like *Strange as news from Bree* is not only an incredulous comment on the Shire's dubious nearest neighbours, but also an ingrained attitude to anything outside of the norm.

> *'Elves and Dragons! I says to him. Cabbages and potatoes are better for me and you. Don't go getting mixed up in the business of your betters, or you'll land in trouble too big for you.'*[49]

This proverb-laden paragraph is the Gaffer's spluttering response to the (apparently terrifying) news that his son Sam has been 'learned his letters.' And while this small-mindedness might be laughed at, he is proved right: Sam ends up in trouble far too big for him. It would have been far more sensible and safe to stick to cabbages and potatoes. Similar proverbs of warning and distrust range from cross-cultural cynicism (*Each to his own fashion*) to suspicion of all strangers (*Fair speech may hide a foul heart,* and *Folk are not always what they seem*), while *Handsome is as handsome does* professes scepticism as the correct first port of call when faced with the impressive or beautiful.

The underlying philosophy behind these statements is a gnarled and rather fatalistic pessimism about the world at large, akin to that of the similarly nature-centric Ents but balanced by the Hobbits' unwearying appetite for simple pleasures. Sam's *Apples for walking, and a pipe for sitting*, Bilbo's *A little sleep does a great cure*, Frodo's marvellously vivid *Short cuts make delays, but inns make longer ones*, all hint at the same delight. *Proper fourteen-twenty!* they say, when drinking good ale.

Due to their humble rootedness in nature and tradition, and their faithfulness to the job at hand (interspersed with the occasional beer, apple, and pipe), the Rustics remain incorruptible. Having grown up being told that *You'll come to a bad end if you don't watch your step*, Sam easily overcomes temptation when it comes, while Gentlehobbits like Lotho Sackville-Baggins and Peregrin Took both experience disastrous failures of character. In particular, we are shown that those hobbits with a 'close

49 Tolkien, *The Lord of the Rings*, p. 24.

friendship with the earth'[50] (in contrast with the ilk of Ted Sandyman and his foul, smoke-belching mill) have a particular degree or depth of insight that is unavailable to those who have not had their advantages. There's earth under their feet, clay on their fingers, wisdom in their bones, and both their eyes are open.

Sam Gamgee and the Gaffer

> *'You're nowt but a ninnyhammer, Sam Gamgee: that's what the Gaffer said to me often enough'*[51]

To be raised as 'Samwise'—a modernization of Old English *Samwís*—is not an easy start in life, since the name means 'halfwit.'[52] Saddled with this preposterous moniker, and a father who saw fit to give it, Sam could not have grown up with a high opinion of his intellect. And yet before he had even ventured from the vicinity of the Hill he had learned to read and write, memorised 'The Fall of Gil-galad,' and composed at least one full-length song of his own, 'The Stone Troll.'

Although Sam seems perpetually out of his depth as his beloved Shire is left further and further behind, he is clearly no halfwit—he knows more than he shows. While not a hero or leader in any conventional sense, he overcomes (or muddles through) every test and task he faces, from sleeping in trees to taking on (and giving up) the Ring.

In the despair of Cirith Ungol, forced to take the untameable Burden from the stricken Frodo, Sam is on trial. He is alone, with no leader to follow and no one to ask for advice as the Ring's power waxes 'gnawing at his will and reason.' But Sam passes the test, partly because to him it was no test at all.

> *'In that hour of trial it was the love of his master that helped most to hold him firm; but also deep down in him lived still unconquered his plain hobbit-sense… The one small garden of a free gardener was all his need and due, not a garden swollen to a realm; his own hands to use, not the hands of other to command.'*[53]

50 Tolkien, *The Lord of the Rings*, p. 1.

51 Tolkien, *The Lord of the Rings*, p. 594.

52 Similarly, the name 'Tolkien' derives from German 'tollkühn'—'foolhardy.'

53 Tolkien, *The Lord of the Rings*, p. 881.

Handsome is
as handsome does.

Loving service and fruitful labour are the ethical core of Sam's life. Hobbit-sense and love of Frodo pierce the wild fantasies of 'Samwise the Strong' and a flowering Gorgoroth, while healthy self-deprecation keeps him firmly in his right and proper place—a place of servanthood. In doing so, he saves the entire Quest.[54]

> *'I am learning a lot about Sam Gamgee on this journey. First he was a conspirator, now he's a jester. He'll end up by becoming a wizard—or a warrior!'*
> *'I hope not,' said Sam. 'I don't want to be neither!'*[55]

The Wisdom of the Unlearned

In correspondence, Tolkien described Sam as 'a reflexion of the English soldier, of the privates and batmen I knew in the 1914 war, and recognised as so far superior to myself.'[56] The kind of selfless service he had in mind does not require a great store of insightful wisdom, only the will to keep going and not give up. Sam will keep going 'if it breaks my back and heart,'[57] and the majority of the proverbs he uses aid this endurance.

Sam's sayings appear to be mostly spoken to himself; muttered with a shrug and a shake of the head (as with *Live and learn* and *Talking won't mend nothing*, or the idiomatic *As hopeless as a frost in spring* and *A tight belt and a light tooth*), but sometimes delivered with the cautious hope of an optimistic hobbit (*Trust to luck* and *Where there's life there's hope*). There is little poetry or high wisdom in these sayings—Sam would be embarrassed if Gandalf or Elrond heard him use them—but there is encouragement to the flagging spirit.

> *'I don't want to give up yet. It's not like me, somehow'*[58]

Sam is the epitome of the faithful servant: he has complete trust in Frodo's wisdom and judgement, and carries *Never leave your master* as his mantra.[59] This philosophy of service, and of finding fulfilment through

54 As argued by Michael Stanton, who credits the Gaffer's teaching for the achievement. (Stanton, *Op. Cit.*, p. 341.)

55 Tolkien, *The Lord of the Rings*, p. 203.

56 Carpenter, *Biography*, p. 81.

57 Tolkien, *The Lord of the Rings*, p. 918.

58 Tolkien, *The Lord of the Rings*, p. 929.

59 The only person over whom Sam regards himself as senior is Gollum, the recipient of Sam's only proverb-based instructions or commands: *Third time pays for all*, *Turn over*

submission rather than individualistic success, is one of which the Gaffer (who tended the garden at Bag End for the best part of eighty years) would approve.

Gaffer Gamgee, as Michael Stanton notes, 'is a prime examplar of the wisdom of the unlearned. His words are shrewd, concrete, and intensely practical.'[60] He is also, in Tom Shippey's estimation, one of those few who have the wisdom and authority to change and shape inherited proverbs to their own context.[61] Others (eg. Bilbo in *The Hobbit*) may say *Where there's life there's hope*, but the Gaffer adds *and need of vittles*. *All's well as ends well*, says a Rustic proverb in the mouth of Farmer Maggot, but the Gaffer makes it *All's well as ends Better!*

These examples show an intuitive understanding of the purpose of proverbs: they are not museum pieces to be brought out mechanically, looked at, and then put away. Rather, inherited sayings are emblems of a living tradition, through which multiple experiences and multiple wisdoms are fitted to the present moment and the immediate need. To someone like the Gaffer, tradition is not a musty old artefact but is constantly being created, added to every second (though in light of what has gone before). Tradition is an ongoing story, in which the Gaffer and his son are characters and contributors.

From Rustic to Worldly-wise

The Gamgees' narrative arc is an ugly duckling story. The tenants[62] and employees of the Bagginses 'arise from their quiet fields to shake the towers and counsels of the Great.'[63] From a thoroughly insignificant start—growing up as a gardener's son in a small village in a powerless country—Sam grows to become 'one of the most famous people in all the lands'[64] as well as a beloved civic leader.

The Gaffer—or 'Master Hamfast' as Bilbo very properly calls him[65]—had moved to Hobbiton when young to be apprenticed to Holman Green-

---

a new leaf, and keep it turned, and *Each to his own fashion*.

60 Stanton, *Op. Cit.*, p. 337.

61 Shippey, *Roots & Branches*, p. 308 footnote.

62 That the Gamgees' home on Bagshot Row is owned by the Master of Bag End is implied by the authority Lotho Sackville-Baggins has to turn the Gaffer out of his house. (Tolkien, *The Lord of the Rings*, p. 988-989.)

63 Tolkien, *The Lord of the Rings*, p. 264.

64 Tolkien, *The Lord of the Rings*, p. 991.

65 Shippey observes that the nomenclature of this exchange—between '*Mister* Bilbo'

hand, the gardener at Bag End, and not shifted since. *Hamfast* is a Saxon word meaning 'stayathome' and fits the Gaffer to a tee—'I can't abide changes'[66] he says—though he fails to pass that trait on to Sam.

Gardening and rope-making are the family trades, and Sam follows his father into the former. So far, so safe. But when he begins to visit Mr Bilbo (in order to hear the 'stories of the old days') and is 'learned his letters,' Sam steps outside the proper limits of his vocation and class. This is clearly an issue for the Gaffer. 'I hope no harm will come of it,' he comments, as if reading and writing are all one and the same with wearing ironmongery and fighting in battles.

The entrance of literacy and learning into the Gamgee family fundamentally changed the course of their story. Long before he'd ever left the Shire, Sam was enthralled by fireside-tales of dragons, oliphaunts, walking trees and the like, a fascination that was fed by Mr Bilbo. It was that same fascination that suckered him into eavesdropping on a conversation between Gandalf and Frodo. 'Lor bless me, sir, but I do love tales of that sort. And believe them too,'[67] he said when trying to explain himself. He was punished by being sent 'to see Elves.'

Sam leaves Hobbiton as a private servant and returns to become a public servant, following Frodo's advice to *Use all the knowledge and wits you have of your own*. After taking the lead in the cleansing of the Shire, Sam serves as its Mayor for forty-nine years, and his family ascend from the ranks of the Rustics to become civic leaders: Gentlehobbits, in fact. His daughter Elanor's family become Wardens of Westmarch;[68] while another daughter, Goldilocks, marries the son of Thain Peregrin,[69] meaning that Sam's descendents would become the hereditary Thains of the Shire.

In this way, a melding between the three wisdom traditions of the Halflings—Traveller, Educated, and Rustic—is achieved in the person and family of Samwise. One wonders what the Gaffer would have made of this ennoblement—whether he would have been proud, ashamed, or confused. *Elves and dragons!* he may well have said. Not bad for a ninnyhammer.

---

and '*Master* Hamfast'—delineates the class divide (a divide notably marked not by animosity but by mutual respect) between the two. (Shippey, *Roots and Branches*, p. 289)

66 Tolkien, *The Lord of the Rings*, p. 256.

67 Tolkien, *The Lord of the Rings*, p. 62.

68 Tolkien, *The Lord of the Rings*, p. 1077.

69 Tolkien, *The Lord of the Rings*, p. 1072.

The Educated or Gentlehobbits

> *'Bagginses and Boffins... Tooks and Brandybucks, and Grubbs, and Chubbs, and Burrowses, and Hornblowers, and Bolgers, Bracegirdles, Goodbodies, Brockhouses and Proudfoots.'*[70]

The names of the twelve dozen welcomed by Bilbo to the special family dinner at the end of his (and Frodo's) birthday party give us a glimpse of the sphere of Shire society to which the Bagginses belong. No Gamgees, Twofoots, Rumbles, Maggots, Sandymans, or Cottons here: these are the upper echelon, what Shippey calls 'a vestigial upper class.'[71] A remnant perhaps of the Fallowhides—that historic tribe of Hobbitry distinguished by having 'more skill in language and song than in handicrafts' and being 'somewhat bolder and more adventurous'[72]—these Educated hobbits were both the primary landowners and the civic leaders of the Shire, and constituted a distinct subculture of manner and lifestyle within it.

> *'A very nice well-spoken gentlehobbit is Mr Bilbo'*[73]

While not having the airs and graces of what might be called 'gentry,' Gentlehobbits do have a distinct ethos and culture due to their clannish nature and tendency to marry within their 'class.'[74] According to Shippey, what distinguishes a Gentlehobbit is 'wealth (not having to work), accent and education (being 'well-spoken' and widely literate), birth... and a certain steady politeness.'[75] Additionally, Gentlehobbits are clearly more geographically footloose than the Rustics, as is seen by the comings and goings between Hobbiton, Buckland, the Eastfarthing, and Tookland in the friendship between Frodo, Merry, Fatty, and Pippin.

While lettered and generally more sophisticated than the norm, these Educated hobbits are, if anything, presented as less wise (and certainly less responsible) than those who would otherwise have regarded them as their 'betters.' This may be related to the 'something Tookish' of their Fallowhide origins—part of a trait that produced 'strong charac-

---

70 Tolkien, *The Lord of the Rings*, p. 29.

71 Shippey, *Roots and Branches*, p. 288.

72 Tolkien, *The Lord of the Rings*, p. 3.

73 Tolkien, *The Lord of the Rings*, p. 22.

74 The tendency to intermarry is shown by the fact that Bilbo, Frodo, Meriadoc Brandybuck, Peregrin Took, and Fredegar Bolger are all related to one another in multiple ways.

75 Shippey, *Roots and Branches*, p. 296.

ters of peculiar habits and even adventurous temperament'[76]—but it is also the unavoidable result of their indolent lifestyles: when there is no adversity and no great issues to overcome, the need for wisdom ceases to be pressing. As a result, the Shire's educated class are not great proverb-makers.

Those sayings that do apparently originate with Gentlehobbits tend to be limited to their pet subjects: the dining table (eg. *Drink is not enough for content*); manners and propriety (eg. Bilbo's *Dwarves are sometimes politer in word than in deed* or Merry's *Mind your Ps and Qs*); and leisurely inactivity (*If you sit on the door-step long enough, you will think of something*). Elsewhere in Middle-earth, elders and leaders recite axioms and maxims concerning courage, hope, paradox, and warcraft, but the upper echelon of the Shire has no such heritage.

One result of this dearth of oral tradition amongst the Educated is the development of a very sensible habit: tapping into the wisdom of others. But rather than only learning from the Big People they encounter, Bilbo (*Don't let your heads get too big for your hats*), Frodo (*It's no good worrying about tomorrow*), Merry (*Share pipes, as good friends must at a pinch*), and Pippin (*Handsome is as handsome does*) each utilise sayings that bear all the hallmarks of originating not from Outside, nor from within their Educated sphere, but from the Rustics. The Gentlehobbits might have been privileged and wealthy, yet they still had to borrow from the treasure trove of their employees and neighbours.

Peregrin Took

'A fool, but an honest fool, you remain'[77]

When the people of Minas Tirith mistake Pippin for *Ernil i Pheriannath*[78]—the 'Prince of the Halflings'—they are not as far from the mark as might have been thought. Pippin might be the youngest member of the Conspiracy and the youngest member of the Fellowship, but he is also the eldest son of Paladin II, the Thain of the Shire.[79]

76 Tolkien, *The Lord of the Rings*, p. 9.

77 Tolkien, *The Lord of the Rings*, p. 579.

78 Tolkien, *The Lord of the Rings*, p. 751.

79 Paladin was of a cadet branch of the family, but when his cousin Ferumbras III died unmarried and childless, he became the Took and the Thain. The twenty-five year old Pippin, in the midst of his irresponsible 'tweens,' would instantly have been thrust to the forefront of Hobbit society, heir to a legacy as old as any in the Shire.

The role of Thain was created after the demise of the North Kingdom, when the son of the last king chose to be only an ethnic chieftain—Lord of the Dúnedain—rather than continue as ruler of other former subjects, such as those in the Shire and the Bree-land. The Thain held 'the authority of the king that was gone,'[80] though this was only rarely asserted, as when Bullroarer Took led an armed brigade in the Battle of Greenfields[81] and when Thain Paladin took up arms against the ruffians of Lotho Sackville-Baggins.[82] But such cases were highly exceptional. Generally, The Rules (ie. laws inherited from the time of the kings) were universally obeyed as a matter of free will, leaving the Thainship as little more than 'a nominal dignity.'[83]

The original thains were of the Oldbuck family—subsequently called Brandybuck after crossing the Brandywine to colonise Buckland—but by the time of Paladin II the title had long since passed to the Tooks, so that 'the Thain' and 'the Took' were practically interchangeable terms. The Took family was large, wealthy, and influential (even outside of the Tookland), as well as educated and literate—they even kept a library! But in spite of the Tooks' status as one of the 'great' or aristocratic Hobbit clans, they were commonly treated with more suspicion and scepticism than respect, due to their propensity to 'go and have adventures.'[84] This 'Tookish' streak is the 'something that was not entirely hobbitlike'[85] which set the Tooks apart. And it seems that they were far from ashamed of this tendency: 'Peregrin,' a name that means no less than 'pilgrim' or 'traveller in strange countries,' was apparently considered completely appropriate for a child of the family.

Raised in or near Great Smials, the ancestral home of the Took clan in Tuckborough, Pippin would have been the recipient of every material advantage that was available to a hobbit, in the Shire or out of it. By the time that he helped his cousin Frodo to move from Bag End to Buckland (and prepared to follow him out of the Shire and into the Fellowship) Pippin was free from any responsibility or complication—he had no profession, nor was apprenticed to any, due to his impending future as

80 Tolkien, *The Lord of the Rings,* p. 5.

81 Tolkien, *The Hobbit,* p. 22.

82 Tolkien, *The Lord of the Rings,* p. 986.

83 Tolkien, *The Lord of the Rings,* p. 9.

84 Tolkien, *The Hobbit,* p. 5.

85 *Ibid.*

landowner (of 'the lands round Whitwell'[86]) and Shire-chieftain. He had never known hardship or difficulty or danger, having never had to go out of his comfort zone. His idiomatic proverb, *We may stand, if only on one leg, or at least be left still upon our knees* (spoken to Beregond on the walls of Minas Tirith) may reflect Hobbits' dogged unwillingness to give in to adversity, but adversity was something that Pippin had never tasted.

> *Little people should not meddle in affairs that are too big for them.*

Whilst he may have a flawed view of his own intellect ('There must be someone with intelligence in the party'[87]), Pippin is no simpleton or mere passenger, as is shown when he and Merry are kidnapped by Saruman's Orcs. A helpless captive, nonetheless he manages to run away from the Orc-troop (to drop his Lórien brooch for the pursuing Aragorn to find), before disguising his cut bonds and even pretending to have the Ring in order to rile and confuse Grishnákh and so to escape. These are not the acts of an indolent imbecile. However, his subsequent stealing of the palantír from Gandalf joins with telling a Baggins-centric story in Bree and dropping a stone down the guardroom well in Moria as exploits of absurd thoughtlessness. It is not, perhaps, that Pippin is without wisdom, more that, in his own words, 'I am not much more than a boy.'[88]

There is little or nothing of the philosopher in Pippin and his proverbs, which are few and tend to be limited in range. *Don't believe what strangers say of themselves* and *Hobbits ought to stick together* contrast the perils of mixed company with the trustworthiness of the known, while *Folk are not always what they seem* and *Handsome is as handsome does* are standard Shire scepticism, unwilling to be cowed or swayed by surface appearances.

These sayings are 'low culture' and therefore very probably rustic in origin; borrowed due to the dearth of lore in the Educated sphere. This borrowing of a proverb can also alter its meaning: in the mouth of the Gaffer or Tom Cotton, *Short cuts make long delays* would be an admonishment against slipshod work, pointing out that doing something badly often means doing it twice; but coming from Pippin, who has no work to do, it becomes a warning to cross-country ramblers.

---

86 Tolkien, *The Lord of the Rings*, p. 752.

87 Tolkien, *The Lord of the Rings*, p. 265.

88 Tolkien, *The Lord of the Rings*, p. 745.

The only occasion when Pippin's proverbs stray from the pragmatic into the pensive or poetic is when, having come into the presence of the grieving Denethor, Pippin delicately describes the death of Boromir:

> *Pippin flushed and forgot his fear.*
> *"The mightiest man may be slain by one arrow," he said; "and Boromir was pierced by many"*[89]

In the judicious use of a proverb to describe a scene of great pain and tragedy, Pippin displays the potential of a poetic axiom to soften a heavy blow, whilst also revealing his own growing wisdom. The heightened language, the employment of a (presumably) non-Hobbit proverb, and the tactful offer of service that follows, all mark Pippin's transition from an irresponsible youth who has 'walked all these days with closed ears and mind asleep'[90] to something more resembling the 'lordly' figure he is later seen to be.[91] As one of the returning Travellers, even other Hobbits come to admire the Prince of the Halflings.

Meriadoc Brandybuck

> *Great heart will not be denied.*

The Brandybucks are 'queer.' So says Old Noakes, so says the Gaffer, so too says Daddy Twofoot. They live on the wrong side of the Brandywine River, fool about with boats, and are right next to that 'dark bad place' the Old Forest.[92] But more than all those things, the most incomprehensible aspect of the Brandybucks of Buckland to most Hobbits is that they have chosen to leave the Four Farthings of the Shire and live Outside.[93]

Brandy Hall, the vast ancestral home of the wealthy Brandybuck clan, is also heartbeat of a 'small independent country.'[94] Buckland was originally settled by Gorhendad Oldbuck, who built Brandy Hall—'a regular warren' never containing 'fewer than a couple of hundred relations'[95]—

89 Tolkien, *The Lord of the Rings*, p. 739.

90 Tolkien, *The Lord of the Rings*, p. 737.

91 Tolkien, *The Lord of the Rings*, p. 1002.

92 Tolkien, *The Lord of the Rings*, p. 22.

93 Buckland was not part of the Shire as originally gifted by the Kingdom of Arthedain, and may not have been formally added until the edict of King Elessar in the Fourth Age. (Tolkien, *The Lord of the Rings*, p. 9.)

94 Tolkien, *The Lord of the Rings*, p. 96.

95 Tolkien, *The Lord of the Rings*, p. 23.

and established what was in effect a family-run fiefdom. Oldbuck changed his name to Brandybuck, and his descendents presided over Buckland from then on.

Merry, as the eldest son of the eldest son of Old Rory—Rorimac Brandybuck, the Master of Buckland—would have grown up with the expectation of one day becoming the head of the family and Master himself. For him to naturally fall into roles of leadership and even bravery is therefore less surprising than would be the case with other hobbits.

He starts simply—sneaking a look at Bilbo's secret book, and forming a Conspiracy with Pippin, Sam, and Fatty Bolger—but that is only the start. Having organised the ponies and supplies required to leave the Shire, and led the Company into the Old Forest, he rises to heroic heights: cutting off arms and hands of Saruman's Orcs; wounding the Witch-king (to save the life of Éowyn and to allow her to strike the mortal blow); and finally coordinating and commanding Hobbit-forces in the Battle of Bywater.

In contrast to other Gentlehobbits like Pippin or the young Bilbo, it is clear that from an early age travelling and other minor adventures were perfectly normal for Merry—as he says, *No Took ever beat a Brandybuck for inquisitiveness*. By the time the four hobbits set out from Crickhollow, Merry had been in the Old Forest several times,[96] knew all about Bree and the *Prancing Pony*, and had developed a better head for maps and geography than the norm.[97] Frodo may be the most educated and widely-informed of the Company, but Merry is the most experienced.

In spite of his leadership qualities, Merry makes little use of proverbs, perhaps because his upbringing had taught him to lean on factual knowledge rather than received wisdom. The proverbs that Merry does use fall into two distinct categories: the practical and the reflective. The practical ones are mainly concerned with food and comradeship (*Drink is not enough for content*, he explains as Isengard concerning Ent-draughts, and *Share pipes, as good friends must at a pinch*), but also include *Mind your Ps and Qs*, an idiomatic saying of uncertain provenance still common in modern English.

96 Tolkien, *The Lord of the Rings*, p. 105.

97 As he later shows by identifying the River Entwash, Fangorn Forest, and Mount Methedras from memory. (Tolkien, *The Lord of the Rings*, p. 470.)

These proverbs exhibit that, to a Gentlehobbit, 'practicality' mainly implies the serious issues of vittles and good manners, and that ethics (or the serious dissection of morality) rarely rears its awkward head. Not that Merry is by any means unethical, only that he has never been in any difficulty great enough to reveal what the ethos underlying his actions might be. The Brandybucks have not had to blow the Horn-call of Buckland for over a century, and regard being 'in a pinch' as no more than the necessity to share pipes. Their lives are ethical, in the sense that they are filled with an apparent goodness and *bonhomie*, but they have no distinct philosophy underpinning their good acts. Kreeft, quoting Cicero, argues that 'not to admit you have a philosophy is to have a bad one,'[98] but a lack of a formal moral system may also imply childlike innocence, and that seems closer to the mark in this case.

> *'His grief he will not forget; but it will not darken his heart, it will teach him wisdom.'*[99]

Whatever his inherited ethical underpinnings, leaving the Shire changes Merry—having been a Gentlehobbit, he becomes one of the Travellers. In the quiet hours of recuperation after the Battle of the Pelennor Fields, sharing a pipe with Pippin, Merry is able to consider this transformative process and his reflective proverbs emerge. He strings together three beautifully thoughtful adages: *It is best to love first what you are fitted to love*, he says, and *You must start somewhere and have some roots*; before concluding *The soil of the Shire is deep*. This is quite a contrast from his previous engagement with proverbs, but then Merry catches himself and stops short, saying, 'I don't know why I am talking like this.'[100]

Merry clearly finds something slightly embarrassing about reflecting in poetic and philosophical language, as if it is unfitting for a hobbit, even a hobbit of a great family. But, as he says, 'it is the way of my people to use light words at such times and say less than we mean. We fear to say too much. It robs us of the right words when a jest is out of place.'[101] This is the heritage he is outgrowing.

98 Kreeft, *Op. Cit.*, p. 13.

99 Tolkien, *The Lord of the Rings*, p. 851.

100 Tolkien, *The Lord of the Rings*, p. 852.

101 *Ibid.*

The Travellers

'But if I may be so bold, you've come back changed from your travels, and you look now like folk as can deal with troubles out of hand.'[102]

If the wisdom of the Rustics may be characterised as a grizzled pragmatism, and that of the Gentlehobbits as polite (but mostly vacuous) frivolity, the effect of leaving the Shire is harder to sum up. The results are wide-ranging: Bilbo returns from his adventure a poet, a coiner of phrases, and a budding polymath; Frodo is wizened but weary and wounded; Merry and Pippin change physically (in both height and garb) and cut a dash with their fair-speech and 'lordliness'; while Sam exchanges private servanthood for public service, restoring the Shire and becoming its Mayor. They no longer fit their former categories, Gentlehobbits or Rustics; they are transformed.

In the strata of the Shire, everyone has their place and should stick to it; the Travellers are the exceptions and therefore become exceptional. After Sam becomes Mayor, Merry the Master of Buckland, and Pippin the Thain, it appears that the Shire-hobbits do manage to make peace with their 'lordly' manner—their exotic clothes, songs, and stories—making it easy to forget how outlandish and disreputable it had formerly been for a hobbit to travel at all, let alone befriend Big People.

Having once been wandering tribes, accustomed to all the hardships and dangers of Middle-earth, the hobbits of the Shire had long since forgotten their former life: they were comfortable, settled, and fat. Everything beyond the Towers to the West and Bree to the East had become alien and untrusted, and leaving the Four Farthings behind was not merely outside the norm or unrecommended, but virtually a death (as it had proved for Bilbo's eccentric Tookish uncles, whose fate was 'hushed up'[103] to avoid public scandal). The Outside and the Big People had become such uncomfortable, disquieting subjects that they began to carry almost the same weight of mysterious unease as Lothlórien did to the Men of Gondor, or the Paths of the Dead to the Rohirrim. Perhaps an occasional Bucklander might still spend a night or two in Bree, but even that was becoming a rarity,[104] making the Wide World a closed book to Shire-hobbits.

102 Tolkien, *The Lord of the Rings,* p. 973.

103 Tolkien, *The Hobbit,* p. 5.

104 Tolkien, *The Lord of the Rings,* p. 147.

Bilbo was first. With a 'Tookish' streak at war with his comfortable Gentlehobbit self-satisfaction, his recruitment by Gandalf and Thorin thrust him out into the Wide World. That he returned from his journey to find his home and belongings being auctioned is far less of a surprise than the fact that it had taken so long for the locals to stop waiting for his return. And when he not only returned, but continued his affiliation with Big People beyond the borders—learning Elvish, and quoting foreign sayings and stories—Bilbo was confirmed as exceptional. Transformed by the world and its wisdom, Bilbo foreshadowed the similar transformations later undergone by Frodo, Sam, Merry, and Pippin.

Due to his ongoing unhobbitlike affiliations, Bilbo brought into the Shire alien sayings and perspectives, and started teaching them. In this way Frodo, having only left Bag End the day before, could use a proverb—*Go not to the Elves for counsel, for they will say both no and yes*—which is clearly imported, since the Shire knows nothing of Elves or their advice.

Frodo learned widely from Bilbo, and after leaving the Shire all four Travellers eagerly absorbed new information: Sam wanted to be taught Gimli's song *In Moria, In Khazad-dûm*, and memorised sayings from Gildor and Haldir; while Pippin was fascinated by Gandalf's rhymes of lore. And as they learned they found guidance and consolation through the folk heritage of lands beyond the Shire.

The proverbs the Travellers learned are distinguishable from Shire-wisdom in several ways. The most easily-recognised are those clearly marked as alien by the speaker, such as *Do not meddle in the affairs of Wizards, for they are subtle and quick to anger*—a saying of Gildor, repeated by Merry, 'which Sam used to quote.'[105] Likewise, *A rope may be a help in many needs* is used by Sam but credited to 'Haldir, or one of those folk,'[106] while the Gaffer's *It's an ill wind as blows nobody any good* is presumably an import from the Elvenking, who said it to Bilbo nearly eighty years earlier. Other Travellers' proverbs can be identified by the sheer unlikeliness of their ever having originated in the Shire. Pippin's *We may stand, if only on one leg, or at least be left still upon our knees* may chime well with Hobbit doggedness, but can have no source from amongst the lived experience of any Shire residents, while Frodo's *The Shadow... can only mock, it cannot make* speaks of a subject so far beyond the comprehension of the gaffers and gammers as to be a fairy-tale.

105 Tolkien, *The Lord of the Rings*, p. 576.

106 Tolkien, *The Lord of the Rings*, p. 595.

Waking Up

> *'If you have walked all these days with closed ears and mind asleep, wake up now!'*[107]

A key fact to recognise is that the Travellers, while never relinquishing their Rustic or Educated roots, are to a degree forced to change. The Rustic philosophy—to do the task at hand and to distrust the unknown—is hopelessly limited outside of the Shire's sheltered existence, while Gentlehobbits' emphasis on well-mannered enjoyment makes them excellent company but of little practical use outside their comfortable lives. 'This is a serious journey not a hobbit walking-party,'[108] as Gandalf admonishes Pippin in Moria.

The Travellers have to adjust and to adapt in order to be more than passengers, and this involves a change in perspective: a recognition of a wider context. This is most clearly seen when Sam describes to Frodo the story they have fallen into—a story that the Shire has all-but ignored, yet goes all the way back to Eärendil, the Silmarils, and beyond. These hobbits are no longer small-minded and self-centred but can acknowledge 'that there is a story behind their story' and that 'what has been gives meaning and context for what is.'[109] Likewise, Merry and Pippin discover that, in comparison to their cosy privileged upbringing, 'There are things deeper and higher; and not a gaffer could tend his garden in what he calls peace but for them, whether he knows about them or not.'[110]

These meditative words show a thoughtfulness that was previously unpresent or unseen, particularly in Merry and Pippin. Merry's wry saying *It's not always a misfortune being overlooked* deserves to be seen in this light: that of a bourgeois hobbit awakening to the bigger picture. The proverb sounds simple enough, but it has multiple applications. Having been unfortunately overlooked for service by Théoden, Merry is then fortunately overlooked by the Witch-king, but only because he was first overlooked (or intentionally ignored) by Elfhelm and others during the ride from Rohan. Yet Merry's journey places the proverb in an even wider context, one in which the mere existence and endurance of Hobbits and their land stems from their being overlooked: Sauron had never

107 Tolkien, *The Lord of the Rings,* p. 737.

108 Tolkien, *The Lord of the Rings,* p. 305.

109 Kurt Bruner & Jim Ware, *Finding God In The Lord of the Rings,* (Tyndale House, 2001), p. xii.

110 Tolkien, *The Lord of the Rings,* p. 852.

heard of the Shire until the imprisonment of Gollum,[111] and Saruman had considered that 'Hobbits are... of no concern.'[112] *It's not always a misfortune being overlooked* is Merry recognising that his personal and physical insignificance, and that of his people, may well be a most fortunate feature.

Returning home, the Travellers become guardians of the wider perspective they have learned. The gaffers and gammers of the Shire may not need to know the full meta-narrative of Middle-earth, but it is important, as Frodo says, for somebody to 'keep alive the memory of the age that is gone.'[113] This becomes the Travellers' task. Pippin and Sam respond by giving significant names to their children,[114] while all five returning hobbits are engaged in the writing of books.[115]

Bilbo Baggins

> *'My dear Bilbo! Something is the matter with you! You are not the hobbit that you were.'*[116]

On the quiet morning when Gandalf first accosted the owner of Bag End outside his round green front door, Bilbo was an overweight, bourgeois stay-at-home (albeit one with a 'Tookish' streak). But in the years between the Unexpected Party and the Long-Expected Party, he had been transformed, becoming the nearest thing to a polymath that the Shire had ever produced. Hobbiton and Bywater looked up at the Hill with distrust and a shaking-of-the-head: the Rustics saying *Bag End's a queer place, and its folk are queerer,* while the Gentlehobbits sighed 'He's mad,' 'mad Baggins,' and 'silly old fool.'[117]

An adventurer, storyteller, scholar, translator, poet, and chronicler, Bilbo started out as none of these things. More silly than sage, there is no

111 Tolkien, *The Lord of the Rings,* p. 58.

112 Tolkien, *The Lord of the Rings,* p. 47.

113 Tolkien, *The Lord of the Rings,* p. 1006.

114 Sam's children include Elanor, Frodo, Merry, Pippin, and Bilbo, while Pippin's only named child is called Faramir.

115 *The Red Book* is written by Bilbo, Frodo, and Sam, and Pippin commissions a copy, named *The Thain's Book,* as well as collecting historical manuscripts from Minas Tirith. Merry is the author/compiler of several volumes, mainly on social history. (Tolkien, *The Lord of the Rings,* p. 14-15).

116 Tolkien, *The Hobbit,* p. 347.

117 Tolkien, *The Lord of the Rings,* p. 30.

sign of the archetypal Traveller that he would become. Before leaving Bag End, Bilbo has little wisdom to share and uses just one proverb—*If you sit on the door-step long enough, you will think of something*—a saying that springs from no greater source of profundity than his regular post-breakfast repose at the entrance of Bag End blowing smoke-rings (though it does happen to prove inadvertently prophetic). But such is the wisdom of the Gentlehobbits.

When Bilbo quotes family sayings—like *Every worm has his weak spot* and *Never laugh at live dragons*—they are more comic than wise, and certainly not learned through hard experience. Far more useful to Bilbo are Rustic-sounding axioms like *A little sleep does a great cure* and *Answers [are] to be guessed not given*. In using them, Bilbo is quoting unsophisticated 'Hobbit-sense'—most likely the words of his tenants and gardeners—and it is clear that, in spite of their vulgar origins, these proverbs travel rather better than the picturesque but frivolous sayings of his own class.

Bilbo's use of proverbs mirrors his development as an individual. As his adventure with the dwarves develops and his experience widens, not only does he increasingly dip into his culture's fund of wise sayings, but he also starts to add to them. This begins up a tree in the shadows of the Misty Mountains (*Escaping goblins to be caught by wolves*, we are told, 'became a proverb'[118]) and continues inside the Lonely Mountain itself (where *Never laugh at live dragons* 'became a favourite saying of his later, and passed into a proverb.'[119]) In both cases, significant lessons are enshrined as memorable sayings. Then, on the return leg of the journey, Mr Baggins changes tack: *Even dragons have their ending* and *Roads go ever ever on* are the wistful, reflective thoughts of the transformed Traveller. But these are just the start.

The Tradition-maker

> *'He was mighty book-learned was dear old Mr. Bilbo. And he wrote poetry.'*[120]

---

118 Tolkien, *The Hobbit*, p. 115.

119 Tolkien, *The Hobbit*, p. 263. Olga Trokhimenko observes that this latter account 'is nothing less than a description of an evolution of a proverb in a nutshell' (Olga Trokhimenko, 'The Function of Proverbs in J.R.R. Tolkien's *Hobbit*,' *Proverbium 20*, (University of Vermont, 2003), p. 374), detailing the process by which a phrase or exclamation becomes part of oral tradition.

120 Tolkien, *The Lord of the Rings*, p. 181.

The Travellers are each affected in different ways by their experiences. Bilbo leaves behind Shire parochialism and embraces an ongoing engagement with the Outside, becoming a learner and writer of significance. As well as coining proverbs, his affinity for telling stories (not least of his own escapades) in turn leads him into discovering, translating, and writing a great number of songs and poems.

While some of Bilbo's verses are standard Shire-fare, dealing with baths, inns, and hearty fireside meals, there are others with which no Gentlehobbit would feel at home. 'The Fall of Gil-galad' (sung by Sam at Weathertop) and 'Eärendil was a Mariner' (debuted by its writer in the Hall of Fire at Rivendell) present ancient historical fact anew, while 'The Road Goes Ever On and On' is an entirely new invention and each of its three versions reflect Bilbo's changing worldview and philosophy. It is first heard as 'Roads Go Ever Ever On' in the final pages of *The Hobbit*, and is principally about returning home from the wonders of the Wide World. The second version appears twice in the early chapter of *The Lord of the Rings*, recited once by Bilbo and then by Frodo, and reflects the understanding of life as a journey, with a rarely-predictable route and an unknown destination—the core philosophical lesson learned in common by the Travellers. The third version, spoken by Bilbo in Rivendell after the destruction of the Ring, speaks of leaving the Road for others to follow, and turning instead to 'evening-rest and sleep,' imagery of peaceful death.

The highpoint, both of Bilbo's proverb-making and his verse-writing, comes late in life, in exile in Rivendell; a place in which the only other mortal he might regularly see is Aragorn. After meeting the *Dúnadan* and hearing his story, Bilbo writes an eight-line poem for him, a poem made up of four proverbs and four prophecies:

'All that is gold does not glitter
Not all those who wander are lost;
The old that is strong does not wither,
Deep roots are not reached by the frost.

From the ashes a fire shall be woken,
A light from the shadows shall spring;
Renewed shall be blade that was broken:
The crownless again shall be king.'[121]

121 Tolkien, *The Lord of the Rings*, p. 241.

The Bilbo of these lines is a far cry from the ridiculous host of the Unexpected Party. Each word carries weight and each line stands alone. We do not know the source of the poem's proverbs, but they are rooted in common imagery—gold, walking, growing—to express the truth that even familiar items may be assessed inaccurately.

Aragorn, the poem says, is easy to underestimate: he is royal but has no crown; he is heir to a kingdom but wanders in homelessness; he is the last smoking embers of a once-great fire; he is a deeply-rooted tree forced to survive the frosts of winter.[122] As one of an underestimated, overlooked people, Bilbo may have sympathised with the lowly reception given to this son of kings. These four proverbs are an attempt to redress this misjudgement, by undermining the assumption that 'what you see is what you get.'

As the poem shifts from proverb to prophecy, it mirrors the shift in subject matter from the general to the specific—from principles to the person whom the principles describe. The proverbs, as proverbs should, deal with and describe truths that should apply anywhere, but the second stanza describes the foreseen return of the King, concluding with two lines that relate solely to Aragorn.

The result is so effective that Gandalf and Aragorn both have the poem memorised, and its recitation at the Council of Elrond suggests that it is also familiar to all the community of Imladris. Having been 'the wonder of the Shire for sixty years'[123] Bilbo has also become the wonder of Rivendell.

Tempting and Warning

Bilbo never aspires to be anything other than a Hobbit, and sayings of both the Rustics and the Gentlehobbits remain on his lips throughout his later life, but in many ways he outgrows them. The extra width of his worldview means that practical advice (like *Don't let your heads get too big for your hats,* given to Merry and Pippin in Rivendell) and simple, joyful truths (like *A loon is he that will not sing,* from the Bath Song)

122 Tom Shippey takes this thought further by identifying the proverb-stanza as 'anti-gnomic'—when something is described through what it isn't (or what it fails to do) rather than what it is. (Shippey, *Roots and Branches*, p. 310.) By contrast, Treebeard's song that begins 'Learn now the lore of living creatures' is an example of a gnomic poem, with its definition by description.

123 Tolkien, *The Lord of the Rings,* p. 1.

that reflect the priorities of the Shire come to take second place to the deeper life-lesson he seeks to convey: that *It's a dangerous business going out of your door.*

> *You step into the Road, and if you don't keep your feet, there is no knowing where you might be swept off to.*

Bilbo (with a little nudge from Gandalf) had been swept away, and in using such a saying to Frodo, he is both tempting and warning—it is clear that the Tookish streak and solid, respectable Baggins are at war in his heir as well. *The Road goes ever on and on,* Frodo is told, and the warnings continue in *When pools are black and trees are bare 'tis evil in the wild to fare* and *Surely there are many perils in the world* (the latter used by Frodo, but presumably learned from his uncle).

Piecing these proverbs together, a coherent message emerges: quests come with a cost. Bilbo has had his life transformed, and though he doesn't regret that change he is determined to make it clear to those hobbits who would follow him, and especially to Frodo, that *Adventures are not all pony-rides in May-sunshine.* Once you step into that Road, saying yes to the dormant Tookish streak and to the lure of the world Outside, *There is no real going back.*

Frodo Baggins

One of the great proverbial moments of *The Lord of the Rings* occurs when Frodo, Pippin, and Sam encounter Gildor Inglorion and his company in the Woody End. Despite having never left the Shire, Frodo is well enough equipped to greet these High-Elves with *Elen sila lumenn' omentielvo* and to thank them at dinner in their own language. Moreover, he has learned enough proverbial wisdom to spar playfully with Gildor:

> 'It is said: *Do not meddle in the affairs of Wizards, for they are subtle and quick to anger.* The choice is yours: to go or to wait.'
> 'And it is also said,' answered Frodo: '*Go not to the Elves for counsel, for they will say both no and yes.*'
> 'Is it indeed?' laughed Gildor.[124]

124 Tolkien, *The Lord of the Rings,* p. 82-83.

Gildor responds to Frodo's use of a proverb—a proverb of unknown provenance, but almost certainly brought into the Shire by Bilbo—with an onslaught of his own sayings: *Seldom give unguarded advice*; *Advice is a dangerous gift, even from the wise to the wise*; and *All courses may run ill*. The effect is partly rhetorical: any one of these sayings would have sufficed, but by using all three Gildor can gently put the hobbit in his place by hinting that he has 'plenty more where that came from.'

Gandalf aside, this is Frodo's first real engagement with non-Shire culture, and it sees him both honoured and humbled. He is honoured because Gildor has no obligation to justify himself before a mere hobbit, and in choosing to do so therefore raises Frodo to the status of peer. And he is humbled because in that single moment Frodo exchanges his status as most worldly-wise hobbit in the Shire—a big fish in a small pond—for the realisation that he is a rank beginner when it comes to life Outside. Frodo doesn't use proverbs with Big People thereafter.

Having been orphaned at a young age and brought up 'any old how' in Brandy Hall, Frodo had been an irresponsible youth—'one of the worst young rascals of Buckland'[125] according to Farmer Maggot. That he comes to be considered, by Elrond at least, as among the great of the elf-friends—Beren, Túrin and all—is a testament to the transformative effect of his experiences, but also to the formative role of Bilbo. Frodo not only becomes the confidant of Bilbo, learning the truth about the Quest of Erebor and the Ring, but also his pupil and the heir to the old hobbit's learning. He is instructed in Elvish,[126] has been taught a good deal of history (at least enough to know about Gil-galad and the Last Alliance), and receives an inheritance of experience and wisdom unprecedented in the Shire.

A Mine of Wisdom

Unlike the extroverted Bilbo, Frodo is not an outward-processor; he is quiet, wistful, often solitary, and keeps his thoughts to himself. Between Bree and Rauros—the period during which he is a follower, not the leader—Frodo only gives his opinion twice, and on each occasion (on the pass of Caradhras, and at Parth Galen) he has to have it demanded from him. But this is not because he has nothing to say or no wisdom to offer.

125 Tolkien, *The Lord of the Rings*, p. 91.

126 His greeting to Gildor is in Quenya, while he is expected to understand the Sindarin *Dúnadan* when he meets Aragorn in Rivendell.

'He was seldom moved to make song or rhyme... though his memory was stored with many things that others had made before him.'[127]

Frodo is a mine of wisdom, but this only becomes apparent when he is burdened with the responsibility of leadership. Specifically, it is in the context of his inward debates that we see his most thoughtful applications of proverbs, as he turns them over in his mind, seeking guidance. On the long march from Emyn Muil to Mount Doom, Frodo knows that he cannot rely on Sam for more than companionable stolidity, and he is wary of trusting Gollum at all. Proverbs therefore become his primary counsellor at need. *Better mistrust undeserved than rash words,* he reminds himself when longing and fearing to open up to Faramir; *Do not be too eager to deal out death in the name of justice* rings through his memory when presented with the chance to kill Gollum; and *The servant has a claim on the master for service, even service in fear* comes to mind when wishing to be free of his wretched guide. These sayings are unspoken—they are reported as thoughts, not speech—but their use appears instinctive to Frodo, even in moments of great stress, suggesting that it must be a long-learned trait.

Proverbs clearly play a fundamental part in Frodo's decision-making, but he does not quote tradition in conversation as part of an effusive vocabulary (as do Gandalf or Faramir), or as a means of presenting his perspective to others (like Boromir or Gimli). Frodo's wisdom heritage is practical guide to determining a course of action, but is only used when there is no other person to consult. When authority to make decisions lies with him, Frodo uses proverbs; and when it doesn't, he doesn't.

A Jewel Among Hobbits

The name Frodo comes from the Old English *Fróda*, meaning 'wise by experience' or 'the wise one.'[128] It is fair to say that even before leaving the Shire, Frodo is wise beyond the scope of most of his contemporaries, due to his awareness of the high, the noble, and Middle-earth's meta-narrative of good and evil, but his experiences outside the Four Farthings stretch and deepen his wisdom. Frodo changes.

To take the example of motivation, Frodo's decision to accept the burden of the Ring is initially motivated by love for his home, and the deter-

127 Tolkien, *The Lord of the Rings,* p. 350.

128 Shippey, *The Road to Middle-earth*, p. 206.

mination to safeguard and preserve the Shire.[129] But as the Quest continues, Frodo's purposes change. Even in the House of Elrond he foresees no ending other than the dark and unpleasant,[130] and by the time he reaches Ithilien his motivating factor is no longer success, but obligation: 'I am bound, by a solemn undertaking to the Council, to find a way or perish in the seeking'[131] he says to Faramir.

This change—from pursuing a Happy Ending to remaining faithful to a vow—is a matter of moral philosophy. Frodo's ethos, originally based on pursuing ideal results and consequences, has swung in the direction of Deontological ethics, meaning that he is now motivated principally by doing his duty.[132] Crawling through Mordor, and even up Mount Doom itself, Frodo embodies this dutiful worldview. He has promised, therefore he has to fulfil his promise. 'Can you manage it?' asks Sam. 'I must' is the reply.[133]

> *'I am commanded to go to the land of Mordor, and therefore I shall go… What comes after must come.'*[134]

The proverb *What comes after must come* is what might be expected from one of the more fatalistic peoples of Middle-earth—Treebeard and the Ents perhaps—not from one of the Halflings, who are optimistic and practical, and who say *All's well as ends well.* But Frodo has outgrown satisfaction-through-results and ceased to be goal-oriented, instead seeking only to fulfil his present obligation. As for results? Well, *It's no good worrying about tomorrow,* Frodo's philosophy now tells him, *it probably won't come.*

In the event, Frodo fulfils his vow and achieves the desired result as well—the Ring is destroyed, the Enemy is defeated, and the Shire is saved. Yet this is a Pyrrhic victory for Frodo, who is both wounded beyond healing and uncelebrated by the Shire-folk he had set out to save. Having given

129 'I should like to save the Shire, if I could' he says when still in Bag End. 'I feel that as long as the Shire lies behind, safe and comfortable, I shall find wandering more bearable: I shall know that somewhere there is a firm foothold.' (Tolkien, *The Lord of the Rings,* p. 61.)

130 Tolkien, *The Lord of the Rings,* p. 266.

131 Tolkien, *The Lord of the Rings,* 677.

132 In the view of Immanuel Kant, this would make Frodo truly virtuous, since 'Moral worth exists only when a man acts from a sense of duty.' (Bertrand Russell, *The History of Western Philosophy,* (Psychology Press, 2004), p. 644).

133 Tolkien, *The Lord of the Rings,* p. 913.

134 Tolkien, *The Lord of the Rings,* p. 624.

up the pursuit of a happy ending, he does not receive one, though he does achieve it for others. 'I tried to save the Shire,' he says, 'and it has been saved, but not for me.'[135]

After returning, Frodo may even go so far as to believe that he has not kept his vow. In his darker moments, he appears to see himself as a failure, because he could not ultimately give up the Ring of his own choice and is tempted to regret its destruction. His name may mean 'wise by experience' but it is hard to see any of his companions recognising these post-Quest thoughts as wisdom. Frodo cannot enjoy the Shire, and his final proverb explains the twin senses of hollowness and fulfilment he feels:

> *It must often be so, when things are in danger: some one has to give them up, lose them, so that others may keep them.*

The Hobbits: Remembering the Greatness of the World

The Shire is 'full of riddles, proverbs, and proverbial expressions,'[136] and yet, in spite of their oral traditions, the Hobbits 'had begun to forget: forget their own beginnings and legends, forget what little they had known about the greatness of the world. It was not yet gone, but it was getting buried: the memory of the high and the perilous.'[137]

In the Shire-society of Bilbo's early years, the high is shunned and the perilous kept beyond the borders by the Rangers' unseen guard. The Shire may be protected but it is also emasculated, producing Rustics with practical wisdom but small minds, and an effete class of Gentlehobbits who have records of former days but who rarely bother with them. Gandalf, as a steward of 'all worthy things that are in peril,'[138] describes in *Unfinished Tales* his intention to put this problem right. 'But' he observes 'you cannot teach that sort of thing to a whole people quickly... you must begin at some point, with some one person.'[139]

---

135 Tolkien, *The Lord of the Rings*, p. 1006.

136 Trokhimenko, *Op. Cit.*, p. 367.

137 JRR Tolkien, *Unfinished Tales of Númenor and Middle-earth* (Houghton Mifflin, 1980) p. 331.

138 Tolkien, *The Lord of the Rings*, p. 742.

139 Tolkien, *Unfinished Tales*, p. 331.

That person is Bilbo, and with him the wider story of Middle-earth is reintroduced into the Shire, later to be enlarged through the other Travellers. But remembering the greatness of the world does not devalue the place of the diminutive and meek; the Hobbits' simple contribution is affirmed as an integral and value-bringing part of the heroic whole. Without the uncluttered simplicity of the Shire to fight for, the high and heroic lacks meaning.

Merry and Pippin recognise that Tooks and Brandybucks 'can't live long on the heights'—they are not kings or wizards or warriors, and don't want to be. 'But' says Merry, 'we can now see them, and honour them.'[140] In becoming aware of the Big Picture, they perceive the valued place of Rustics and Gentlehobbits within it.

In a world containing not only Elves, Dwarves, and Men, but also Ents, Eagles, Istari, and the Powers, the Shire-folk do not need to emulate (or dominate) bigger people in order to fulfil their task or achieve their potential. In fact they benefit from their smallness: Smaug's stronghold is penetrated by the quiet feet and unfamiliar smell of a Hobbit burglar; Saruman is swept away by an Entish avalanche started by the 'small stones' of a Took and a Brandybuck;[141] and Sauron is defeated because of Frodo and Sam's insignificance; they succeed while the eyes of the great are elsewhere.

In the Quest of Erebor and the War of the Ring hobbits play roles of such unforeseen significance that Gandalf's original stewardly purpose is obscured, but it is not forgotten. As Frodo, Sam, Merry, and Pippin finally leave Bree and head for home, the wizard informs them that he will not be returning to the Shire, and that they must now settle its affairs themselves. 'That's what you've been trained for,' he says. 'Do you not understand?'[142] That training, beginning with Bilbo nearly seventy years earlier, becomes the Travellers' responsibility to pass on.

The leaf-mould of Tolkien's early years in rural Warwickshire gave life to a unique people, culture, and wisdom. Hobbits would never be so presumptuous or highfaluting as to call their proverbs a 'philosophical heritage,' but that is what 'Hobbit-sense' is. Supplemented by the accounts of their friends and the learning of the Wise, Shire-wisdom becomes perhaps the most grounded and well-rounded of Middle-earth's oral

140 Tolkien, *The Lord of the Rings,* p. 852.

141 Tolkien, *The Lord of the Rings,* p. 485.

142 Tolkien, *The Lord of the Rings,* p. 974.

traditions. Heroic but humble, educated but pragmatic, parochial yet aware of the great tale into which it has fallen, Hobbit-sense is rooted in the soil of the Shire, but has grown.

> *'You are grown up now. Grown indeed very high; among the great you are, and I have no longer any fear at all for any of you.'*[143]

143 *Ibid.*

CHAPTER TWO

BOMBADIL AND GOLDBERRY

'Tell me, if my asking does not seem foolish, who is Tom Bombadil?'
'He is,' said Goldberry… smiling.[144]

An old battered hat with a long blue feather stuck in the band bobs into view: the mysterious Tom Bombadil. Who is he? Elrond names him *Iarwain Ben-adar*, 'oldest and fatherless,'[145] but Bombadil himself gives no answer, only repeating his name and continuing on his sing-song way.

Tom does not age or change, he has neither father nor children, armour nor weapons, but he can speak with authority to Barrow-wights and to bad-hearted trees, and even appears unaffected by the Ring.[146] He is a delightful mystery with a long story.

'Eldest, that's what I am. Mark my words, my friends: Tom was here before the river and the trees; Tom remembers the first raindrop and the first acorn. He made paths before the Big People, and saw the Little People arriving. He was here before the Kings and the graves and the Barrow-wights. When the Elves passed westward,

144 Tolkien, *The Lord of the Rings*, p. 122.

145 Tolkien, *The Lord of the Rings*, p. 258.

146 Leading Jonathan Witt and Jay W. Richards to speculate that he may be 'an exercise in one of the great theological what ifs'—an entirely unfallen or uncorrupted creature (Jonathan Witt & Jay W. Richards, *The Hobbit Party* (Ignatius Press, 2014), p. 37).

> *Tom was here already, before the seas were bent. He knew the dark under the stars when it was fearless—before the Dark Lord came from Outside.'*[147]

A teller of long tales and a singer of ridiculous songs, Bombadil's words carry weight, in spite of their almost-constant silliness. Having lived through the great story of Middle-earth—seeing it, enduring it, and flourishing in the midst of it—he can speak with authority.

As with the Ents, the Istari, and the Elves, Bombadil's ageless longevity (and that of his wife, the similarly mysterious River-daughter, Goldberry) makes something of a mockery of the idea of an 'oral tradition.' Poems, stories, and songs are constantly in his mouth, but since he has no previous generation to receive them from and no new generation to teach them to, we are left to wonder why such vessels of transmission are being used at all.

And then there are the proverbs themselves. *Heed no nightly noise*, says Tom at bedtime, and *Some things are ill to hear when the world's in shadow*, as if being scared of the dark is a deep matter for lore. But then again, maybe it is. After all, Tom had lived through the 'terror of darkness,'[148] when the primeval trees that originally lit the world were destroyed and the harmless twilight beneath the stars became 'a cloak of darkness... an Unlight.'[149] Bombadil therefore remembers that darkness and shadow may be more than an absence of illumination: they can be a malevolent force in themselves, worthy of warning—worthy of a proverb.

The Power of Light and Colour

Old Tom Bombadil is a merry fellow;
Bright blue his jacket is, and his boots are yellow.

The Ring is on its way to the Land of Shadow, where the Dark Lord sits in his Dark Tower. The hobbits have fled from the Black Breath of the Black Riders into the tangled gloom of the Old Forest, where 'some shadow of the Great Darkness'[150] remains. Frodo is beset by the same darknesses Bombadil remembers. In the absence of a Star-glass or a White Rider, into

147 Tolkien, *The Lord of the Rings*, p. 129.

148 JRR Tolkien, *The Silmarillion* (Houghton Mifflin, 2001), p. 95.

149 Tolkien, *The Silmarillion*, p. 74.

150 Tolkien, *The Lord of the Rings*, p. 457.

his darkness comes a different light, a light resplendent in colour: yellow boots, blue coat, long brown beard, bright blue eyes, and face as red as a ripe apple. No shadowy evil can come near such bright vivacious colour.

Likewise, Goldberry—her name itself colour-filled—is described primarily for her hue: the yellowness of her hair, the reed-green and dew-silver of her gown, the forget-me-not blue studding her golden belt. She sits enthroned in the midst of bright white lilies floating in their brown and green vessels, recognising in Frodo an elf-friend by the light in his eyes and the ring in his voice.

> *'Here's my Goldberry clothed all in silver-green with flowers in her girdle! Is the table laden? I see yellow cream and honeycomb, and white bread, and butter; milk, cheese, and green herbs and ripe berries gathered. Is that enough for us?'*

With such constant splashes of light and colour, the house of Tom Bombadil appears at first to be cartoonish and garishly gaudy. The reality, however, is far deeper, though hidden in plain sight. Holding in memory the reality of darkness as a malevolent force, Tom and the River-daughter see light and colour as an absence of evil, and have consequently filled their home with the full spectrum, making it a fortress against the encroaching dark of the Forest, the Downs, and the world Outside. Their colours—and the colourful nature of their melodic speech—become weapons, beating back the black of evil with fearless merry brightness.

Get out you old Wight! Vanish in the sunlight!

The power of this vivacious light is demonstrated when Bombadil rescues the hobbits from the 'Night under Night' of the Wight's barrow. Having been brought back out into the light of the Sun, 'the horror faded out of their hearts as they looked at him, and saw the merry glint in his eyes.'[151] Dread and fear cannot abide old Tom's melodies and colours. Indeed, Glorfindel implies that, in spite of appearances, Bombadil could resist the strength of the Dark Lord longest of all—longer even than Galadriel, Elrond, Gandalf, and Círdan—but not for ever. And if he fell, light itself would cease:

> *'Could that power be defied by Bombadil alone? I think not. I think that in the end, if all else is conquered, Bombadil will fall, Last as he was First; and then Night will come.'*[152]

151 Tolkien, *The Lord of the Rings*, p. 140.

152 Tolkien, *The Lord of the Rings*, p. 259.

Rhyme and Reason

In Tom's hands, the simple matter of light and colour is revealed to be a topic of profound gravity, and other hidden depths also emerge, for example in Goldberry's cheery proverb *Make haste while the Sun shines!*[153] This appears at first to be nothing more complex or profound than an encouragement to make the most of fine travelling weather, but when taken in conjunction with her longevous perspective it can also become a reminder of a far weightier concept: the brevity of mortal life.

The River-daughter is almost certainly a Maia[154] and hence older than the Sun itself, meaning that all the years since it[155] first rose to light the world are short to her. She knows that the Sun has not shone forever, nor will it continue perpetually—time is short. Hobbits, like all mortals, know little of the nature and origins of the Sun and cannot conceive of the world before it, let alone after it. Their lives are, in comparison to Bombadil and Goldberry, brief to the point of insignificance, but they do not know it; it makes sense that there should be a proverb to remind them. While the mortal and immortal live on different time-scales, both have lives that will end in darkness: either the darkness of death or of the end of days. They must each make haste before the light fails.

Whilst such profundities as these are occasionally perceivable, giving more purpose to their proverbs, at other times it seems that the sayings and songs of Bombadil and Goldberry have no intent behind them at all. Instead of teaching, the mercurial couple delight in the poetic rhythms of proverbs for the same reason they constantly break into song: for the sheer joy of it.

Hey dol! Merry dol! Ring a dong dillo!
Ring a dong! Hop along! Fal lal the willow!
Tom Bom, jolly Tom, Tom Bombadillo!

But what is the source of this melodic joy? Ursula K Le Guin observes that Bombadil's patterns of speech are insistently lyrical and rhythmic because he is 'profoundly in touch with… the great, natural rhythms of day and night, season, growth and death.'[156]

153 A variation of the old saw 'Make hay while the Sun shines.'

154 Possibly one of those who entered Middle-earth in the First Age, as did Melian the wife of Thingol.

155 Or more properly 'she.'

156 Ursula K Le Guin, 'Rhythmic Pattern,' *Meditations on Middle-earth*, Karen Haber, Editor (Byron Press, 2001), p. 103.

Long tales
are thirsty,
and long listening
is hungry.

It might be said that Bombadil and Goldberry are so in step with the macro-rhythms of the natural world that their house has become a concert hall of micro-rhythms, of rhymes and songs and dances. Rather than being an exercise in Lore, the poetic inflections and cadences of their axioms are employed because they are enjoyed, and the hobbits soon fall into song themselves 'as if it was easier and more natural than talking.'[157] In a world like Arda, which was sung into being, it is fitting that the most entirely uncorrupted of its inhabitants are still continuing that heritage of joyous melody.

Cynical Silliness

More than just being in step with it, Bombadil and Goldberry appear to be a personification of the natural world: its rhythms, colours, and melodies. They have no angst, built on the kind of indifference to civilisation that might be felt by a tree or river, and is indeed felt by the Ents of Fangorn and Wild-men of Drúadan Forest. When Shippey describes Bombadil's major quality as an unpremeditated naturalness,[158] it therefore suggests the philosophical tradition of Diogenes and the Cynics, those ancient Greeks who sought to expose the falsehoods and conceits of conventional society by living according to nature.

The school of thought propagated by the Cynics 'did not teach abstinence from the good things of this world, but only a certain indifference to them.'[159] Cynics were therefore ascetics, owning little and desiring no more, and—echoing Bombadil's flippant attitude to the Ring—they rejected the things other people found valuable. While Bombadil and Goldberry never go to the extent of living in a ceramic jar and surviving on onions *á la* Diogenes, their 'naturalness' is certainly Cynical (in the Classical sense), and proverbs like *Clothes are but little loss, if you escape from drowning* reflect a choice to focus on things of deeper worth and reject the superfluous.

157 Tolkien, *The Lord of the Rings*, p. 123.

158 Shippey, *The Road to Middle-earth*, p. 106.

159 Russell, *Op. Cit.*, p. 223.

Bombadil and Goldberry: the shallow deeps

There is a paradox at the heart of this happy couple: the 'deeper things' upon which they focus do not appear to be deep. In avoiding what they consider superfluous, they have chosen to take silliness seriously, capering and chorusing in unabashed childlike joy. Tom refuses to travel with Frodo and Company to Bree, in spite of their peril, because he has 'important' work to do: 'my making and my singing, my talking and my walking.'[160] To Tom and the River-daughter, the Ring—upon which the fate of Middle-earth hangs—is not a matter of great significance.[161]

Frodo and Company are left scratching their heads at the absurdity of these ancient children and their gaudy, melodic, merry wisdom. The proverbs they hear are not worldly-wise and offer very little practical assistance in the Wild—*Be bold, but wary* and *Sharp blades are good to have* are as helpful as Tom's words go. Instead of profound counsel to navigate the vagaries of existence, the subjects with which Bombadil and Goldberry's wisdom concerns itself are the simple things of their simple lives. Eating and drinking, entertaining and being entertained are the weighty philosophical activities that abound in their home. Courage, war, justice, death, and the wider world are off the radar.

So, Tom Bombadil: Who is he? What is he? We are never told, only shown. With an armful of lilies and a mouthful of song, the first Edenic colours and melodies of creation live on in his house, and darkness is kept at bay. But Tom has renounced power and influence, shutting himself in a little land[162] where all things 'belong each to themselves.'[163] These geographical limitations release him to relish and revel in the simple unadorned beauty he sees: his wife and his horse, food and drink, lilies and light and laughter. They are all he wants or needs. To Tom, the serious tasks of life—the matters for deep lore—are flower gathering and the bright colours of his clothes, while *Goldberry is waiting* is argument enough to excuse him from all the quests, adventures, and activities of the world.

160 Tolkien, *The Lord of the Rings*, p. 142.

161 Gandalf warns the Council of Elrond that were they to entrust the Ring to Bombadil, he would probably lose it or even throw it away (Tolkien, *The Lord of the Rings*, p. 259).

162 Excepting his brief excursions down the Withywindle to Buckland and the Marish—where he evidently knew Farmer Maggot—as versified in 'Bombadil Goes Boating' from *The Adventures of Tom Bombadil*.

163 Tolkien, *The Lord of the Rings*, p. 122.

CHAPTER THREE

THE BREELANDERS

Strange as News from Bree

While the peoples and nations of Middle-earth maintain varying degrees of interdependence—the trade-links between Dorwinion and Esgaroth, the collaborative relationship between Eregion and Moria, and the military pact between Rohan and Gondor to name but three—the general rule is for separateness, not intermingling. Sometimes this self-sufficiency and self-reliance is caused by distrust, betrayal, or conflict,[164] but more often it is no more than an outworking of geographic isolation or a healthy sense of liberty. And just as the languages Sindar and Quenya became distinct due to the geographical separation of the Grey-elves and the High-elves, the prevailing spirit of independence and autonomy in Middle-earth contributes to its diversity of cultures and worldviews. Every nation has a differing philosophy, and no universally-held *lingua franca* of wisdom has developed—the peoples of Middle-earth simply differ too much and congregate too little for that.

But one truly 'mixed society' did exist. At the confluence of the two great highways of Eriador, a little land lay that was not only a geographical crossing-point but also a cultural one. Four villages and the small, cultivated region around it; a home to hobbits, men, and news from distant countries: the Bree-land.

164 Such as the estrangement between the Rohirrim and their neighbours the Dunlendings.

'Nowhere else in the world was this peculiar (but excellent) arrangement to be found.'[165]

Bree-men

This territory, and more specifically its main township of Bree, was by the end of the Third Age one of the oldest continually-occupied settlements of Men in Middle-earth, and the most westerly of all.[166] The Men of Bree—short, fat, and cheerfully independent—appear not to have been numbered among the Edain, but to be descended from lesser peoples from whom also came the Dunlendings and other non-Númenórean inhabitants of Eriador. They 'belonged to nobody but themselves'[167] and had endured, according to their own accounts, since the Elder Days.

The Bree-men had settled at the intersection of the Greenway and the Great East Road, and these two thoroughfares provide a glimpse of what their land became. The former, running from Fornost Erain in the north to Osgiliath in the south, was built by the Dúnedain to link their capital cities of Arnor and Gondor; while the latter had been constructed by the Dwarves in the First Age in order to speed travel between their settlements in Lune and those in the distant East. Two highways, two distinct cultures; one crossing-point.

Bree-hobbits

The Bree-land was also believed to be the oldest permanent settlement of hobbits in the world, although the subsequent colonies of the Shire and Buckland were much larger. By the time of Frodo's visit hobbits had been living in the Bree-land for around seventeen hundred years, primarily in holes dug into the Bree-hill itself.[168] It was at Bree that the three tribes of the *Holbytlan*—Stoors, Fallowhides, and Harfoots—first re-amalgamated, having lived scattered throughout Eriador and Wilderland over previous wandering centuries, and the 'Little-folk' were considered an intrinsic part of Bree life.

165 Tolkien, *The Lord of the Rings*, p. 146.

166 *Ibid.*

167 *Ibid.*

168 'Bree-hill' is a tautology, since the word 'Bree' is a variant on the Old English word for 'hill.'

Whilst not being particularly remarkable in other ways, the Bree-hobbits were famous for, and proud of, being the originators of an addictive art: the smoking of *sweet galenas* or 'pipe-weed.'[169] This habit, championed in Bree, spread around the known world from that acknowledged epicentre.

These men and hobbits were not in competition, but had come to regard each other as mutually-exclusive but necessary parts of the Bree-folk. Their relationship is expressive of the nature of their land: accepting and welcoming, but still maintaining an independent identity.

BARLIMAN BUTTERBUR

> *'A worthy man, but his memory is like a lumber-room: thing wanted always buried.'*[170]

It seems that Bree—and in particular its inn, *The Prancing Pony*—had by the end of the Third Age learned the trick of hearing all the news of all the lands. The Outsiders passing through the *Pony*'s common room passed on their outlandish tales, songs, and sayings, to the point that, when confronted with anything odd or peculiar, Shire-hobbits were accustomed to shrug their shoulders and say *Strange as News from Bree*.

The likelihood is that Bree owed its continued existence to being a staging post on the trade-routes of Eriador: its strategic location meant that virtually everyone on the road would have stayed there. The consequent wealth of the nations passing through would have guaranteed a degree of prosperity to Bree in peace-time, though the demise of Arnor, Tharbad, Eregion, and Moria meant that by the time of Frodo's visit, Bree's fortunes had long been in decline.

We are told that the Bree-folk 'were more friendly and familiar with Hobbits, Dwarves, Elves, and other inhabitants of the world about them than was (or is) usual,'[171] but the plain fact is that they had to be. With its prosperity tied to travellers, Bree had to be a place of welcome or it would not have survived. And as the principal hub of hospitality and community life, *The Prancing Pony* and its proprietor came to epitomise Bree's attitude to outsiders.

---

169 Tolkien, *The Lord of the Rings*, p. 8.

170 Tolkien, *The Lord of the Rings*, p. 167.

171 Tolkien, *The Lord of the Rings*, p. 146.

Barliman Butterbur's profession is welcoming people: providing them with food and fire, privacy if necessary, company if willing. All-comers are made at home, and Butterbur (who inherited *The Pony* as the family business) would have grown up familiar with a scene wherein locals mix with adventurous Bucklanders, mysterious Rangers, émigré Dunlendings, tramping companies of dwarves, and other travellers—not to mention Gandalf.

Whilst playing host to this melting-pot of influences, it is also clear that Butterbur and his contemporaries do not travel, are not particularly learnéd, and are thoroughly suspicious of, and easily alarmed by, the unknown. Indeed, even the words 'history' and 'geography' are rare in the Bree-dialect.[172]

Having lived his entire life in the cosmopolitan world of *The Pony*'s common-room, Butterbur would have had ample opportunity (had he the inclination) to learn all that could be learned—to become an amateur lore-master like Bilbo or Frodo. But in that he had no interest. 'I'm all for Bree'[173] he declares in his defence. Like the other locals in the common-room, Butterbur may hear the proverbs of other lands but he has no desire to learn them, and this leaves Bree with an unexpectedly meagre wisdom tradition.

'One Thing Drives Out Another'

On the arrival of Frodo and his friends, the innkeeper's world is presented to them: warm and kind, but narrow and hurried. Butterbur's conversation—an endless stream-of-consciousness gallop of gossiping chitchat—is dominated by small worries and the practicalities of the daily grind, and the proverbs he uses are of the same ilk; obviously not glamorous imports from far nations. For example, in the hustle and bustle of the inn *It never rains but it pours*, and, as a consequence, *One thing drives out another* (including things of obvious importance like Gandalf's letter, or the damage done to the Shire). Butterbur loves to sigh and grumble, but with a shake of the head and a shrug of the shoulders he keeps plodding onwards, saying *What's done can't be undone*.

These proverbs are all truisms—they describe reality but contain neither particular insight nor poetic value—and are limited to the narrow scope

172 Tolkien, *The Lord of the Rings*, p. 152.
173 Tolkien, *The Lord of the Rings*, p. 969.

of Butterbur's interests. And as native Bree-wisdom, they also exhibit the village's attitude to the outside world. One moment the inn-keeper is inviting his guests to join the company, assuring them that 'We like to hear a bit of news, or any story or song you may have in mind,'[174] and the next he is explaining 'We're a bit suspicious round here of anything out of the way.'[175] This contradiction is perplexing. Does Bree really have an appetite for the unusual, or does it only want news that isn't actually new?

The roaming ranger, Strider—one of the main contributors of the out-of-the-way to the *Pony*—is apparently both shunned *and* eagerly listened to; valued as a news-source or story-teller but not as a person. Likewise, Mr Underhill's company are afforded a chorus of welcome to the common-room, but within minutes of taking Frodo to their hearts the locals completely withdraw their warmth, and in the end no one even bids the guests goodnight. Butterbur's stock-phrases express the same contradiction: *Make yourselves at home!* he says, and *As you please!*—the classic axioms of an hospitable nature. But he is just as likely to warn *There's no accounting for East or West* ('meaning the Rangers and the Shire-folk, begging your pardon'[176]) or to repeat the Bree-land mantra, *We want to be let alone!*

Butterbur and Bree therefore have a paradox at their heart: they are open yet closed; hospitable yet suspicious; well-informed yet small-minded and ignorant. This incongruity is not without its causes. Bree is a welcoming place because it has to be—valuable income is generated from the business of Outsiders—but at the same time, Outside is also where all things dark and dangerous originate, things to be avoided at all costs. Pulled in both directions at once (and with no military strength nor any other means by which to defend themselves), the underlying fears of the Bree-folk cause them to hold anything untoward or alien—such as Mr Underhill's 'accident'—at arm's length; something to be feared, not understood or braved.[177]

Due to this wariness and distrust of all things Outside, Butterbur (like his beloved land) is far less than the potential sum of his parts. Clearly a

174 Tolkien, *The Lord of the Rings*, p. 151.

175 Tolkien, *The Lord of the Rings*, p. 158.

176 Tolkien, *The Lord of the Rings*, p. 153.

177 It is worth noting that when danger does come to Bree, the locals choose to stay at home and bar their doors rather than attempt any more courageous response. (Tolkien, *The Lord of the Rings*, p. 970.)

good person—and trusted by Gandalf, who says, 'He thinks less than he talks, and slower; yet he can see through a brick wall in time (as they say in Bree)'[178]—he nonetheless aspires little higher than Aragorn's scornful characterisation: 'A fat innkeeper who only remembers his own name because people shout it at him all day.'[179]

Bree-Sense

'Do not spoil what you have by desiring what you have not'[180]

The Bree-folk will never be great or influential, since they do not aspire to significance, only survival. Had they chosen to absorb the wealth of wisdom that passed through their little land, Bree could feasibly have been one of the most nuanced, erudite, and well-informed cultures of its age—a cosmopolitan hub of cross-pollination. But if it had, it is also likely that it would have been endlessly fought over; conquered, re-conquered, and ultimately laid waste.

Bree therefore chose to avoid ambition in an attempt to steer clear of trouble, rooting itself in a wisdom of not aiming too high. What might be thought small-minded and humdrum is actually the secret of the village's enduring success. Whilst providing the history books with no great figures or events, Bree outlasts the kingdoms of Númenor and Arnor combined. The Breelanders survive the ravages of the ages, living to tell the tale—and provide a place for others to tell theirs—simply through keeping their heads down and avoiding trouble. This is their wisdom. No solutions are proposed by Bree-proverbs, only the characteristic shrug of a people who have survived by weathering storms, not attempting to understand, control, or direct them.

In shunning ambition and instead choosing to indulge only those desires that can easily be satisfied—be they pipe-smoke, beer, or news—the Bree-folk find themselves within the Epicurean philosophical tradition. Unlike the stereotype of Epicureans as hedonists and pleasure-seekers, their figurehead Epicurus taught that great excess leads to great dissatisfaction, and instead pointed to the cultivation of 'quiet joys' as the

---

178 Tolkien, *The Lord of the Rings*, p. 215.

179 Tolkien, *The Lord of the Rings*, p. 165.

180 Epicurus, as quoted in Jeremy Harwood, *Philosophy: A Beginner's Guide to the Ideas of 100 Great Thinkers* (Quercus Publishing, 2012), p. 47.

means towards achieving tranquillity.[181] The temperate pleasure that is found in peace and in freedom from fear is the Epicurean goal, and is sought by valuing friendship,[182] rejecting fame and power,[183] and recognising absence of pain as the greatest pleasure.[184]

> *'There was hot soup, cold meats, a blackberry tart, new loaves, slabs of butter, and half a ripe cheese: good plain food'*[185]

The Prancing Pony is a hub of Epicurean 'quiet joys': of 'drink, fire, and chance meeting'; of songs and tales; and of hospitable pipe-smoke. The meal served by Butterbur to the hobbits is a study in temperate enjoyment, as is his common-room's beer, firelight, and friendly warmth. Significantly, the *Pony* also reflects another Epicurean value in that it is a place where all things and subjects that might cause fear or pain or even disappointment are studiously avoided. 'Dreadful things that it makes the blood run cold to think of'[186] are shut out.

While there may be strong similarities between the worthies of Bree and the Epicurean Greeks, the parallels are not exact. Epicurus taught that pleasure of the mind trumps pleasure of the body, and that freedom from fear is attained through a thorough knowledge of the world, but the Bree-folk pay little or no attention to their cerebral development. Closing their minds to wider knowledge, they appear to prefer living in bewilderment (or mysterious fear) about the very things that many of their guests count as normal, so that even the doings of a place as unexotic and predictable as the Shire are steered away from. *Your business is your own*, says Harry at the gate, the very picture of the indifferent disinterested mind.

The result of these choices is far from the *ataraxia*—tranquillity characterised by freedom from fear—that Epicurus sought. Beneath its joviality and warmth, Bree is a place of perpetual anxiety, convinced that *It never rains but it pours* but never stopping to ask why. If anything, the Breelanders' fear of the world beyond their borders is heightened by their

181 Russell, *Op. Cit.*, p. 233.

182 According to Cicero, Epicurus said that 'Friendship cannot be divorced from pleasure, and for that reason must be cultivated, because without it neither can we live in safety and without fear, nor even pleasantly.' (Russell, *Op. Cit.*, p. 234)

183 Epicurus advised abstinence from public life, as encapsulated in the Epicurean maxim 'Live unknown!' (Russell, *Op. Cit.*, p. 234.)

184 Russell, *Op. Cit.*, p. 233.

185 Tolkien, *The Lord of the Rings*, p. 151.

186 Tolkien, *The Lord of the Rings*, p. 971.

ignorance of it. Due to their lack of knowledge, they habitually direct a distrustful *There are queer folk about* at the very people, the Rangers, who have for generations anonymously guaranteed their quiet safety. They receive only a wry, knowing smile in response.

And yet Bree survives and its folk endure, whilst greater, wiser civilisations crumble. With no pretentions to prominence or influence, Bree (and *The Prancing Pony* in particular) continues to fulfil its one great purpose: as an important meeting-place for others.

It is at Bree that Gandalf first meets Thorin, and the Quest of Erebor is planned,[187] and it is at Bree that the Ring-bearer and future King of Gondor are brought together. Without the plodding, small-minded survival of the Bree-land, Smaug may never have been defeated, the Ring might have been lost to the Nazgûl, and disaster would have come to all. *The Pony* more than earns the seven-year 'enchantment of surpassing excellence' that Gandalf lays upon its beer.

187 Tolkien, *The Lord of the Rings*, p. 1052.

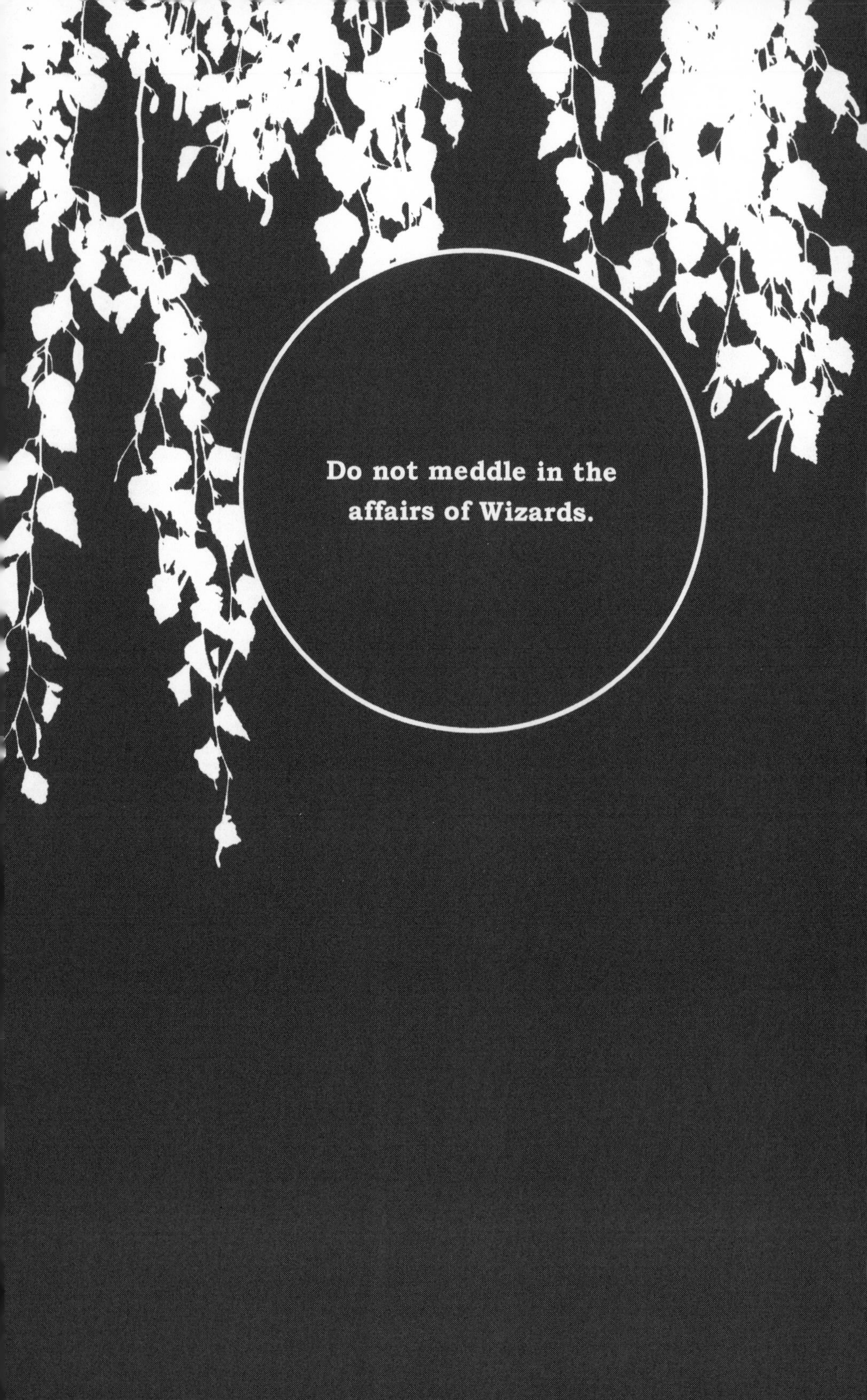
Do not meddle in the
affairs of Wizards.

CHAPTER FOUR

THE ISTARI

'... members of a high and ancient order, most excellent in Middle-earth'[188]

The arrival in Middle-earth of the *Heren Istarion*—the Order of Wizards—is one of the great turning points of the Third Age. A thousand years after the victory of the Last Alliance and the loss of the Ring, a new shadow fell on the Greenwood, which (amid other indications) intimated that Sauron was returning. Although intervening only rarely in Middle-earth, the Valar summoned a council to determine a response.

Rather than attempting to confront and overthrow the Darkness directly (as they had in the War of Wrath), the Powers chose instead a more subtle riposte: they would send representatives to Middle-earth, agents through whose support and encouragement the Free Peoples might resist and thwart the Dark Lord of their own volition.

Several of the Maiar—immortal semi-divine spirits dwelling in Valinor—were nominated for the task, and five were ultimately chosen. These were:

Saruman the White
Alternative names: Curumo,[189] Curunir
Nominated by: Aulë the Smith

188 Tolkien, *The Lord of the Rings*, p. 567.
189 Tolkien, *Unfinished Tales*, p. 393.

Gandalf the Grey
Alternative names: Olórin, Mithrandir, Tharkûn
Nominated by: Manwë, Lord of Air

Radagast the Brown
Alternative name: Aiwendil[190]
Nominated by: Yavanna, Queen of the Earth

Alatar and Pallando,[191] the Blue Wizards
Alternative names: Morinehtar and Romestamo[192]
Nominated by: Oromë the Huntsman

The name *Istari* means 'wise ones.'[193] The defining characteristic of the Wizards therefore was (or should have been) wisdom—the ability to discern good sense from bad, sagacity from stupidity—and to influence others appropriately. As Maiar they were significantly more powerful than the native inhabitants of Middle-earth, but were forbidden to use their power to dominate others or to contest Sauron directly. Apart from this obligation—of concealing their power and influencing rather than dominating—the Wizards appear to have been at liberty to strengthen the resistance of the good in whatever way seemed best to them.

All five Wizards shared a common origin and calling, but each apparently had his own areas of special interest; proficiencies through which he sought to contribute to the freedom of Middle-earth. The task remained the same but the methods differed, methods best understood in light of the Vala under whom each of the five had served in Valinor. For example, the Blue Wizards, Alatar and Pallando, focused their attentions on the far reaches of Middle-earth, a choice reflective of their relationship with Oromë, who (alone of the Valar) had travelled widely in those regions. Likewise, Radagast's attempts to resist Sauron through devotion to nature appear to be a manifestation of his loyalty to Yavanna, the Vala of flora and fauna.

---

190 Tolkien, *Unfinished Tales*, p. 393.

191 Tolkien, *Unfinished Tales*, p. 393-4.

192 The various names of the *Ithryn Luin*, the Blue Wizards, are debatable since Tolkien had not published his further speculations on them by the time of his death. The alternative names given above are from *The Peoples of Middle-earth,* Christopher Tolkien, Editor (Houghton Mifflin, 1996*)*, pp. 384-5.

193 Tolkien used the word 'wizard' because of its etymological association with 'wise.'

These immortal, 'angelic' beings took on the physical form of old men, concealing their heritage and power, and entered Middle-earth. The two greatest of the Order, Saruman and Gandalf, laboured for over two millennia, until all their efforts culminated in the War of the Ring. With vast knowledge and insight, gleaned both from long life in Middle-earth and previous ages in the Blessed Realm, these two were great among the Wise and uniquely placed to fulfil their roles. But they were also susceptible to failure; corruption by evil was just as possible for them as it had been for Morgoth and Sauron. Through the lens of their proverbial wisdom, the philosophical and sociological reasons for Saruman's fall and Gandalf's triumph become evident.

Saruman the White

> *'Curunir 'Lân, Saruman the White, fell from his high errand, and becoming proud and impatient and enamoured of power sought to have his own will by force'*[194]

Pride and impatience, leading to imposition of power by force; that the head of the Order established to counter the Dark Lord should fall into serving (or at least emulating) him is both tragic and ironic. But it is also a reflection of the similarities between the two figures—similarities with deep roots. Before being commissioned as one of the Istari, Saruman was a Maia of Aulë the Smith, the craftsman of the Valar, maker of the Sun and Moon, creator of the Dwarves, and tutor of the Noldor. So too was Sauron.

The Aulëan Achilles Heel

> *'Of [Aulë] comes the lore and knowledge of the Earth and of all things that it contains: whether the lore of those that make not, but seek only for the understanding of what is, or the lore of all craftsmen'*[195]

Aulë is described as the Lord of matter—of the world's raw materials—and hence of the techniques by which it can be shaped or knowledge about it discovered. As progenitor of all tool-bearing arts and sciences, Aulë's delight is in shaping the unprocessed into beautiful and useful

194 Tolkien, *Unfinished Tales*, p. 390.

195 Tolkien *The Silmarillion*, p. 39.

forms. But in the early days of Arda, his impatience for pupils to instruct led to him creating his own people, the Dwarves, against the will of Illúvatar. Although Aulë repented and the Dwarves were allowed to live, his potent combination of skill, ambition, and impatience was passed on to them, and to all those others whom he taught.[196]

Of the Maiar who attached themselves to Aulë, two of the greatest were Mairon and Curumo. Mairon soon fell into evil, joining Melkor's rebellion and becoming his greatest lieutenant, Sauron. Curumo remained faithful but, having been nominated by Aulë to the Order of Wizards, later fell by seeking to become a Power himself.

Names are always significant in Arda.[197] Saruman received the name *Curumo* from the Quenya-speaking Elves of Valinor, and was likewise titled *Curunir* by the Sindarin speakers of Middle-earth. Both names mean 'Man of Skill' or 'Skilful One,' showing that from the first this wizard was recognised for, and associated with, dexterous ability.

The name *Saruman* itself—given by the Rohirrim and linguistically rooted in their Mercian dialect of Old English—'implies cleverness' according to Tom Shippey. Shippey observes that, to the Anglo-Saxons, the element *Searu* commonly meant 'device, design, contrivance, art,' but where the word appears in *Beowulf* it additionally denotes 'cunning' and 'is nearly always linked with metal.'[198] In describing their nearest notable neighbour as the 'metal-device-cunning man,' the Rohirrim had correctly identified the Man of Skill's core: great dexterity and technological ability, but with a scheming nature. *The Men of the Mark do not lie, and therefore they are not easily deceived*. Indeed.

In the estimation of Treebeard, Saruman 'has a mind of metal and wheels.'[199] In his impatience to achieve his ambitious ends, and to achieve them quickly, he turns to industrial technology. Peter Kreeft, explaining the link between technology and domineering control, says that 'Every technological power is a power over time, a way of saving

196 In addition to the Dwarves, these students were principally the Noldor (including Fëanor, the creator of the Silmarils, and Celebrimbor, the forger of the Elven-rings) and a subsection of the Maiar.

197 John Garth goes as far as asserting that 'For Tolkien, to a greater extent even than Charles Dickens, a name was the first principle of story-making.' (Garth, *Op. Cit.*, p. 63.)

198 Shippey, *The Road to Middle-earth*, p. 170. Likewise, Saruman's tower Orthanc (from Old English *Orþanc*) translates as 'cunning device.'

199 Tolkien, *The Lord of the Rings*, p. 462.

time.'[200] The Istari had been given a long, slow task—to be influencers, not imposers—and Saruman ultimately proves a bad fit for it. He lacks patience.

While Gandalf faithfully aids others, commanding no army and refusing the Ring, though with either he could have instantly contested the power of Sauron, Saruman's haste and ambition seeks immediacy and direct rule. Through large-scale industrial strength—the blasting fire, wheels, and machines of Isengard—and an army of faceless slave labour, Saruman rejects his commission to serve and seeks instead to dominate.

Ambition and craft taking precedent over humility and wisdom is the tragic repeated motif of Aulë's family tree: the sad story of Fëanor's rise and fall; the Dwarves' dragon-baiting wealth and their insatiable Balrog-waking delving; and the emergence and destruction of the ring-forging smiths of Eregion. Fall after fall follows this Aulëan heritage. As Shippey observes, those in Middle-earth who are most susceptible to evil are 'equatable with industrialism, or technology.'[201] And Aulë is their patron. Even those with no link to Aulë but who share his loves and gifts are under threat: Ted Sandyman's unashamed appetite for Bywater's new smoke-belching mill shows that even a hobbit can choose ugly technology over things more in tune with the unhurried beauty of the natural world.

The Proverbs of Isengard

Proverbs are not Saruman's strong point. Having apparently spent insufficient time with (or shown enough respect for) any particular people group to learn their traditions, Saruman appears ignorant of Middle-earth's fund of wise sayings. His use of proverbs is minimal, and when they are employed they often reflect the most base 'eye for an eye' school of rough justice:

> *One thief deserves another.*
> *One ill turn deserves another.*
> *A beggar must be grateful, if a thief returns even a morsel of his own.*

Elsewhere, Saruman's sayings act as a rhetorical technique to shut down debate and to silence others. In this way, he tells the future king of

200 Kreeft, *Op. Cit.* p. 140.
201 Shippey, *The Road to Middle-earth,* p. 170.

Rohan *Meddle not in policies which you do not understand*, and has the gall to address *Does an unarmed man come down to speak to robbers out of doors?* to the wizard whom he imprisoned and the king whose kingdom he invaded.

The only genuinely insightful proverb Saruman is recorded as using is *To every man his part*—a simple yet perceptive saying, explicitly valuing the role of every person of every stature. In the mouth of Elrond such a truth might underpin the collaborative multiculturalism of the Fellowship, and for Gandalf it would justify his time spent away from the centres of power, building relationships with the less-significant: Hobbits, Breelanders, Ents, and Eagles. Yet when Saruman uses it, the context is not honouring but is patronising and dismissive, turning the proverb on its head. Quoting it from the balcony of Orthanc, he exposes his contempt for those who are indeed satisfied by playing their part: Hobbits ('these… small rag-tag'[202]), the Rohirrim ('What is the house of Eorl but a thatched barn…?'[203]), and even Aragorn, Gimli, and Legolas ('these lesser folk'[204]). He may cite the proverb, but Saruman does not believe it.

This is not the only example of Saruman misusing proverbial wisdom. Armed with a truism like *What was lost may yet be found*, Saruman is able to justify his role of information-gatherer *par excellence*: he is Middle-earth's great accumulator of knowledge. A studier, and an amasser of data, he seeks to know all that can be known and is accustomed to justify his counsel with an masterful 'Have I not earnestly studied this matter?'[205]

But 'knowledge puffs up,'[206] as the Biblical proverb warns, and Saruman becomes a case in point: the arrogant pride that grows alongside his intellectual and technological advancement is the very thing that keeps him from wisely applying it. His accumulated cleverness gives him the tools to make himself a power, but it also gives him the foolish pride to want to be one.

> *'His knowledge is deep, but his pride has grown with it.'*[207]

---

202 Tolkien, *The Lord of the Rings*, p. 569.

203 Tolkien, *The Lord of the Rings*, p. 567.

204 *Ibid*.

205 Tolkien, *The Lord of the Rings*, p. 244.

206 1 Corinthians 8:1, from *Holy Bible, New International Version* (Hodder & Stoughton, 1984).

207 Tolkien, *The Lord of the Rings*, p. 47.

The great temptation of data-rich cleverness is to trust itself beyond question. Having amassed an arsenal of clear, clean 'scientific' answers, Saruman starts to believe that he himself is the answer to Middle-earth's problems. His quest—for 'Knowledge, Rule, Order'—is self-aggrandising and egocentric, and flies in the face of Kreeft's warning that sometimes it is better not to know; that 'sometimes knowing is dangerous.'[208] And in over-trusting himself, he distrusts others, preferring to work alone and use his own tools—beginning with the power of his voice and the propaganda of Wormtongue, and ending with the direct power of industrial warfare—rather than collaborating with others or appealing to received wisdom.

In *Unfinished Tales*, we are told that Saruman was 'so far fallen that he believed all others of the Council had each their deep and far-reaching policies for their own enhancement.'[209] In Gandalf, for example, he sees a rival with the same priorities that motivate him, whose ambitions will only be satisfied by 'the Keys of Barad-dûr... the crowns of seven kings, and the rods of the Five Wizards.'[210]. Gandalf simply laughs at this, saying 'I fear I am beyond your comprehension.'[211]

The Will To Power

> *'Our time is at hand: the world of Men, which We must rule. But we must have power, power to order all things as we will'*[212]

'We must have power'[213] are the words of Saruman to Gandalf, but '*I* must have power' is what he means. Saruman seeks no community, only leadership; he studies privately and secretively, keeping his knowledge to himself; and as he finally comes to see himself as the sole solution to Middle-earth's problems, he builds up a personal powerbase, aided by increasingly industrialized might. He still seeks the destruction of Sauron, but only in order to replace him.

> *'We can keep our thoughts in our hearts, deploring maybe evils done by the way, but approving the high and ultimate purpose:*

208 Kreeft, *Op. Cit.*, p. 120.
209 Tolkien, *Unfinished Tales*, p. 349.
210 Tolkien, *The Lord of the Rings*, p. 569.
211 Tolkien, *The Lord of the Rings*, p. 568.
212 Tolkien, *The Lord of the Rings*, p. 252.
213 *Ibid.*

Knowledge, Rule, Order; all the things that we have so far striven in vain to accomplish'[214]

These high-sounding words expose Saruman's ethical core: that the ends justify the means, whatever those means may be. Breeding Orcs, attacking Rohan, allying with Mordor, and seeking the Ring for himself may in themselves be deplored, but if the correct results are achieved, then no matter. This makes Saruman a Consequentialist, but Saruman's school of morality is not Utilitarian: he does not seek the greatest good for the greatest number, only for himself. His dog-eat-dog ethos is an ethic of competition and rivalry, and it leads him away from collaboration and coalition and into self-centred individualism.

Saruman would have affirmed Friedrich Nietzsche's assertion that the right and correct state of the world is a cosmic competition in which the strong rise and rule, vanquishing the weak and the meek.[215] In this view, traditional virtues such as mercy and compassion are seen as weaknesses, since they perpetuate the survival of the powerless and restrain the emergence of the *Ubermensch*—the 'superman.' This *Ubermensch* is what Sauron is and what Saruman has sought to be. All others are by comparison mere worms, as indeed Wormtongue becomes.

'He was great once, of a noble kind that we should not dare to raise our hands against.'[216]

Saruman's story ends at the door of Bag End, the *Ubermensch* killed by his own worm. Having been sent to Middle-earth as the head of the Order charged with inspiring and encouraging the fight against the Enemy, the sole remaining satisfaction of his final months is in spiting those who succeeded where he failed.

Hobbits have no will to power, so when they finally catch the petty and vindictive Sharky, they offer him the things he most despises: mercy and compassion. He repays it by attempting murder. *One ill turn deserves another*, he says, attempting to justify himself, only to be defeated again, this time in use of proverbs, as Frodo counters that *It is useless to meet revenge with revenge: it will heal nothing*.

214 Tolkien, *The Lord of the Rings*, p. 253.

215 Russell, *Op. Cit.*, p. 690.

216 Tolkien, *The Lord of the Rings*, p. 996.

Looking around at the ravages of what, in the final stage of his corruption, Saruman had devoted himself to, Frodo responds not with anger but with pity and sadness. 'This is Mordor,' he says. 'Saruman was doing its work all the time, even when he thought he was working for himself.'[217]

Gandalf the Grey

'I am Gandalf, and Gandalf means me!'[218]

In the summer of 1911, Tolkien went on a walking holiday in the high Alps, during which he bought a postcard reproduction of a painting called *Der Berggeist*, 'The Mountain Spirit.' The painting shows an old man with a white beard and long cloak sitting on a rock under a pine tree, and from whose hand a young deer is eating. According to Humphrey Carpenter, Tolkien 'preserved this postcard carefully, and long afterwards he wrote on the paper cover in which he kept it: 'Origin of Gandalf.''[219]

If Saruman is the case study of wisdom-gone-wrong, of craft and cleverness twisted into arrogance and power-grabbing, then *Der Berggeist* is the origin of the antidote: the Grey Pilgrim,[220] 'an old man in a battered hat,'[221] unpresumptuous and unimpressive, but deeply good.

Gandalf is good. It is sometimes hard for goodness to feel vibrant and exciting, but he achieves it. His goodness is not a bland, watered-down facsimile—the sickly-sweet, the cloyingly sentimental, or the puritanical and moralistic—it is the real thing: rich and inspiring and enjoyable. Gandalf's goodness goes far beyond 'doing the right thing'; it is the virtue that moral systems intend to point towards.

Proverbs And The Big Picture

'If individuals could see more widely... they would realise the cause-and-effect logic, though there are so many causes that perhaps no one but God can ever see them all at once. The world is a Persian carpet, then, and we are ants lumbering from one thread to the other...

---

217 Tolkien, *The Lord of the Rings*, p. 994.

218 Tolkien, *The Hobbit*, p. 8.

219 Carpenter, *Biography*, p. 51.

220 The literal translation of the Sindarin *Mithrandir*.

221 Tolkien, *The Lord of the Rings*, p. 351.

> *That is why one of Gandalf's favourite sayings is 'Even the wise cannot see all ends' and why he often demonstrates its truth himself.'*[222]

While Gandalf is good, he is not primarily a moral teacher; he is a describer of reality. It is the Persian carpet of deeper reality that Gandalf's wisdom unveils. While direct instructions do exist in his proverbs—*Do not be too eager to deal out death in judgement*, for example, or *Put all the rats in one trap*—these are rare exceptions. Statements of principle abound—*Wonder makes the words of praise louder*, or *Hope is not victory*, for example—but pride of place is given to insights into the otherwise unknown or unguessed nature of things: what Tom Shippey describes as 'the relationship between reality and our fallible perception of it.'[223] All the while Gandalf keeps at least one eye on the grand narrative of Arda: Providence, the Powers, and the faintly-perceivable tapestry of their subtle influence. Middle-earth itself is only part of the story, not the whole.

In line with the Wizards' commission to encourage and influence others rather than to directly employ their power, Gandalf is rarely explicit about who he is and what he knows. When this is done, the references are usually obscure and missable[224]—perceivable only by those with eyes to see. But there are also exceptional moments of 'emergency' as well, in which a palpable supernatural (or Valinorean) dynamic is revealed. For example: on the Bridge of Khazad-dûm, Gandalf reveals himself as 'a servant of the Secret Fire';[225] on the Pelennor, resisting the Nazgûl, he rides forth with 'a light starting from his upraised hand';[226] and when, in easily lifting the prone Faramir from his pyre, Gandalf 'revealed the strength that lay hid in him; even as the light of his power was hidden under his grey mantle.'[227]

These hints of Gandalf's true 'angelic' nature give to his use of proverbs a distinctive element. While axioms like *There are many powers in the world, for good or for evil*, and *It is not our part to master all the tides of the world*, might appropriately be spoken by a number of different

222 Shippey, *The Road to Middle-earth*, p. 165.

223 Shippey, *The Road to Middle-earth*, p. 140.

224 Such as when he hints at the Valar's influence by saying, 'I can put it no plainer than by saying that Bilbo was *meant* to find the Ring, and *not* by its maker… and that may be an encouraging thought' (Tolkien, *The Lord of the Rings*, p. 54-55).

225 Tolkien, *The Lord of the Rings*, p. 322.

226 Tolkien, *The Lord of the Rings*, p. 802.

227 Tolkien, *The Lord of the Rings*, p. 834.

people, in Gandalf's mouth they take on a spiritual or theistic dimension.[228] Likewise, when he says to Théoden, *You are not without allies, even though you know them not*, Gandalf speaks not only as one with first-hand knowledge of all the Free Peoples of Middle-earth, but also as an emissary of the West. Whilst never overt in his references to Illúvatar and the Valar, Gandalf sees their influence around him and is confident of their aid.

The Wandering Philosophy

Gandalf's proverbs and the philosophy they espouse are undeniably theistic, yet Middle-earth is not a 'religious' place—there are no priests or temples, and few references to spiritual things.[229] Gandalf has been commissioned by the Powers, and therefore can be seen as something of a prophetic messenger—retelling the ancient-but-true and repeating things easily forgotten—but he is not a 'Thus says the Lord...' prophet. In fact, he is almost the opposite, choosing not to teach directly about Illúvatar or the Valar.

Gandalf's proverbs exemplify this choice. Many of them are ethical—*Be not unjust in your grief*, or *Generous deed should not be checked by cold counsel*—and therefore carry an appeal to the obligations of right-living, and Michael Stanton points out that these insights (especially those regarding the self-defeating nature of evil) 'imply the existence of a kind of world-wide justice,'[230] but Gandalf makes no reference to the Powers who presumably administer this justice. No recognition of, or obedience to, the Valar is ever demanded by his teaching. Instead Gandalf encourages in others the willingness to courageously do the right or the noble thing, even without any expectation of a 'happy ending'—success or salvation. He prefers (what Shippey identifies as) the Old Norse ethic of courage: commitment to virtue without any offer of lasting reward.'[231]

Results are never emphasised in Gandalf's ethics; he is emphatically not a Consequentialist like Saruman, and the ends never justify the means.

228 For example, *There are many powers...* can be taken as a reference to the Powers themselves.

229 Exceptions include the songs of the High-elves and Gondor's Standing Silence before meals.

230 Stanton, *Op. Cit.*, p. 344.

231 Shippey, *Roots and Branches*, p. 191. Alongside this Norse ethic, it is worth recognising that the name Gandalf itself is Old Norse, taken (along with the names of all the dwarves in *The Hobbit*) from *Völuspá*, the Nordic creation myth.

Likewise, Gandalf never makes promises or predictions about how things will turn out. The present tense is always what counts:

> *'It is not our part to master all the tides of the world, but to do what is in us for the succour of those years wherein we are set, uprooting the evil in the fields that we know, so that those who live after may have clean earth to till. What weather they shall have is not ours to rule.'*[232]

Gandalf declares that the world is too wild to predict or control, so that *Even the very wise cannot see all ends*. Many proverbial expressions in Middle-earth deal with this issue of unpredictability—of the deceptiveness of appearances—and Gandalf uses the most. First impressions should not be trusted, warns the angel in the body of an old man. Through his proverbs, optimistic bravado is tempered and those who lose heart are strengthened. *Hope is not victory*, he reminds the cocksure, while to the disheartened he says, *Despair is only for those who see the end beyond all doubt.*

In the midst of this wariness of presumption, a clear ethic emerges: avoid looking too far ahead; do the task at hand. *Go where you must go*, Gandalf says, *One must tread the path that need chooses.* Because ultimately *All we have to decide is what to do with the time that is given us.*

The Proverbious Lore-master

Whilst being a reteller of the ancient and a hinter of the eternal, it is clear that Gandalf's memory is by no means foolproof. At the doors of Moria he says, 'I once knew every spell in all the tongues of Elves or Men or Orcs,'[233] implicitly admitting that he no longer does. Even a wizard can forget.

On the journey to Minas Tirith, Pippin discovers how Gandalf boosts his recollection. He overhears the wizard 'singing softly to himself, murmuring brief snatches of rhyme in many tongues.'[234] This is the sound of study: Gandalf is reciting rhymes of lore—those songs or poems intended to transmit traditional knowledge orally[235]—as an aid

232 Tolkien, *The Lord of the Rings*, p. 861.

233 Tolkien, *The Lord of the Rings*, p. 299.

234 Tolkien, *The Lord of the Rings*, p. 582.

235 Other rhymes of lore include *The Long List of the Ents* ('Learn now the lore of living creatures'), *Athelas* ('When the black breath blows'), and the *Verse of the Rings* ('Three

to memory. The assumption is that this private discipline has been the pattern of many solitary journeys; over the course of Gandalf's wandering centuries the lore-master has had few companions, but his oral tradition has been ever-present.

In his discussion of Middle-earth's 'wise sayings,' Tom Shippey identifies a key role that is occasionally played in wisdom traditions: that of the 'proverbious' person.[236] While many individuals may respect, consult, and transmit their oral heritage, the proverbious person is so rooted and confident in it as to bend, stretch, play with, and otherwise modify what has been inherited. Gandalf is the prime exemplar of such a person. Not only does he reshape the proverbs he hears—such as instantly changing *The hands of the king are the hands of a healer* to *The hands of the king are the hands of healing*—but he also allows them to shape him.

A proverbious person becomes a lore-master through first being a lore-servant. There are over four hundred proverbial sayings in *The Lord of the Rings*,[237] and around 15% of them come from the mouth of this one wizard. To Gandalf, rhymes of lore, proverbs, songs, and words of command are not vessels by which to convey his own message; instead, he is the vessel for theirs. Gandalf is a conduit through which proverbial sayings flow, to the point that his very speech patterns resonate with their rhythms and cadences. As a result, Gandalf uses so many proverbs that at times he appears to do so without even realising it, meaning that (as Shippey says) 'you cannot always tell what is a proverb and what is not.'[238]

To take one example among many:

> *'Many folk like to know beforehand what is to be set on the table; but those who have laboured to prepare the feast like to keep their secret; for wonder makes the words of praise louder.'*[239]

From one perspective, there appears to be three separate proverbs in this single sentence, yet at the same time it is unclear as to whether

---

Rings for the Elven-kings under the sky').

236 The case-study offered by Shippey is Gaffer Gamgee, since he adds '...and need of vittles' to *Where there's life there's hope*, and changes *All's well as ends well* to *All's well as ends Better!* (Shippey, *Roots and Branches*, p. 308.)

237 Not to mention a mass of others in *The Hobbit*, *The Silmarillion*, *Unfinished Tales*, and other writings of Tolkien.

238 Shippey, *Roots and Branches*, p. 307.

239 Tolkien, *The Lord of the Rings*, p. 949.

Gandalf is quoting established sayings or is speaking *ex tempore*. Either conclusion can be reached, and this is what makes identifying Gandalf's proverbs so problematic. Michael Stanton suggests that in this case we are witnessing 'a Gandalfian creation'[240]—that the Grey Wanderer is inventing proverbs, not quoting them—but it is just as likely that the three sayings pre-existed, and the proverbious wizard is stringing them together like a preacher whose speech is laden with snatches of scripture. But we cannot know. Gandalf rarely marks the presence of a proverb with a formal 'It is said...' or 'Remember that...,' possibly because he is so rooted in wise sayings that he is not consciously quoting at all.

Examples of this habit of quoting without signalling a quotation abound, providing multiple opportunities to play proverb hide-and-seek. For example, in Rivendell, supporting the inclusion of Merry and Pippin in the Fellowship, Gandalf says: 'I think, Elrond, that in this matter it would be well to trust rather to their friendship than to great wisdom.'[241] A less proverbious person might have replied 'But Elrond, as it is said, *Trust rather to friendship than to great wisdom*,' drawing attention to the proverb as a rhetorical tool. Gandalf, however, trusts his listener to recognise the saying, or at least the value of its wisdom, rather than spoon-feeding a lesson.

Humble Greatness

There is no patronising or condescending side to Gandalf, no sense of superiority by which he might 'talk down' to his audience. He has been commissioned to walk among the peoples of Middle-earth, kindling hearts into resisting the Shadow. He succeeds, not because of his own greatness, but because of his humility.

In *The Silmarillion* Gandalf is described as the wisest of the Maiar,[242] but rather than trumpeting or glorying in his greatness, he dwells on his own shortcomings, distrusts his strengths, and (as a result) appreciates the value of the rustic, the royal, and everyone in between. This humble wisdom allows Gandalf to happily learn from the traditions of lesser people because, unlike Saruman, he doesn't consider himself superior to them.

240 Stanton, *Op. Cit.*, p. 343.

241 Tolkien, *The Lord of the Rings*, p. 269.

242 Tolkien, *The Silmarillion*, p. 30.

In this way—both in wilfully quoting proverbs, and by subconsciously being guided by their influence—Gandalf becomes an embodiment of wisdom; he is a fount and a conduit of traditional sayings, as well as an encapsulation of their truth. In making wisdom his master, it has formed him into the 'wise one' that he is. Alone of the Istari, he fully embodies the title of Wizard.

THE ISTARI: CONCLUDING CONTRAST

Tolkien believed that the most improper job for any man was bossing others around. He concurred with the ancient view that *nolo episcopari*—'I do not want to be a bishop'—is the only true qualification for becoming one.[243] The Mediaevals used the phrase to show that that it is those who are ambitious for power who must be frustrated, and Tolkien's most intense distaste was reserved for those who attempted (even with good motives) to achieve their objectives by recourse to control or domination.

In Middle-earth, the desire to rule is never a healthy one, and the renunciation of power (and specifically of the Ring) a trustworthy sign of wisdom and virtue. This pattern is fleshed out throughout the history of Arda: from Morgoth to Lotho Sackville-Baggins, it is power—or the longing for power—that corrupts. The only person in whom strength of authority can wisely be vested is the one who does not want to wield it.

> *'Who would go? For they must be mighty, peers of Sauron, but must forego might'*[244]

Gandalf and Saruman—or, more precisely, Olórin and Curumo—provide the principal case study in the power of power, due to their comparable origins, duties, and abilities. While Curumo originally served Aulë the Smith, the craftsman of the Valar, and thereby became 'skilled in all the devices of smithcraft,'[245] Olórin dwelt in the Valinorean realm of Lórien, with Irmo, the Vala of dreams and visions.[246] We are also told that he often went to the house of Nienna, who is the Vala of grief and mourning, and that 'all who hearken to her learn pity, and endurance

243 Humphrey Carpenter, *The Letters of JRR Tolkien* (Houghton Mifflin, 1981), p. 64.

244 Tolkien, *Unfinished Tales*, p. 393.

245 Tolkien, *The Silmarillion*, p. 300.

246 Tolkien, *The Silmarillion*, p. 28.

in hope.'[247] Gandalf's character was therefore founded on a combination of these two influences—of revelatory vision on the one hand and compassionate tender-heartedness on the other. *The Silmarillion* records that, even in Valinor, 'those who listened to him awoke from despair and put away the imaginations of darkness.'[248]

Olórin did not wish to be a wizard. Although counted wisest of the Maiar, when the Powers debated the need to counter Sauron and came to nominate members to form the *Heren Istarion*, he was apparently absent from the council and had to be called for. It was Manwë himself who nominated him, but Olórin 'declared that he was too weak for the task, and that he feared Sauron.'[249] In line with the wisdom of *nolo episcopari*, this reluctance served only to confirm to Manwë the aptness of his choice, thus Olórin became one of the Five. And although Saruman was the Order's acknowledged leader, it was to Gandalf that Círdan gave the Elven-ring Narya, it was Gandalf whom Galadriel nominated to be the head of the White Council (he declined[250]), and it was Gandalf to whom Frodo offered the One Ring.

Though less is known of Saruman's early tutelage in the West, it seems apparent that the skills and affinities he gained from Aulë and brought to the Order of Wizards contrast strongly with those of Gandalf. In particular, it should be noted that while Gandalf's focus is always on people, Saruman is primarily a lover of things, of artefacts and the raw materials from which they can be made.

This love is not a shortcoming in itself. Indeed, it is a key to understanding the reason for Saruman's selection as a wizard. He was nominated by his tutor, the craftsman of the physical world, who had already spent much of his time labouring to repair 'the tumults and disorders of Melkor' in the earliest days of Arda.[251] The evils of the Third Age, as in those primeval conflicts, caused physical damage to the world, and Aulë would have mourned over this chaotic ugliness. Proposing Curumo, a lieutenant who cared with similar depth about the disorder of Middle-earth (and was suitably skilled to engage in a mission of physical reparation), was therefore a completely reasonable step.

247 Tolkien, *The Silmarillion*, p. 28.

248 Tolkien, *The Silmarillion*, p. 31.

249 Tolkien, *Unfinished Tales*, p. 393.

250 Tolkien, *The Silmarillion*, p. 300.

251 Tolkien, *The Silmarillion*, p. 27.

The ideal Saruman—the Saruman perhaps of his first thousand years in Middle-earth—would therefore have been a second (lesser) Aulë. He would have been a mender and a reforger of the broken or twisted, labouring to undo the destructive work of the Dark Lord. In this way, without breaking the Istari's ban against directly confronting Sauron, Saruman could have played a significant part in restoring the beauty and order of Aulë's original intention for the physical world.

Had Saruman remained true to his task, it is conceivable that even the worst of Sauron's devastations—the choking desert of Gorgoroth, the poisoned Morgal Vale—could have been made habitable and (perhaps in collaboration with Radagast) fruitful once more. It was with such reparations in mind that Curumo was appointed to the Order of Wizards. He was great among the Wise, but ultimately came to believe too much in his own greatness and to desire power.

The Desire to Dominate, the Temptation to Tyrannize

It is too simple to say that Saruman had an inherent, fatal 'will to power' and that Gandalf did not. Indeed, in the process of refusing the Ring Gandalf makes it clear that the ability it affords does attract him strongly:

> *'Do not tempt me! For I do not wish to become like the Dark Lord himself. Yet the way of the Ring to my heart is by pity, pity for weakness and the desire of strength to do good. Do not tempt me!'*[252]

There is no doubt that it would have been perfectly possible for Gandalf to fall (and, conversely, for Saruman to remain faithful). However, Gandalf's tutelage under Irmo and Nienna gave him one great advantage to aid his resistance: he was never self-centred. His compassionate core kept his eyes away from himself and on the needs of others, whilst also keeping his attitude cooperative and collegiate. In this way Gandalf was never tempted to build up a personal powerbase, and while Saruman's abilities were both good and great, to him they served only as a beginning. Further empowering an already powerful figure, they led him to seek solutions solely within himself—to seek mastery. Gandalf knows that this is a dangerous desire:

> *It is not our part to master all the tides of the world, but to do what is in us for the succour of those years wherein we are set.*

252 Tolkien, *The Lord of the Rings*, p. 60.

The Wandering Friar and the Enthroned Prelate

If, to extend Tolkien's comparison, Saruman is one who wanted to be a bishop (and whose desire for power therefore marks him as ripe for corruption), the equivalent image for Gandalf is that of a wandering monk; a greyfriar perhaps, in the mode of the Franciscans. Like St Francis, Gandalf chooses to own little and to depend on others for shelter, and whilst having great influence he never attempts to seize power. His self-imposed dependency on others safeguards him from the temptation to coerce or compel.

Saruman started in similar fashion, but after fifteen hundred years spent in comparable wandering he decided that to bring order amidst the destructive and growing power of Sauron, he needed a stronghold. The benevolent manner in which took Isengard hid his purpose: 'building up a power of his own.'[253] Subsequent events show how this choice accelerated Saruman's decline: he discovers and uses the palantír; he starts searching for the Ring and attempting to make his own; he begins to oppose the White Council; and finally he builds an army. Having desired to become a 'bishop,' to have authority and power over others, his cathedral of Orthanc becomes 'a place of guarded strength and fear, as though to rival the Barad-dûr.'[254] Gandalf, meanwhile, continues in the mode of *Der Berggeist*.

The Gandalf–Saruman contrast is therefore between the wandering friar and the enthroned prelate; between the penniless pilgrim wrapped in grey and the masterful figurehead in shimmering robes, safe in his impregnable tower. In the great war against the Enemy, it is easy to see where common sense might put its hopes, but *Even the very wise cannot see all ends*. When the war is over, it is Gandalf who crowns the king—fulfilling a bishop's traditional role—and of whom Aragorn says, 'this is his victory.'[255]

253 Tolkien, *The Lord of the Rings*, p. 1042.

254 *Ibid.*

255 Tolkien, *The Lord of the Rings*, p. 946.

CHAPTER FIVE

THE HALF-ELVEN

Eala Earendel engla beorhtast
[Hail Earendel, brightest of angels]
Ofer middangeard monnum sended
[Above Middle-earth sent unto men]

In his early twenties, Tolkien read the above lines for the first time. They are part of an eighth century devotional piece called *Crist* ('Christ'), written in Anglo-Saxon by the poet Cynewulf, in which the planet Venus is described in personal and angelic terms, using the name *Earendel*. 'I felt a curious thrill,' Tolkien later remembered, 'as if something had stirred in me, half wakened from sleep. There was something very remote and strange and beautiful behind those words, if I could grasp it.'[256]

Forty years later, now in Quenya, Cynewulf's line reappears in *The Two Towers*: Frodo, holding the Starglass in the great darkness of Shelob's Lair, cries out *Aiya Eärendil Elenion Ancalima!*—'Hail Eärendil, brightest of stars!'—a prayer to the mariner who sails the skies with a Silmaril on his brow. The journey from a fragment of Old English to the pass of Cirith Ungol mirrors the journey of Tolkien's legendarium as a whole.

According to John Garth's chronology,[257] Tolkien made his first excursion into what became Middle-earth on 24 September 1914, by writing a

256 Carpenter, *Biography*, p. 64.
257 Garth, *Op. Cit.*, p. 45.

poem—'The Voyage Of Earendel The Evening Star'—inspired by the line from Cynewulf. After reading the poem to his friends of the TCBS,[258] one of them, GB Smith, asked what it was actually about. Tolkien replied, 'I don't know, I'll try to find out.'[259] An understanding of the Half-elven, of Eärendil and his family, is incomplete without the acknowledgement that every facet and feature of Middle-earth grew from this 'finding out' process.[260] As Tolkien sought to grasp the beauty behind the words, a single Anglo-Saxon spark developed into a great heavenly light: Eärendil the Mariner, the 'great intercessor between gods and Middle-earth.'[261] But who were the Half-elven, and what is the light that they bring?

Cross-cultural Amalgamation

Every child conceived has some degree of mixed heritage, however similar the parents, yet some receive roots that are far more cross-cultural. The twin brothers Elrond and Elros have a unique lineage: neither wholly Elves nor Men, but the progeny of both, due to mixed marriages in both their paternal and maternal bloodlines. In consequence, they are known as the *Peredhil*—the Half-elven—but they were not the first Half-elven in Middle-earth.

The first union of the Eldar and the Edain occurred when Beren son of Barahir, a man of the House of Beor, married Lúthien Tinúviel.[262] They had one son, Dior, who for a time was the King of Doriath. The second such union was that between Tuor son of Huor of the House of Hador, and Idril Celebrindal, daughter of Turgon the Elven King of Gondolin. When their son Eärendil married Beren and Lúthien's grand-daughter Elwing, the two 'Half-elven' family lines were united, with a heritage including not only all three houses of the Edain, the Fathers of Men, but also the royal houses of all three Elf kindreds: the Vanyar, Noldor, and Teleri. Consequently, when Eärendil and Elwing sailed to Valinor to

---

258 The Tea Club and Barrovian Society, consisting of close friends from King Edward's School, Birmingham. Only Tolkien and Christopher Wiseman survived the Great War.

259 Garth, *Op. Cit.*, p. 53.

260 This word-based 'finding out' process became standard for Tolkien. As observed by Gilliver *et. al*. 'painstaking consideration of an individual word would often be the precursor to the unlocking of his imagination, and the development of a new facet of his created world.' (Peter Gilliver, Jeremy Marshall, & Edmund Weiner, *The Ring of Words* (Oxford University Press, 2006), p. 57.)

261 Shippey, *The Road to Middle-earth*, p. 298.

262 Lúthien was herself of mixed heritage, since her mother was one of the Maiar of Valinor and her father King of the Elves of Doriath.

petition the Valar for their help against Morgoth, they did so as fitting representatives of both Elves and Men.

In this hybrid line of Half-elven lived an amalgamation of their ancestors' strengths: the courage, loyalty, and ambition of the Edain, and the knowledge, craftsmanship, and longevity of the Eldar. The cross-pollination between peoples did not diminish these virtues, but brought out what was best in both. So when Eärendil and Elwing's petition to the Valar was successful and Morgoth defeated, their twin sons Elros and Elrond belonged wholly to neither Elves nor Men, but were pre-eminent amongst both.

After the War of Wrath and the reshaping of Middle-earth, the Valar set before the two remaining *Peredhil* an irrevocable choice as to which people they should belong. As their father began sailing the skies with the last Silmaril on his brow, Elros chose the Gift of Men (death) and became the first King of Númenor, while Elrond chose the life of the Eldar and remained in Middle-earth.

In Númenor, Elros founded a nation, a people (the Dúnedain or 'Men of the West'), and a legacy that ultimately lasted until the reunification of the Kingdoms of Arnor and Gondor, over six thousand years later. Elrond lived through those intervening millennia, serving as counsellor and herald of Gil-galad, the last High King of the Noldor, before founding Rivendell and becoming guardian of the Elven-ring Vilya. When Elrond finally passed over the Sundering Sea at the beginning of the Fourth Age, the Half-elven legacy endured through his sons Elladan and Elrohir, and in the marriage of his daughter Arwen to his foster-son Aragorn, descendant of Elros and King of the Númenóreans.

Elrond

> *'He was as noble and fair in face as an elf-lord, as strong as a warrior, as wise as a wizard, as venerable as a king of dwarves, and as kind as summer.'*[263]

If Eärendil was an anthropological intermediary (between Elves and Men, and between both peoples and the Valar), and Elros' kingdom of Númenor was a geographical intermediary (between Middle-earth and the West), it is important to recognise that Elrond Half-elven fulfils

263 Tolkien, *The Hobbit*, p. 61.

the role of intercessor or intermediary as well. While ostensibly living among the Elves (and especially the Noldor), Elrond is a counsellor to all the Free Peoples. He offers a longevous and pan-cultural perspective to the mortal, with whom Elvish collaboration is otherwise rare, as well as sitting on the White Council and harbouring the heirs of Elendil.

The extent of Elrond's fame as Middle-earth's preeminent counsellor is shown by the fact that even far-off Gondor, whose men rarely seek any advice but their own, has a proverb specifically about him: *The might of Elrond is in wisdom, not in weapons*, they say. But Elrond is not, to use another of Boromir's phrases, the 'greatest of lore-masters'[264] simply because he has studied widely. In representing and interpreting 'the ancient wisdom' to the present world, Elrond typifies the crossing point between fact and application, between knowledge and insight. He is a wisdom tradition made flesh, a living repository of the accumulated truths of Men and Elves. His memory alone reaches back six millennia—beyond the foundations of every extant mortal civilisation. Elrond does not merely recite history; he recalls it.

> *'I have seen three ages in the West of the world, and many defeats, and many fruitless victories.'*[265]

Learning from Tradition

> *'Humility entails learning from others. Learning from others entails respect for tradition, for tradition is simply learning from dead others.'*[266]

'Learning from dead others' is something that abounds in Tolkien's world. Even without including sayings, songs, riddles, and other pieces of oral inheritance, there are over five hundred references to the first two ages of Middle-earth in *The Lord of the Rings* alone. This multitude of references is the inherited tradition, a 'vast sea of wisdom underlying the story.'[267] Elrond's counsel is always given in light of this legacy, since he regards tradition as the most trustworthy source of knowledge. Due to his enormous personal experience, supplemented by the 'storied and

264 Tolkien, *The Lord of the Rings*, p. 240.

265 Tolkien, *The Lord of the Rings*, p. 237.

266 Kreeft, *Op. Cit.*, p. 134.

267 Kreeft, *Op. Cit.*, p. 122.

figured maps and books of lore'[268] of Imladris, Elrond could easily have sought to do without oral tradition, yet proverbs—the wisdom of dead others—are in evidence whenever he speaks.

While others recite sayings when lacking assurance or seeking guidance, in Elrond's mouth they are primarily a tool of transmission: to teach or convince others by appealing to tradition. This approach emphasises Elrond's intermediary role since, in spite of his natural authority of experience and position, he, like Gandalf, prefers to build consensus than to issue commands. Proverbs are the consensus view of a culture, and they allow Elrond to steer clear of directly stating (and thereby imposing) his own opinions. It is common therefore to see Elrond build his counsel around proverbs and other appeals to precedent.

While providing perspectives on evil, on wisdom, and on oath-taking, Elrond's main use of proverbs is to warn others of the limits of their knowledge. In philosophical terms, Elrond's role is that of the epistemologist—someone concerned with distinguishing justified belief from opinion, and thereby determining what can and cannot be known. As a result, his advice is often couched in caveats against presumption and conjecture.[269] Proverbs used by Elrond during the Council—such as *None can foretell what will come to pass, if we take this road or that*, and *Look not too far ahead*—display his misgivings and mistrust of prediction, leaving straightforward suggestions (such as *Fear the many eyes of the servants of Sauron*) as rarities.

Elrond's caveats do not make him a Sceptic—someone who believes that there is nothing that can be truly known—but he does share something with the methodology of the rationalist René Descartes, which states that everything which can be doubted should be.[270] Elrond never goes as far as to question his own senses as Descartes did, but he is concerned that too many things are considered 'known' when in fact they are only believed or inferred from immediate experience. Elrond refuses to take anything for granted. In his hands, a simple geographical truism such as *Anduin the Great flows past many shores* becomes a warning against any presumptions the members of the Fellowship might have about their path, amidst the unknowns of the Wide World.

268 Tolkien, *The Lord of the Rings*, p. 270.

269 A response to 'the familiar fact that sometimes I turn out not in fact to know something that I thought that I knew.' (Laurence BonJour, *Epistemology: Classic Problems and Contemporary Responses* (Rowman & Littlefield, 2009), p. 5.)

270 BonJour, *Op. Cit.*, p. 11.

Elrond's unwillingness to presume leads him away from certainty and into caution. Those who receive his counsel go away better informed, but often less assured: more aware of the world, but especially its vagaries and volatilities. Often they appear to know more of what *not* to do than what they must do. Such paradoxes are at the heart of Elrond's wisdom.

When Philosophies Disagree

Elrond's abilities as a cross-cultural communicator come to the fore when confronted by Gimli in Rivendell. With the Fellowship about to depart, Gimli disagrees with Elrond's decision not to require its members to swear a binding oath—in fact, Elrond goes as far as to expressly give permission for any member (barring Frodo) to turn back or turn aside at any time. This scope for infidelity is anathema to the dwarf, in whose values system loyalty ranks alongside courage as the greatest of virtues. The never-shy Gimli, unsurprisingly, chooses to voice his disagreement, though significantly he chooses not to argue in the first person, but only to quote a proverb:

> *Faithless is he that says farewell when the road darkens.*

It is possible that Gimli believes that he is kindly correcting an oversight, rather than confronting the most-trusted counsellor in Middle-earth. In either case, Elrond could dismiss the objection, citing his authority, his experience, or his learning. Instead, he chooses to honour the dwarf, replying with a proverb of his own:

> *Let him not swear to walk in the dark, who has not seen the nightfall.*

Elrond's use of a proverb to cast aspersions about the value of vows comes as no surprise when his heritage is considered. On both sides of his Half-elven nature, Elrond has inherited highly relevant warnings from history. On the one hand he is descended from the Noldor, whose experience with vows is tragic: Fëanor and his sons swore to recover the stolen Silmarils at all costs, and their oath resulted in the three kin-slayings[271] and centuries of hopeless war. And on the mortal side of his heritage Elrond counts as a forefather Beren, who swore to Thingol that

271 The first was at Alqualondë, where the Noldor fought the Teleri for use of their ships; the second was when Doriath was destroyed by the sons of Fëanor; and the third was at the Havens of Sirion, where the final refuge of Elves in Beleriand was obliterated in a failed attempt to regain the last Silmaril from Elrond's mother Idril.

'when we meet again my hand shall hold a Silmaril.'[272] Beren fulfilled his oath, but it was twisted: when he returned the Silmaril was indeed in his hand, but the hand was in the belly of Carcharoth the wolf. Warned by this heritage, Elrond is fully aware that vows—even those sworn in good faith—are perilous; to be feared, not encouraged.[273]

Stubborn as only dwarves can be, Gimli remains unbowed before Elrond's judgement. Perhaps cynical at the prospect of working with peoples whose endurance and loyalty he regards as suspect, he insists on the value of oath-swearing by quoting a further proverb. Elrond's response reflects both his compassionate nature and his epistemological scepticism:

> *Sworn word may strengthen quaking heart.*
> *Or break it. Look not too far ahead.*

Gimli's implication—that some members of the Fellowship (not himself!) could do with strengthening—is countered by a straightforward appeal to emotional well-being. Elrond is commissioning the Fellowship to attempt a task whilst admitting that he does not know how it will be achieved. His consideration of the psychological health of the group is pastoral and kind, especially to the hobbits.

The final warning—*Look not too far ahead*—is typical of Elrond's cautious attitude towards the future. Just as vows are dangerous because they are presumptuous, so even the most well-informed assumptions can be proved false. The next step is the only step on which one should put their weight.

The Half-elven: the weight of history

> *'May the stars shine upon your faces!'*[274]

Leaving Imladris as evening falls, the members of the Fellowship walk into the shadows of night and of impending evil. But in the sky above them the Silmaril shines in the darkness, bound to the brow of the star-sailor Eärendil and serving both as a guide for the present and a reminder

272 Tolkien, *The Silmarillion*, p. 168.

273 A further example of the 'twisting' of oaths is found in that made by Gollum: he unwittingly fulfils his promise 'to serve the Master of the Precious' by taking and destroying the Ring when Frodo could not.

274 Tolkien, *The Lord of the Rings*, p. 274.

of the past, when even greater darknesses were overcome. Eärendil's son Elrond, standing as the inheritor and interpreter of this heritage, bids the Fellowship farewell. He stands in the midst of the peoples of Middle-earth, not fully belonging to any of them but somehow representing the combined wisdom of all, just as his father once stood before the Valar as Middle-earth's representative. The journey to a December night in Rivendell from a snippet of Old English poetry—the process of 'finding out,' of grasping the elusive beauty of the star-angel Earendel—led Tolkien through the whole history of Middle-earth, and culminated with Elrond and the Fellowship of the Ring.

In the person of Elrond, as well as in his children, much of the highest and best of Middle-earth's history is embodied—the beauty of Melian and Lúthien, the royal kingdoms of Doriath and Gondolin, the valiant courage and faithfulness of Beren and Tuor, and so on. But when he speaks of the 'many defeats, and many fruitless victories' he has seen, Elrond reveals the extent to which his wisdom is built not only on the beautiful lessons of history, but also the bitter. The rash pride of his Noldorin forebears, the arrogance of his great-great-grandfather Thingol, the tragic destruction of Gondolin, Menegroth, and the Havens of Sirion: all are just as much the story of Half-elven family tree as its beauty and light.

If, as Søren Kierkegaard asserted, 'life can only be understood backwards,'[275] then Elrond is chief among those seeking to learn from what has gone before. Having grown up balancing the truths and contradictions of his heritage, Elrond makes Rivendell a refuge for the waning wisdom of the Elder Days. There, the good, the wise, and the beautiful endure as he appropriates the past: both the sweet and the bitter. The burden of history appears heavy, but Elrond has an ability to know much whilst holding on lightly to what he knows.

In stark contrast with Saruman and Denethor, the Third Age's other great accumulators of learning, Elrond applies his knowledge with a humility that verges on the self-effacing. He could have become king after the fall of Gil-galad, but chose instead to be a counsellor; he could have built a great stronghold, but preferred to found a refuge; he could have commanded others, but opted for counsellors like Erestor and Glorfindel rather than yes-men or slaves. And significantly, Elrond learns from his

275 As quoted in Alastair Hannay, *Kierkegaard: A Biography* (Cambridge University Press, 2001), p. 113.

proverbs. *It is perilous to study too deeply the arts of the Enemy, for good or for ill*, he says, whilst Denethor probes the palantír and despairs, and Saruman becomes enamoured of power having 'long studied the arts of the Enemy himself.'[276]

Instead of seeking power, Elrond's desire is for a synergy between Middle-earth's various cultures. His greatest contribution to the War of the Ring—the bringing together an unprecedented Fellowship of divergent peoples—is a direct outworking of his collaborative mediating role. Having inherited an intermediary status, Elrond's humility and collegiate instincts help him recognise the value of diversity and collaboration; that truth is greater than the perspective of any single person or people. He may be the greatest of lore-masters, but it is in the joining together of disparate peoples that hope is found. The Wise have their part to play, but Elrond is unsurprised that it is a hobbit who is chosen to bear the Ring and, with it, the fate of all.

> *Such is oft the course of deeds that move the wheels of the world: small hands do them because they must, while the eyes of the great are elsewhere.*

The light of Eärendil, brightest of stars, is therefore more than literal illumination. It is the combined wisdom of Men and Elves, embodied in Elrond, and enlightening Middle-earth. The days are dark and in need of something to drive back the Shadow, just as the Dark Ages of the poet Cynewulf needed heavenly radiance. The days may be dark, but they are lit by the wisdom of the Half-elven, just as *Middengeard* was once lit by the celestial Earendel.

276 Tolkien, *The Lord of the Rings*, p. 251.

CHAPTER SIX

THE ELVES

'I reckon there's Elves and Elves. They're all Elvish enough, but they're not the same.'[277]

By the time that Tolkien had begun trying to find out what his first fictional creation, the star-mariner Earendel, was really about, he had already been inventing languages for at least a decade—indeed, he later asserted that he had been doing so since he could write.[278] Beginning with 'Nevbosh' (co-created with cousin Mary Incledon) and the Spanish-based 'Naffarin'[279] during childhood days, he continued the craft into adulthood.[280]

As an undergraduate, Tolkien's linguistic creativity was primarily devoted to a Finnish-based language called 'Quenya,' which had developed to the point where he could even write poetry in it. But as he worked at this private hobby, he discovered that 'you cannot have a language without a race of people to speak it.'[281] Additionally, since peoples and

277 Tolkien, *The Lord of the Rings*, p. 351.

278 Carpenter. *Letters*, p. 143.

279 Carpenter, *Biography*, p. 36-7.

280 CS Lewis, on first meeting Tolkien in 1926, had clearly been made aware of his linguistic pastime, recording in his diary that 'Technical hobbies are more in his line. No harm in him' (as recorded in Carpenter, *The Inklings*, p. 23.)

281 Carpenter, *Biography*, p. 75.

languages do not materialise out of thin air, Tolkien also needed to 'create for the languages a 'history' in which they could develop.'[282]

It was in this process of reverse-engineering a people from their language that the speakers of Quenya emerged: the *Quendi* or Elves; beautiful and wise creatures, immortal within the life-span of the world. Out of the soil of an invented tongue, a people had emerged—no other beings in all literature had previously been birthed in such a way.

For a man with such vast creative energy, one language was never going to be enough. Soon a second was devised, different but etymologically linked to the first. 'Sindarin' naturally demanded its own distinct speakers, as well as a collection of satisfying historical reasons for its similarities to and differences from Quenya. It was therefore out of a technical linguistic division that the Sundering of the Elves emerged: the tale in which the Valar summon the newly-awakened Quendi to join them in the Blessed Realm, but many refuse.[283] Tolkien's language-making hobby had brought forth both people and plot, whilst simultaneously setting the stage for all the subsequent drama of Middle-earth.

The Undying Tradition

'We still remember, we who dwell
In this far land beneath the trees
The starlight on the Western Seas'[284]

Frodo, Pippin, and Sam, walking through the Woody End at dusk, are saved from the attentions of a Black Rider by a group of High-elves, Quenya-speaking exiles from the West. The great days of this ancient people are so long-gone that they live with a constant burden of sadness and nostalgic regret.[285] They had once been great beyond the Halflings' comprehension: former residents of the Blessed Realm with 'faces that

282 Carpenter, *Biography*, p. 89. Also see Carpenter, *Letters*, p. 219: 'The stories were made rather to provide a world for the languages than the reverse.'

283 The divergence of the two tongues being due to the separation between the *Calaquendi*—the Elves of Light, who reached and lived in Valinor—and those wandering tribes who remained in Middle-earth. John Garth discerningly observes that while Quenya, 'the language of lore,' was devised during undergraduate days at Oxford, Sindarin, 'the language of adventure, tragedy, and war' emerged after Tolkien's experiences in the Battle of the Somme. (Garth, *Op. Cit.*, p. 213.)

284 Tolkien, *The Lord of the Rings*, p. 1005.

285 Carpenter, *Letters*, p. 197.

have seen the Light, and... voices that have spoken with Manwë.'[286] Yet the years had taken their toll, and the Elves whom Frodo greets in their own Fair Speech with the blessing-proverb *elen sila lumenn omentielvo* ('a star shines on the hour of our meeting') had become little more than a living relic, a mummified shadow of their former glory.

Exiles like Gildor Inglorion had lived in the paradise of Valinor and seen perfection. They remembered it. But they were doomed to endure while the world around them diminished, and while their songs and ideals retained a semblance of that ancient unblemished idyll, it was all they could hope for to (as Elrond said) 'preserve all things unstained.'[287] It was to this end that the Three Elven-rings were created, to preserve ancient beauty unstained by creating enclaves of peace where Time seems to stand still.[288] As a result, even the lands in which they no longer live remember them: *Much evil must befall a country before it wholly forgets the Elves*, as Gandalf's proverb says.

While Men and Dwarves desire (or are, at least, fascinated by) Elven immortality, it appears true that, as Shippey says, the Eldar 'had not been punished by death, rather by weariness of life.'[289] Perpetual longevity might have set the Elves free from the restrictions common to mortals, but to what end? Men or Dwarves, had they been uninhibited by old age and death, would have indulged in endless, productive action, but the Elves hold different desires. Gradually fading from the glory of the Elder Days—when, in the first flush of youthful pride they built nations and alliances, and directly contested Morgoth for mastery of Middle-earth—the Elves had turned away from proactive attempts of transformative action.

Shaped by their story of gradual decline, the elves met in the pages of *The Lord of the Rings* are less interested in learning from the past as they are in recreating or preserving it. Humphrey Carpenter draws out a similar feature in Tolkien himself. After losing his parents and many friends to sickness or war, as well as the countryside of his childhood to urban expansion, 'he had a deep sense of impending loss. Nothing was safe. Nothing would last. No battle would be won forever.'[290] The passing of

286 Tolkien, *Unfinished Tales*, p. 67.

287 Tolkien, *The Lord of the Rings*, p. 262.

288 Carpenter, *Letters*, p. 157.

289 Shippey, *The Road to Middle-earth*, p. 241.

290 Carpenter, *Biography*, p. 31.

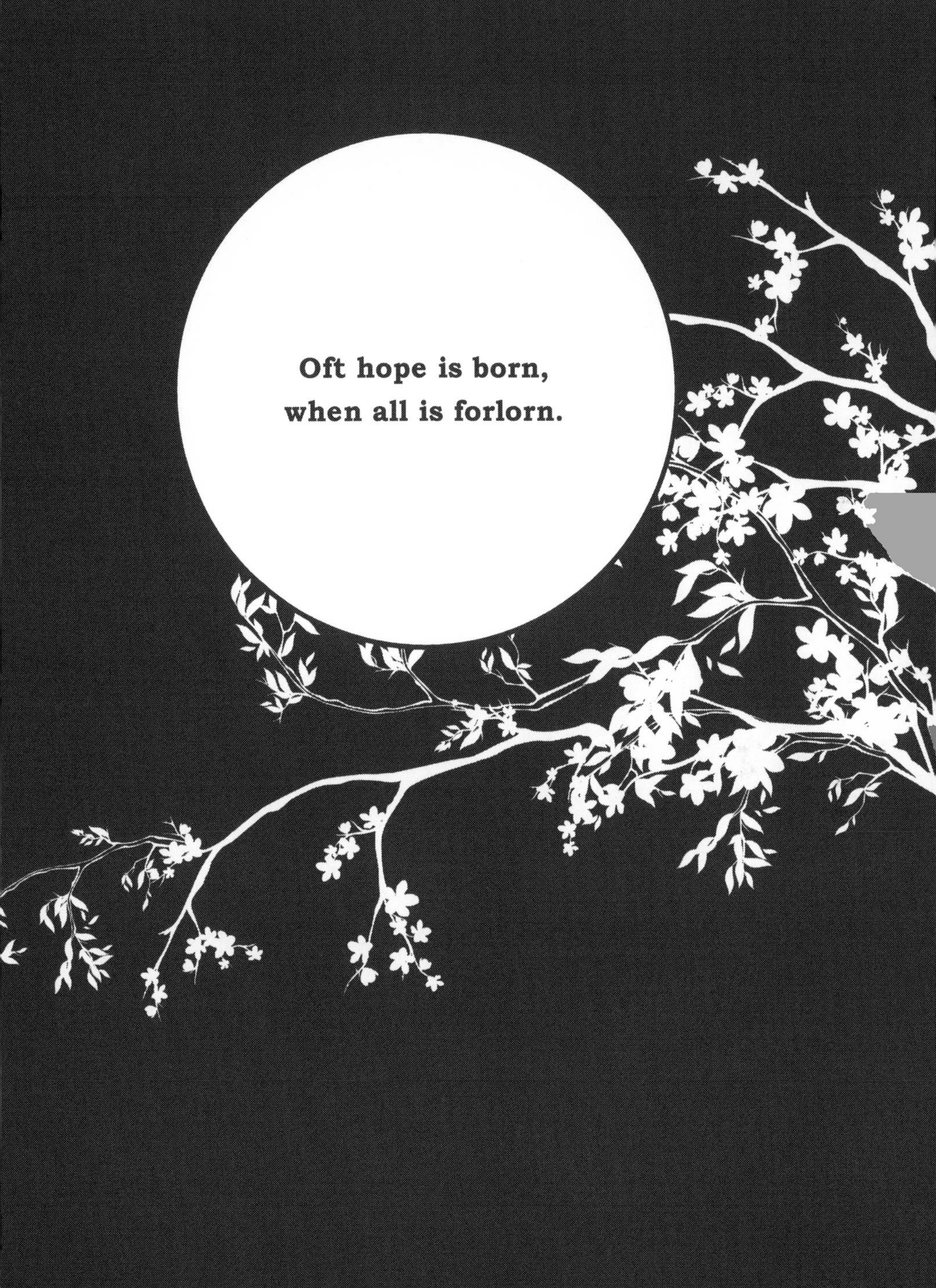
Oft hope is born,
when all is forlorn.

time—what Galadriel refers to as 'the long defeat'[291]—was as grievous a thing to Tolkien as it was to the Elves.

Wider and Deeper

Alone of the peoples of Middle-earth, the Eldar have knowledge (and in many cases, practical experience) of the Valar and the Undying Lands, and as a result carried into the Third Age a wider, deeper understanding of reality than any mortal. Unambitious, embalming, and action-averse they may have become, but like their great forebears these fading Elves still seek to teach those who would learn.

It is in the context of this tutoring that the Elvish use of proverbs comes to the fore. Due to their longevity, the purpose of oral tradition is not primarily used by Elves to pass on knowledge to other generations, but to other peoples, and especially to describe to mortals aspects of reality that their short-lived status cannot observe.

Examples abound. When Celeborn tells the Fellowship that *Maybe the paths that you each shall tread are already laid before your feet, though you do not see them* he is both expressing the Elvish unwillingness to be surprised by the unpredictability of life, whilst also prophetically describing the future of the Quest. Likewise, Galadriel's warning against far-sightedness, *Seeing is both good and perilous,* is tragically proved true by Saruman's corruption and Denethor's descent into despair and madness; both caused by unwise use of the *palantíri*, the seeing-stones.

While these sayings can sound like little more than philosophical platitudes, they repeatedly prove prescient—their truth is born out by later events. Elven proverbs often paradoxically foretell whilst warning against predicting the future; they are far-sighted but wary of far-sightedness. In this vein, Gildor tells Hobbits that *Advice is a dangerous gift, even from the wise to the wise*; and Legolas reminds Man and Dwarf that *Tomorrow is unknown,* and *Few can foresee whither their road will lead them, till they come to its end.*

Hobbits seem particularly eager to learn from the Elven tradition. Sam memorises and repeats Haldir's *A rope may be a help in many needs,* the Elvenking's *It's an ill wind that blows no one any good* reappears in the mouth of the Gaffer, and Gildor's *Do not meddle in the affairs of*

291 Tolkien, *The Lord of the Rings*, p. 348.

Wizards, for they are subtle and quick to anger is remembered and used by both Merry and Sam.

Likewise, the effect of Bilbo's relationship with the Elves of Rivendell is shown in the Elven axioms he learns and passes on to Frodo. *Go not to the Elves for advice, for they will say both no and yes* is an example of this probable loan-work—it must be borrowed since Hobbits have no working knowledge of Elves—as also are sayings like *The Road goes ever on and on* and the first stanza of Bilbo's 'All that is gold...' proverb-poem for Aragorn.

Through maintaining this proverbial tradition, Elves are able to teach and train those others who are willing to learn. But they are not seeking to convert Men or Dwarves into Elves. Having learned to distrust even themselves, the Elves recognise that wisdom is wider than any single philosophy or worldview, however well-informed. Therefore, when Boromir derides his own folk tradition as old and far-fetched—'for the most part old wives' tales, such as we tell to our children'[292]—Celeborn admonishes him, saying *Oft it may chance that old wives keep in memory word of things that once were needful for the wise to know.* To Elves like Celeborn, the wisdom of another tradition, like that of Gondor, is just as worthy of attention as their own.

When the Quendi finally tear themselves away from Middle-earth, passing beyond the walls of the world and into the West, with them leaves the last memory of Valinor and of the Eldar Days. But, in no small part due to their influence and instruction, they leave behind a range of mortal races more able to 'keep alive the memory of the age that is gone... and so love their beloved land all the more.'[293]

Legolas

'Legolas Greenleaf, long under tree,
In joy thou hast lived. Beware of the Sea!
If thou hearest the cry of the gull on the shore,
Thy heart shall then rest in the forest no more.'[294]

292 Tolkien, *The Lord of the Rings*, p. 364.

293 Tolkien, *The Lord of the Rings*, p. 1006.

294 Tolkien, *The Lord of the Rings*, p. 492.

In the First Age, the greatest and most enduring of the Elven kingdoms in Beleriand was that of Doriath: a hidden woodland realm ruled from an underground stronghold excavated beside a forest river. The death of its king, Thingol, and the Sack of Doriath were at the hands of the Dwarves, originating the enmity between two peoples that had previously been allies.

Six and a half millennia later, Thranduil the Elvenking (whose father Oropher was probably an escapee of Doriath[295]) rules a similarly hidden woodland realm, again with an underground stronghold excavated beside a forest river. Legolas is the king's son, the inheritor of the high legacy of Thingol, the Wood-elves' devoted love of the physical world, and an abiding suspicion of Dwarves.

> *'[The Wood-elves] are not wicked folk. If they have a fault it is their distrust of strangers... and after the coming of Men they took ever more and more to the gloaming and the dusk. Still elves they were and remain, and that is Good People.'*[296]

Having been sent by his father to the Council of Elrond, Legolas is thrust into the cross-cultural context of the Fellowship, and into awkward comradeship with other peoples. Although otherwise calm and self-possessed, this is a wholly alien position and his frustrations, particularly with Gimli, occasionally spill over. In such moments, not only is Legolas' exasperation revealed, but also the proverbs of a people who have never trusted Dwarves, do not like them, and do not desire to understand them.

> *Dwarves are strange folk.*
> *A plague on Dwarves and their stiff necks!*

The contrast between the elegant, graceful, woodland elf and his gruff, hyper-masculine,[297] stone-hewing companion is stark, with distrust and wariness on both sides. An elf like Legolas would never have been comfortable submitting to the authority of a dwarf, but he does appear at ease under the leadership of other races, whether the Half-elven Elrond at council, or Gandalf (and latterly Aragorn) in the Fellowship.

---

295 Tolkien, *Unfinished Tales*, p. 259.

296 Tolkien, *The Hobbit*, p. 194.

297 Dwarves as a race conform to masculine stereotypes, as well as having few (and bearded) females. Elves, by contrast, are beardless, fair of face, and can be seen as generally fitting feminine stereotypes.

Since he so rarely seeks to impose, or even raise, his own perspective—he has to be asked directly for an opinion on whether to risk entering Moria, for example—it is easy to forget that Legolas is a royal prince (with all the inherited seniority of position that implies). He is accustomed to leadership and to being obeyed. When Legolas submits to the authority of others, it should therefore not be mistaken for passivity, but as wise deference to those more able than he.

The reverse is also true: when he is the most appropriate person to provide leadership, Legolas is not backwards in coming forwards. On entering Lothlórien, for example, which to the Elves of Mirkwood is a sister-kingdom, he immediately takes the lead, guiding the Fellowship over Nimrodel while telling its story in word and song, and negotiating with those of the Galadhrim whom they encounter. In this Legolas proves himself as a trustworthy leader, to the extent that, when he proposes that they enter Fangorn on the trail of Merry and Pippin, Gimli is willing to say one of the humblest things a dwarf can ever say to a non-dwarf: 'Where you go, I will go."[298]

But when not required in a leadership role, Legolas appears loath to offer his opinions; remaining silent or proffering an occasional proverb. *Let a ploughman plough, but choose an otter for swimming*, he says on snow-bound Caradhras, and *Let us first do what we must do*, when debating how to respond to the death of Boromir. These are pragmatic sayings and display no particular philosophical perspective, only the Wood-elves' basic understanding of practical necessity. But a coherent philosophical worldview does underlie them.

The Mirth and Melancholy of Mirkwood

Unlike the hidden inhabitants of Lothlórien, the Elves of the Woodland Realm are not isolationists. They enjoy trade relationships with Lake Town and Dorwinion, willingly form a military pact with Bard the Bowman, and hold such figures as Gandalf, Radagast, and Aragorn in honour. That the Elves of Mirkwood had developed a vocabulary of proverbs may, in part, be due to these cross-cultural relationships and the consequent need to communicate their nature and worldview to outsiders.

Sam's confusion over the length of the Fellowship's stay in Lothlórien provides a context for these sayings to be used, as Legolas explains the

298 Tolkien, *The Lord of the Rings*, p. 480.

Elvish perspective on time with a string of proverbs. *Time does not tarry ever,* he says, *but change and growth is not in all things and places alike.* To the unaging Elves, *The passing seasons are but ripples ever repeated in the long long stream*, and yet their immortality is only limited to the span of the world itself, and *Beneath the Sun all things must wear to an end at last*.

The way in which the Wood-elves utilise natural, organic imagery in their proverbs is striking: simple concepts of growth, streams, boats, and water are employed to explain perspectives that are otherwise mysterious to mortals. While drifting down Anduin, Legolas compares the flow of time to the movement of a great river against which no one can ultimately fight, and the consequent heartbreak of letting go of that which is past:

> *Such is the way of it: to find and to lose, as it seems to those whose boat is on the running stream.*

There is an underlying sadness in many of these sayings, reflecting the melancholic disposition of all latter Elvish civilisations. While there are exceptions—Galion's *There is nothing in the feeling of weight in an idle toss-pot's arms* comes out of the Wood-elves' proclivity for feasting—the tone is generally one of pessimism. The Elves are committed to loving and preserving Middle-earth, but they are doomed to lose that which they love. Whatever choices they make, the fading process of decline will continue. It is for this reason that *Deep in the hearts of all [Elves] lies the sea-longing, which it is perilous to stir*. Escape (or return) to the West, making way for the Age of Men, lies inexorably ahead. The sense of impending loss is palpable.

Nevertheless, Legolas has a wisdom tradition that also recognises the foolishness of presuming too much about the future. *Tomorrow is unknown*, he warns, *Few can foresee whither their road will lead them, till they come to its end*. As a result, he is never in despair: at times he resembles an Elven Phileas Fogg, stoically unwilling to waste emotional energy (whether anger or anguish) on things that are outside his control. Instead he responds with hope: *Oft hope is born, when all is forlorn*, he reminds Gimli, and *Rede oft is found at the rising of the Sun*.

Elves like Legolas do not base ethical choices on the impact those choices will have: they are not Consequentialists, and in all his proverbs, Legolas exhibits this deep-seated determination not to be brow-beaten by what ifs and maybes, but to act with hope and nobility however dark the future may appear. This is encapsulated when he and Gimli recount their journey with Aragorn. Having braved the Paths of the Dead, galloped through southern Gondor to Pelagir, and raced up the River in the nick of time to turn the tide of battle outside Minas Tirith, they still know that if Frodo should fail, all their efforts would be in vain. Was all their effort therefore a waste? Legolas says no, on the basis that results neither define nor denigrate virtue.

> '*Follow what may, great deeds are not lessened in worth,*' said Legolas. 'Great deed was the riding of the Paths of the Dead, and great it shall remain, though none be left in Gondor to sing of it in the days that are to come.'[299]

The Galadhrim

> *'Whether they've made the land, or the land's made them, it's hard to say... If there's any magic about, it's right down deep, where I can't lay my hands on it, in a manner of speaking.'*[300]

The Elves of the Lothlórien are both similar to, and distinct from, their kindred of the Woodland Realm. Similar because they are, for the most part, rustic Silvan elves with no experience of Valinor, who had come to be ruled by Sindar lords ostensibly from Doriath.[301] But by the time of the War of the Ring, the distinctions between the two realms had grown.

The coming of Galadriel—sister of the King of Nargothrond, bearer of the Elven-ring Nenya, and planter of mallorn trees—dictated Lothlórien's later distinctives.[302] Alongside Celeborn, 'the wisest of the Elves of Middle-earth, and a giver of gifts beyond the power of kings,'[303] Galadriel oversaw the transformation of a small, rustic realm into a stronghold mighty enough to resist all encroachment of the Enemy. In Lothlórien there is no evil, unless a man brings it with him.

299 Tolkien, *The Lord of the Rings*, p. 859.

300 Tolkien, *The Lord of the Rings*, p. 351.

301 According to *Unfinished Tales* these were Oropher, father of Thranduil, and Malgalad/Amdir of Lórien (Tolkien, *Unfinished Tales*, p. 240, 258).

302 Galadriel was by this time the most senior of all the Noldor remaining in Middle-earth—born in the Years of the Trees, daughter of Fëanor's half-brother Finarfin, and sister of Finrod Felagund, King of Nargothrond.

303 Tolkien, *The Lord of the Rings*, p. 347.

Between the Noldorin Galadriel, the Sindarin Celeborn, and the Silvan population at large, Lothlórien does not present a united wisdom tradition or philosophy as such. Instead it is its mixture of embalmed sanctum and time-free enclave that sets it apart. The Elven-ring, wielded by the Valinor-remembering Galadriel, has hallowed the realm, making it an unfallen 'on earth as it is in heaven' land where 'no blemish or sickness or deformity could be seen.'[304]

The distinctiveness of the Galadhrim is therefore more than a higher strain of mere 'Elvishness.' Lothlórien is an unstained Eden, protected from the wider world but also estranged from it, hemmed in within unseen borders. Upon entering the Naith, the Fellowship quickly become aware of an 'otherness' about the place, as if the ticking clock of the outside world has no influence within its bounds.

> *'It seemed to [Frodo] that he had stepped over a bridge of time into a corner of the Elder Days, and was now walking in a world that was no more. In Rivendell there was memory of ancient things; in Lórien the ancient things still lived on in the waking world… on the land of Lórien no shadow lay.'*[305]

Having walked into a corner of Middle-earth where 'the original unmarred goodness of creation'[306] still endures, it is natural that the Fellowship should take especial notice of its inhabitants. Their guide, Haldir, is one of the few of the Galadhrim who still has dealings with the Outside and speaks its common language. Since his life effectively consists of passing between fallen and unfallen worlds, he has a rare perspective to convey.

Haldir's pronouncements, though arguably not proverbs *per se*, resonate with the poetic wisdom of the Elder Days that still lives in Lothlórien. *The light perceives the very heart of the darkness*, he assures the Fellowship, whilst also observing that *In nothing is the power of the Dark Lord more clearly shown than in the estrangement that divides all those who still oppose him*. He also has acquired the habit (previously noted in Gandalf) of building sentences around proverbial phrases, without marking their presence. This lends a feeling of wise weightiness to Haldir's words:

304 Tolkien, *The Lord of the Rings*, p. 341.
305 Tolkien, *The Lord of the Rings*, p. 340.
306 Wood, *Op. Cit.*, p. 20.

'The world is indeed full of peril, and in it there are many dark places; but still there is much that is fair, and though in all lands love is now mingled with grief, it grows perhaps the stronger.'[307]

Dealing With Dwarves

The Elves of the Third Age have a poor reputation—'net-weavers and sorcerers'[308] is the view of the usually generous Éomer, whose people say that *Webs of deceit were ever woven in Dwimordene*—and perhaps they have earned it. Certainly, the Galadhrim are poor in diplomacy. Upon the Fellowship's arrival at Caras Galadhon, bringing the news of Gandalf's demise, Celeborn singles out Gimli as the cause by saying that had he known the tragic news he would have forbidden the dwarf's entrance. Gimli, the first of his people to be admitted to Lothlórien since the glory days of Moria, sits apart, humiliated and alone.

In that moment, Galadriel reveals the value of proverbs as cultural currency. Alone of the Galadhrim, she is one of the Noldor; the branch of Elvendom historically closest to the Dwarves, due to their shared relationship with the Maia Aulë. From this position of kinship, Galadriel reaches out across the cultural divide by quoting *Dark is the water of Kheled-zaram, and cold are the springs of Kibil-nala*, an idiomatic Dwarvish saying about their ancient kingdom.[309] By using a Dwarvish saying (probably learned at least a thousand years before, when Moria was still inhabited), Galadriel is able to demonstrate her knowledge of and esteem for Gimli's heritage in a language the dwarf can understand.

It is this kind of respect that is craved by the Dwarves but rarely received. The bond forged in this single moment of compassion and affirmation is as strong as the Dwarves' legendary stubbornness, and is reinforced as the Fellowship leaves Lothlórien. Galadriel asks Gimli to name his parting-gift, and Gimli refuses. Galadriel commends the grace of his words and re-iterates her request. Gimli stammeringly submits and asks for a strand of her hair, to the astonishment of all. The exchange concludes with Galadriel quoting and refuting a proverb of the Galadhrim's:

307 Tolkien, *The Lord of the Rings*, p. 339.

308 Tolkien, *The Lord of the Rings*, p. 422.

309 Gimli had earlier used the same saying when first drawing near Moria (Tolkien, *The Lord of the Rings*, p. 276).

> 'It is said that *the skill of the Dwarves is in their hands rather than in their tongues*,' she said; 'yet that is not true.'[310]

Finally, Galadriel asks Gimli what he would do with her hair. 'Treasure it, Lady,' he answers, 'in memory of your words to me at our first meeting.'[311] Galadriel's unusual decision to use and honour a Dwarvish proverb at the time Gimli was at his lowest has clearly cut him to the heart. He is changed, not only in terms of his respect for Galadriel but also in relation to his attitude to all Elves: his great friendship with Legolas also stems from this moment of grace.

Elves: the past and the present

> *'Why, to think of it, we're in the same tale still! It's going on. Don't the great tales never end?'*[312]

A central role of all wisdom traditions is the linking together of what was with what is. In the same way, as they live through the great arc of history and pass on its lessons, the Elves represent a 'continuity between the ancient and the modern world' which, as Shippey suggests, Tolkien valued very highly.[313] He loved the interplay between the past and present, the recognition that—as Sam realises on the stairs of Cirith Ungol—all history is one great, ongoing story, and that 'what has been gives meaning and context for what is.'[314]

The Elven cultures of Middle-earth display the full flourishing of wisdom and craft, unhindered by mortality, yet also burdened by the weight of history. Living solely in realms built around preservation,[315] it is perhaps natural that the Elves of the Third Age should reverence the past, aching for what is gone and preserving what is left. But the Long Defeat also means tending the interlocking web of history—in which every part of the Story is understood to be seamlessly connected to every other part—as if it were a living thing.

---

310 Tolkien, *The Lord of the Rings*, p. 367.

311 *Ibid.*

312 Tolkien, *The Lord of the Rings*, p. 697.

313 Shippey, *Roots and Branches*, p. 304.

314 Bruner & Ware, *Op. Cit.*, p. xii.

315 Whether it be Lothlórien, Lindon, Imladris, or the Woodland Realm, all Elven settlements are declining enclaves. Not since the founding of Eregion in the Second Age had a new territory been conquered and settled.

Songs and sayings, passed down from one era to the next, may express and preserve that interconnecting tradition, but no amount of adherence to Celeborn's *Do not despise the lore that has come down from distant years* could transform a land into the unblemished Eden that Lórien is. For that, the Elven-ring is needed.

As foundational as it is to their realm, the Elven-ring is also at the heart of the melancholy of the Galadhrim: they know that even if the Quest succeeds and the One Ring is destroyed, the sustaining power of Galadriel's ring will also end and, with it, Lothlórien itself. Celeborn may say that *Though the world is now dark better days are at hand*, but he is speaking of Middle-earth at large, not his land or his people. For it is not only Lothlórien that is doomed: all Elves are condemned to defeat, diminishing, or departing. There are no other options. *Night must follow noon*, as Galadriel herself says. After the age of the Rings, there was nothing left for them in Middle-earth for them but weariness.[316]

316 *Carpenter, Letters, p. 236.*

CHAPTER SEVEN

THE DWARVES

'The dark filled all the room, and the fire died down, and the shadows were lost… suddenly first one and then another began to sing as they played, deep-throated singing of the dwarves in the deep places of their ancient homes.'[317]

The *Khazad*, the grim figures singing in Bilbo's prim hobbit-hole, are a people apart, neither Children of Illúvatar like Men or Elves, nor tasked emissaries of the Powers as were the Ents, Eagles, and Istari. The Dwarves are different. Fashioned by Aulë the Smith, the craftsman of the Valar, when his intense desire for new created life outgrew his patience, the resulting people reflect their maker: skilled in the finding and fashioning of raw materials; stubborn and stiff-necked; proud and jealous; rash and impatient. And strong.

'Aulë made the Dwarves strong to endure. Therefore they are stone-hard, stubborn, fast in friendship and in enmity, and they suffer toil and hunger and hurt of body more hardily than all other speaking peoples; and they live long, far beyond the span of Men, yet not forever.'[318]

While much of their history, from the Seven Fathers to Thorin and Company, is known, the major problem with discovering the distinctives of

317 Tolkien, *The Hobbit*, p. 17.

318 Tolkien, *The Silmarillion*, p. 44.

the Dwarves' nature is their intense secrecy. Dwarves do not even tell their own true names to non-dwarves, let alone teach their language (which they protect by adopting the tongues of those near whom they live).[319] This means that while, externally, the Dwarves (or *Naugrim*) may be defined by physical strength and obduracy, they also have wrapped themselves around with a strong existential shield of protection. The secrets of Dwarvish hearts remain secret, and non-dwarves are held at arm's length. They are a people apart.

Tolkien compared this idiosyncratic nature with that of the Jewish diaspora: a people apart, at once native and alien, speaking the languages of the surrounding peoples but with a distinctive accent due to their own tongue.[320] Possibly influenced by this thought, he constructed *Khuzdul*, the Dwarvish language, along Hebraic/Semitic lines, with triconsonantal roots[321] and a comparable phonology. The comparison could even be extended, with both Jews and Dwarves at times subject to cartoonish stereotyping, both known for expertise in the working of precious stones and metals, and both recipients of great jealousy and/or distrust. But the central point of resemblance is between two wandering peoples, both severed from their ancestral homelands, and both remaining distinct from the cultures amongst which they settled. However, even this intriguing parallel can only be taken so far; we have to look elsewhere for glimpses of the Dwarves' inner wisdom.

It is a fair assumption to presume that songs and sayings—the truths a people tell of themselves to themselves—should provide the best means of discovering the Dwarves' soul. But we are explicitly told that Khuzdul is primarily 'a tongue of lore,'[322] meaning that most of the Dwarves' proverbs are presumably in that unknown, inaccessible language. If it were not for the helpful fact that the Naugrim are chronically unteachable, the Dwarves' oral tradition would be a closed book to outsiders. But because of their prideful unwillingness to accept any wisdom but their own, it is highly unlikely that the proverbs they do employ when

319 According to some of Tolkien's writings, this mania for secrecy may even have extended to using a rudimentary 'sign language' to communicate privately in the presence of others. (cf. *The War of the Jewels,* Christopher Tolkien, Editor (Houghton Mifflin, 1994), p. 395.)

320 Carpenter, *Letters*, p. 229.

321 Examples of Dwarvish words with triconsonantal roots include *Khazad* (kh-z-d), *Zirakzigil* (z-r-k, z-g-l), and Kheled-zâram (kh-l-d, z-r-m). While there are few Dwarvish words extant, those that are known generally follow this structure.

322 Tolkien, *The Lord of the Rings*, p. 1106.

using the Common Speech are borrowings from other traditions. It is therefore to these Common Speech sayings that we must look for insight into Dwarvish worldview and philosophy.

Stone-hard, Yet Insecure

The central irony about the Dwarves' wisdom tradition is that little or no wisdom is actually displayed. A few proverbs do carry judicious insight—Gimli's *Maybe there is no right choice* can be seen as plaintive and thoughtful, while *Faithless is he who says farewell when the road darkens* is a worthy paean to loyalty—but the majority have no such depth. Why not? Because they are not intended to.

The Dwarvish proverbs that we hear have been translated primarily for the benefit of non-dwarves. This means that their main function is not the passing on of wisdom from one generation to the next, but the proclamation of a message to outsiders, typically one emphasising the Dwarves' own greatnesses, or doing down other races. This smacks of a kind of ethnocentrism—the belief that one's own people or race are the measuring rod by which all others should be assessed—as well as a complete lack of humility. As a result of this self-centredness, the combined wisdom message of the Dwarves is presented as being little more than (as the Scots traditionally say) 'Wha's like us?'

Gimli's words and actions are a case in point. When he says that *The legs of Men will lag on a rough road, while a Dwarf goes on, be the burden twice his own weight*, it is an impudent (and imprudent) display of trumpet-blowing, especially in the company of Aragorn. Likewise, when unable to find fault with the impregnable fortresses of the Hornburg and Minas Tirith, he falls back on criticism of those who defend them: *Men need many words before deeds*, he says, and *It is ever so with the things that Men begin: there is a frost in Spring, or a blight in Summer, and they fail of their promise*.

Throughout the Quest of Erebor and (as represented by Gimli and, to a small degree, Glóin) in the War of the Ring, dwarves appear perpetually brash and boastful, proud to the point of conceit, and guilty of repeatedly showing off or seeking conflict in an attempt to appear impressive. Presumably, young dwarves would have been raised to adulthood surrounded by such sayings, grounded in ethnocentric pride or ancient simmering grudges harboured and passed on.

The psychological implications of such a worldview are intriguing. Beneath the bragging, there appears to be some kind of existential insecurity about the Dwarves. This is highly suggestive.

A comparison could be drawn between this mentality and the younger child of a large family: eternally in the shadow of greater siblings, he falls into the trap of seeking approval by brazenly trumpeting his most meagre triumphs, and when praise is not forthcoming or is lukewarm, he responds by undermining or pointing out the perceived weaknesses of others, to cut them down to size. Perhaps, as children not of Ilúvatar but of Aulë, there is even a feeling of illegitimacy in the Dwarves' perception of themselves, expressed by the need to deligitimise all others.

Whatever the insecurities or vulnerabilities beneath, the desire underlying all their sayings is for retributive scores to be settled and for the Naugrim to be restored to pride of place—at the head of every hierarchy. *The curse of a Dwarf never dies*, said Androg to Túrin in the First Age, or, as Bilbo observes, *There is no knowing what a dwarf will not dare and do for revenge*.

If it is no surprise, given their origins and history, that the Dwarves are dismissive (if not outright distrustful) of others, the degree to which the misgivings and mistrust go both ways should also be noted. This is particularly apparent in the number of proverbs spoken about Dwarves by other peoples. As a rule, it is rare for proverbs to describe whole races, but the Dwarves are such an enigma that several other cultures have developed sayings about them. These range from the Galadhrim of Lothlórien (*The skill of the Dwarves is in their hands rather than in their tongues*) and the Sindar of Mirkwood (*A plague on Dwarves and their stiff necks!* and *Dwarves are strange folk*), to Hobbits of the Shire (*Dwarves are sometimes politer in word than in deed*). Even Smaug himself—a peculiar source of wisdom, but certainly a Dwarf-expert after his long life in the Withered Heath and Erebor—warns Bilbo *Don't have more to do with dwarves than you can help*.

In addition to these examples, several descriptive sayings appear in the mouth of the narrator,[323] uncredited to any particular source:

> *Stone-hard are the Dwarves in labour or journey.*
> *Dwarves make light of burden.*
> *Dwarves are not heroes.*

323 The narrator's voice being assumed to be primarily that of Bilbo or Frodo.

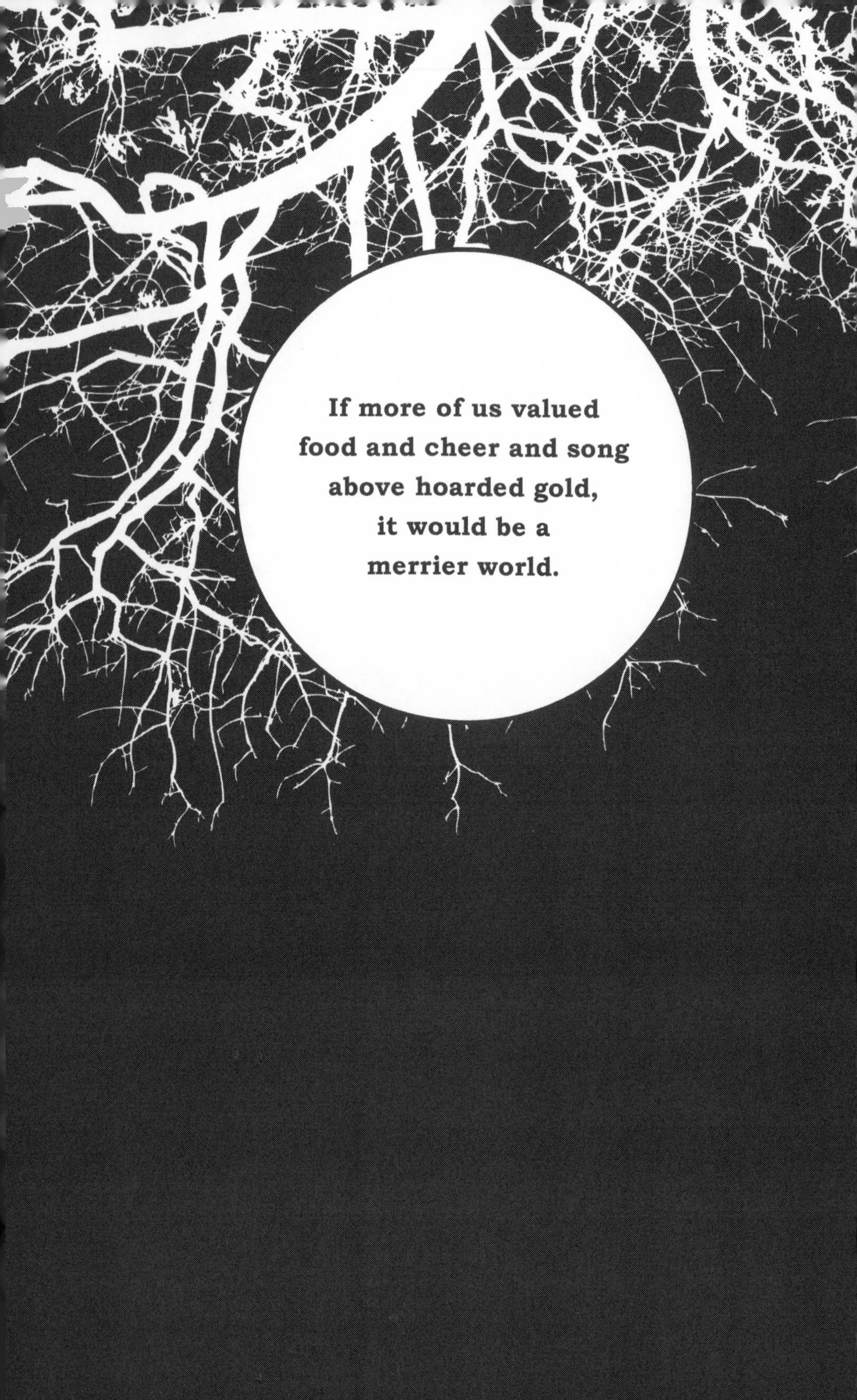
If more of us valued
food and cheer and song
above hoarded gold,
it would be a
merrier world.

These descriptive proverbs are an attempt to fill the vacuum of direct knowledge of the Dwarves. What is known (or guessed) may be passed on through oral tradition, yet the net result of such attempts to define this people is only to magnify the mystery surrounding them.

The Naugrim remain the proverbial riddle wrapped in an enigma: proud but insecure; rich yet never satisfied; desiring respect but rarely giving it. They are a people who parade their (self-perceived) greatness while refusing to disclose their emotional or philosophic core, giving no opportunity for others to learn from or honour the things in which they take so much pride.

THORIN

In 1923, Tolkien contributed a poem of his own composition to a Leeds University magazine. The poem was called 'Iumonna Gold Galdre Bewunden,'[324] a line taken from *Beowulf* that translates as 'the gold of ancient men, wound round with magic.'[325] In it, Tolkien describes the effect of a treasure-trove on its successive possessors, including a dwarf who 'counted the gold things he had got' even as his eyes grew too dim to enjoy them. In the same way that Sauron's precious Ring ends up possessing its possessor, the curse of the poem's hoard is that its owners become its helpless slaves. For Tolkien's dwarf, 'His hope was in gold and in jewels his trust'[326] yet the treasure gives him no satisfaction, nor is it any protection against the subsequent coming of a dragon.

The poem serves as a warning against greed and that 'idolatry of artefacts'[327] which Tolkien and his close friend CS Lewis both hated. While the poem's characters each 'begin with vitality, mirth and courage, they end in age, wealth and squalor.'[328] Gold—and more specifically the love of gold—is their downfall. The message of the poem is identical to the lesson learned from Thorin's life.

---

324 Published in altered form in *The Adventures of Tom Bombadil* as 'The Hoard.'

325 Shippey, *The Road to Middle-earth*, p. 87

326 *Iumonna Gold Galdre Bewunden*, retrieved from http://tolkien.ge/index.php?title=Iumonna_Gold_Galdre_Bewunden

327 CS Lewis, 'The Problem of Pain,' from *The Complete CS Lewis Signature Classics*, (HarperCollins, 2002), p. 591.

328 Shippey, *The Road to Middle-earth*, p. 87.

Thorin Oakenshield was the grandson of Thrór, the last King Under the Mountain before the coming of Smaug.[329] Fabulously rich, Thorin would have been raised with every advantage that a Dwarf could be offered, education included, but was then forced to live the majority of his life in exile and poverty, owning little and commanding few. He was twenty-nine years old when Smaug destroyed the Kingdom of Erebor, and one hundred and ninety-five at the dragon's death, spending the interim years brooding on the 'pale enchanted gold' he had lost and the duty of vengeance he had inherited.

After the death of Thrór was followed by the vengeful glory of the War of the Dwarves and Orcs, and the pyrrhic victory of the Battle of Azanulbizar, Thorin chose to bide his time. Too proud to beg for charity, he chose independence though it required a life of menial labour, including 'blacksmith-work or even coalmining.'[330] His justification—that *The hammer will at least keep the arms strong until they can wield sharper tools again*—is a splendid example of Dwarvish wisdom, emphasising strength, endurance, and a confident expectation of future glory.

Thorin preferred to suffer a century in exile rather than ask for help. Nursing 'a great anger without hope,'[331] he waited and plotted until a chance meeting with Gandalf in Bree led to the two of them formulating the Quest of Erebor.[332]

Strength, And Other Weaknesses

> *'Curb your pride and your greed, or you will fall at the end of whatever path you take, though your hands be full of gold.'*[333]

So Gandalf counsels Thorin, and in doing so identifies the Dwarves' great flaws: the 'deadly sins' of hubris and avarice. Each of Tolkien's peoples appear predisposed to certain moral weaknesses—Men, for example, to impatient lust for power, Hobbits to gluttony and laziness, and Elves to a melancholic tendency to live in the past. Unchecked, these will limit or scupper their potential. Dwarves are brave, fantastically loyal, and know the value of hard work, but they are prone to pride and to greed, and

329 As such he was Heir of Durin and head of the most senior of the Dwarvish houses, the Longbeards.

330 Tolkien, *The Hobbit*, p. 30.

331 Tolkien, *The Lord of the Rings*, p. 1051.

332 Tolkien, *The Lord of the Rings*, p. 1052-3.

333 Tolkien, *Unfinished Tales*, p. 325.

as blind to their own arrogance as they are slaves to their covetousness. They do not see any fault to curb. Michael Stanton's observation, that in Middle-earth 'it is wisdom to recognize one's fallibility,'[334] is both Gandalf's core message and at the heart of all prudence. It is also Thorin's greatest weakness, and the warning goes unheeded.

Like all the Naugrim, Thorin's belief is that he and his people are the envy of everyone else; stronger, braver, better friends, worse enemies, more dexterous, indomitable, and undefeatable. He believes these things because his culture has assured him of their truth. Long grudges passed down from his forefathers have mingled with prideful boasts to form songs and proverbs by which to contrast Dwarven greatness with the perceived weaknesses of everyone else.[335] But it is precisely this faith in his own strength that makes Thorin weak.

By the time of the Unexpected Party, Durin's Folk are at the lowest of ebbs—a militarily weak, wandering diaspora—but the fact that Thorin has no armies, no allies, no lands, and no wealth appears beside the point to him. This king-in-exile still believes that his people are the envy of the world and the greatest force for good within it. He fears no one. 'We have long ago paid the goblins of Moria,' he says, adding with typical hubris; 'we must give a thought to the Necromancer.'[336]

The degree of delusion in this self-assessment is staggering—the thought of the Dwarves defeating Sauron is almost laughable—yet it is matched by the naivety with which Thorin approaches the Quest of Erebor. Ignoring the perils of the Trollshaws, Misty Mountains, Wilderland, and even Mirkwood, he only expects to meet any trouble upon leaving the Long Lake and reaching the Lonely Mountain itself, and his Company comes equipped with musical instruments rather than weapons. Far from encouraging preparedness and research, proverbs like *The less inquisitive you are... the less trouble you are likely to find* have assured the Dwarves that ignorance somehow breeds safety.

Olga Trokhimenko observes that in *The Hobbit* 'The action of the book often fulfils a proverbial saying,'[337] but while this is applicable to Bilbo's proverbs, Thorin's wisdom falls short. There is no foresight or sense of perspective in *It might be worse, and then again it might be a good*

334 Stanton, *Op. Cit.* p. 336.

335 As is shown by Gimli's multiple proverbs of comparison or dismissal.

336 Tolkien, *The Hobbit*, p. 31.

337 Trokhimenko, *Op. Cit.*, p. 369.

deal better, or *There is nothing like looking, if you want to find something*—they are both truisms of the blandest kind—while *Don't start grumbling against orders, or something bad will happen* is leadership by threat rather than example.

In contrast, Bilbo's family sayings prove both useful and true: *Every worm has his weak spot* he says, and is proved right; while *If you sit on the door-step long enough, you will think of something,* though spoken in the comfort and safety of Bag End, exactly predicts the Company's future position on their arrival at the Lonely Mountain. It quickly becomes apparent that the only person with the wherewithal to head the Company is its least-travelled member. Bilbo repeatedly and proactively makes plans and takes personal risks (justifying them with proverbs remembered from home) while Thorin, far his senior in terms of rank and experience, looks on.

Bewundered

Kings-in-waiting are expected to be judicious and learnéd, representing all that is best about their culture. Thorin is therefore a disappointment. Gandalf may call him 'a great Dwarf of a great House'[338] but, having 'no clear idea what to do,'[339] his leadership abilities are painfully and repeatedly exposed. It is only when the Company are in positions of safety—in the Great Hall of Laketown and behind the fortified front gate of Erebor—that Thorin starts to act like a king. His proverbs at these times—the wary *Nothing can escape Smaug once he sees it,* the stirring *Lock nor bar may hinder the homecoming spoken of old,* and the haughty *Winter and snow will bite both men and elves*—become more authoritative. But he does not grow wiser, showing little inclination to shrewd discourse or reflective debate at any stage.

Like his people as a whole, Thorin prefers physical might to strength of wisdom, and endurance to insight; and he prefers gold to all of them. Even with the dragon dead and a river of gold available to heal the hurts caused to all, Thorin allows the 'Iumonna Gold Galdre Bewunden' to guide his policy rather than good sense, neighbourliness, or compassion. His hunger to possess outweighs all other hungers. As

338 Tolkien, *Unfinished Tales*, p. 326.
339 Tolkien, *The Hobbit*, p. 26.

Bilbo tells Bard and the Elvenking, 'He is quite prepared to sit on a heap of gold and starve.'[340]

It is therefore with great pathos that the most memorable and self-evidently true proverb that Thorin uses should be on his deathbed. After a lifetime consumed either by wealth or by its absence, the King under the Mountain sees through his own folly and recognises that Bilbo is an exemplifier of a wise life. *If more of us valued food and cheer and song above hoarded gold, it would be a merrier world,* Thorin says, but it is a lesson that comes late to him.

Gimli

> *'Tell me, Legolas, why did I come on this Quest? Little did I know where the chief peril lay... Torment in the dark was the danger that I feared, and it did not hold me back. But I would have never come, had I known the danger of light and joy. Now I have taken my worst wound... Alas for Gimli son of Glóin!'*[341]

Gimli is an important dwarf. A member of the royal house of the Longbeards,[342] he was considered too young (at sixty-two years of age) to join his father Glóin and the other companions of Thorin Oakenshield in bringing about the reestablishment of the Kingdom under the Mountain, [343] but arrived at Erebor soon after.

Gimli's royal status would have seen him take on a significant role in that first generation of new leaders who directed the great labours of restoration in Dale and under the Mountain described to Bilbo by Balin, and to Frodo by Glóin. Along with his father, he is then sent by King Dáin to Rivendell, to seek wisdom and to warn Bilbo of the repeated visits of a messenger from Mordor looking for news of Hobbits. Having taken part in the Council of Elrond, Gimli is then appointed to the Fellowship of the Ring as the sole representative of his people.

Having grown up in a mostly dwarf-only world, wary of outsiders, Gimli grows to trust other peoples slowly, beginning with the Men of Dale and the Beornings of Wilderland, then Hobbits and—uniquely amongst

340 Tolkien, *The Hobbit*, p. 313.

341 Tolkien, *The Lord of the Rings*, p. 369.

342 Being the great- great- great-grandson of Náin II, Thrór's grandfather.

343 Tolkien, *Unfinished Tales*, p. 336.

his people—Elves.[344] After the defeat of Sauron, it is his inter-cultural collaborations that gain notice. Firstly, he works with the Rohirrim in founding a Dwarvish colony at Aglarond, becoming the Lord of the Glittering Caves. Then he collaborates with the Men of Gondor, crafting new mithril gates for Minas Tirith and helping forge relationships with the new Elvish settlement in Ithilien, established by his friend Legolas. Finally, and most surprisingly of all, Gimli alone in all the history of his people is permitted to join Legolas and cross the Sundering Sea into the West.[345] This is a far cry from his early relationships with non-dwarves. The gradual humbling of the stiff-necked Gimli over the course of the Quest is one of the most subtle character transformations in the story.

Stiff-necked to Something Special

As he is first presented, Gimli seems almost pathologically incapable of accepting his own weakness or the strength of any who are not of his race. He publicly argues with Elrond, before confronting Haldir of Lothlórien with his axe, and preparing even to fight Éomer on the Wold of Rohan. *A plague on Dwarves and their stiff-necks!* cries Legolas in frustration. Gimli's pride is chronic, his attitude unteachable and dismissive. He believes himself rich, and seems set to follow Thorin's path, with conceit and arrogance increasing along the road to spiritual poverty. But he escapes that fate.

It is through the kindness of Galadriel[346] and the friendship of Legolas that Gimli's obduracy slowly softens, along with the mortal blow his pride receives when following Aragorn on the Paths of the Dead:

> *'I was put to shame: Gimli Glóin's son, who had deemed himself more tough then Men, and hardier under earth than any Elf. But neither did I prove'*[347]

In the gradual process of humbling that Gimli undergoes, his use of proverbs is regular but limited. When still in Rivendell, his exchange with

344 He receives a name—'Elf-friend'—that most Dwarves would doubtless have taken as a grievous insult.

345 Tolkien, *The Lord of the Rings*, p. 1072.

346 As discussed in the chapter on The Elves, Galadriel re-uses Gimli's own *Dark is the water of Kheled-zaram, and cold are the springs of Kibil-nala*, to build trust with the dwarf, before arguing against the Elven proverb *The skill of the Dwarves is in their hands rather than in their tongues,* and gifting Gimli three strands of her hair.

347 Tolkien, *The Lord of the Rings*, p. 856.

Elrond (including *Faithless is he that says farewell when the road darkens,* and *Sworn word may strengthen quaking heart*) suggests a proverb-rich person, but this pattern does not continue. Gimli is a wisdom-pauper. Even in Moria, the great home of his forefathers and the source of their wealth, he is impoverished—he may recite a Dwarvish rhyme of lore, saying *Dark is the water of Kheled-zaram, and cold are the springs of Kibil-nala,* but he has nothing further to aid the Fellowship bar staunchness.

Stuck in this prideful poverty, thoughtful reflection takes a consistent backseat to his people's habit of firing disparaging pot-shots at others (including *Strange are the ways of Men, Men need many words before deeds,* and *The legs of Men will lag on a rough road, while a Dwarf goes on, be the burden twice his own weight*). Even as Aragorn and Legolas repeatedly turn to their own proverbs for consolation and counsel after the death of Boromir, Gimli's wisdom tradition offers no contribution beyond a shrug of the shoulders and *Maybe there is no right choice*. Likewise, while proverbial phrases such as *Rest a little to run the better,* and *Mortals cannot go drinking ent-draughts and expect no more to come of them than of a pot of beer,* are true enough, they are not the words and wisdom of the great leaders amongst whom Gimli finds himself.

As the Quest continues and the depth of companionship deepens, the eyes of Gimli are opened to reality: both to the qualities of non-dwarves and to his own limits. Through Galadriel's kindness and affirmation, Gimli's heart is touched and he begins to recognise Elven beauty and light; in friendship with Legolas, this is built upon and expressed in companionship; and in submission to the guidance and counsel of Aragorn and Gandalf, Gimli can start to make peace with his own place in the scheme of things.

Having accepted that others may be more fitted for leadership—and even that the Dwarves may not be the perfect people he had been raised to believe—Gimli's value as a comrade and companion is increasingly revealed. He still may be thrilled to win the Orc head-count at Helm's Deep, but Gimli is also able to sit in Minas Tirith and bond with an elf in reflective conversation, without rushing to assert Dwarvish superiority or needing to win the argument:

> *'It is ever so with the things that Men begin: there is a frost in Spring, or a blight in Summer, and they fail of their promise.'*

> *'Yet seldom do they fail of their seed,' said Legolas. 'And that will lie in the dust and rot to spring up again in times and places unlooked-for. The deeds of Men will outlast us, Gimli.'*
>
> *'And yet come to naught in the end but might-have-beens, I guess,' said the Dwarf.*
>
> *'To that the Elves know not the answer,' said Legolas.*[348]

Quietly exchanging the proverbial expressions of their peoples with both thoughtfulness and respectful humility, the elf and dwarf are clearly close companions—a relationship has been forged which will even outgrow Middle-earth itself. In reaching this point, Gimli has become wealthy in a way few dwarves ever have been. Having recognised a degree of his poverty, he is now rich in cross-cultural experience; rich in humility and self-awareness; and rich in friendship. He goes on to become a great lord with vast wealth, but his wealth of wisdom helps him avoid the idolatry of artefacts, and the words of Galadriel are proven true:

> *'I say to you, Gimli son of Glóin, that your hands shall flow with gold, and yet over you gold shall have no dominion.'*[349]

Dwarves: fanatical lovers of the beautiful

> *'As they sang the hobbit felt the love of beautiful things made by hands and by cunning and by magic moving through him, a fierce and a jealous love, the desire of the hearts of dwarves.'*[350]

Love, beauty, and magic; ferocity, jealousy, and desire. The Dwarves' craving of splendour and magnificence is so fierce within them that it often conceals a more tender core: that they are truly children of Aulë—craftsmen, and fanatical lovers of the beautiful.

This love is both the Dwarves' great strength and their chief weakness. It motivates them to fashion and forge the greatest works of craft, yet by it they are easily enflamed into covetous malice: the killing of Thingol to gain the last Silmaril; the awakening of Moria's Balrog by delving too greedily for mithril; and the stubborn refusal of Thorin to negotiate over the distribution of Smaug's treasure. Dwarvish history echoes the

348 Tolkien, *The Lord of the Rings*, p. 855.

349 Tolkien, *The Lord of the Rings*, p. 367.

350 Tolkien, *The Hobbit*, p. 19.

biblical warning that 'the love of money is a root of all kinds of evil' and that 'some people, eager for money, have... pierced themselves with many griefs.'[351]

Created to be courageous, toughness is the Dwarves' stock in trade, the self-image they extend to the world, though Thorin and Gimli express it in contrasting ways. Thorin is resolute to the point of immovability, but this is often applied unhealthily, by giving short shrift to things or people that could help him. To Thorin's mind, seeking counsel, guidance, or support is to admit weakness, and admitting weakness is itself a weakness.

Thorin is courageous enough to believe that whatever comes, the Dwarves can endure it—but he is wrong. Self-effacing humility, hunger to learn, and willingness to be corrected are never engaged with. That Thorin is mortally wounded by recklessly leaving his stronghold to fight in the open, and also is converted to teachability on his deathbed, are both sadly ironic.

Gimli's story is different. Beginning from a similarly prideful starting point, the process of change is long, slow, and far from smooth. But it is a path walked with courage. From Dwarf-only upringing to cross-cultural bridge-builder, and from obstinate and stubborn to humbly teachable, his is a journey that is completely alien to his people. Seen in this light, engaging and honouring the distrusted and unknown is in itself an act of courage, and undergoing an existential journey of self-discovery requires strength of character. Gimli never becomes less a dwarf—strength and courage are still at the heart of all he does—but he reapplies those traits in a wiser way.

Gimli's acceptance of non-Dwarvish modes of thought and practice is unique amongst his people. Elsewhere, Dwarves are stiff-necked to the point of defiance, immovable in the face of the facts. The fiery love they feel towards their works and possessions has led directly to this state, with delight turning to greed, and defence to distrust. Stubbornness entrenches their estrangement: unwilling to accept as authoritative any source of knowledge but their own, or to admit their own imperfections, the Dwarves are weak in wisdom and poor in prudence. Because of the things they treasure, the Dwarves impoverish themselves. Gimli becomes the exception to this rule.

---

351 1 Timothy 6:10, *Holy Bible, New International Version*.

Tom Shippey asserts that the uniquely Dwarven philosophy of life 'is a kind of unyielding scepticism,'[352] but it could also be said that this is exactly the philosophy that Gimli overcomes. He learns how to learn. But Gimli is no wide-eyed convert. Pragmatism—the school of 'what is good is what works'—is at the heart of his philosophy, and the changes in Gimli can be seen as an extension of this core. If a problem is better solved through recourse to an Elven or Mannish trait than a Dwarvish one, his pragmatism will see that it makes sense to follow that path (whereas a more sceptical dwarf like Thorin might consider it a problem not worth solving).

Gimli's pragmatism recognises that beauty can exist outside of his people—in the Glittering Caves of Aglarond, for example, or the hair of the Lady Galadriel—and as a fanatical lover of the beautiful, this opens to door to respect and friendship with non-dwarves. The new perspectives he learns may be acceptable to him because they work, but their effect is to set him apart from the rest of his race. His death, when it comes, exemplifies this.

Gimli dies, not in Erebor or Moria like his forefathers, nor even in the Glittering Caves where his own Dwarvish colony had been established, but in Valinor. Desiring to walk his friendship with Legolas to its conclusion, and to see the Lady Galadriel again, Gimli passes over the Sundering Seas. After a lifetime of crossing dividing lines, he becomes the first of the Dwarves to reach the Blessed Realm.

352 Shippey, *The Road to Middle-earth*, p. 121.

CHAPTER EIGHT

THE ROHIRRIM

'They are proud and wilful, but they are true-hearted, generous in thought and deed; bold but not cruel; wise but unlearned, writing no books but singing many songs.'[353]

The heart of Tolkien's professional life was as a student, teacher, and lover of the Old English language and mind. In Middle-earth it is the Rohirrim who, 'down to minute details,'[354] most closely embody the peoples of whom he learned and lectured.

When the sons of Eorl speak their own tongue, it is Old English that we hear; and when these brave, high-hearted, unlearned men are described, it is the Saxons of the Dark Ages that provide the mould. With the addition of an equine culture and the panache it brings, the gallant Northmen of Rohan are to the Númenóreans of Gondor as the northern Germanic tribes were to the Greeks or Romans: uncultivated, undomesticated, and untamed. Of all his peoples, it is the Rohirrim whom Tolkien 'regarded with most affection.'[355]

By the time of the War of the Ring, the Eorlingas and their beloved horses had lived in the plains and dales of Calenardhon for five hundred years, having been granted the province in thanks for delivering Gondor in time of war. This northern people, relatives of the Beornings

353 Tolkien, *The Lord of the Rings*, p. 420.

354 Shippey, *The Road to Middle-earth*, p. 117.

355 Shippey, *The Road to Middle-earth*, p. 122.

of Mirkwood, the Bardings of Dale, and the princes of Rhovanion, had changed little in moving south, in spite of the opportunity to intermingle and intermarry with Men of Gondor. As Faramir explains:

> *'Of our lore and manners they have learned what they would, and their lords speak our speech at need; yet for the most part they hold by the ways of their own fathers and to their own memories, and they speak among themselves their own North tongue.'*[356]

The Rohirrim have a brisk, startling energy to them. They are not old and jaded like Gondor but young, confident, and free; longing for no greater glory than to remain so. Faramir describes them as 'Middle Men,'[357] neither of the high culture of Númenor and the Elf-friends, nor related to the Men of Darkness: Easterlings, Haradrim, and the like. As staunch enemies of the Enemy, the Rohirrim are friends and allies of the Wise, but not counted among them.

Evermind

The wisdom of Rohan is not book-knowledge but oral heritage, primarily expressed in Anglo-Saxon meadhall traditions of story and song.[358] This makes the Rohirrim keenly aware of, and emotionally close to, their forebears. Other forms of commemoration abound—wood-carvings, shield and banner emblems, and burial mounds covered in *simbelmynë*, the 'evermind' flower of remembrance[359]—but it is singing that primarily keeps history at the Horse-lords' fingertips.

> *'The whole of their culture is based on song'*[360]

The Eorlingas sing their history,[361] they lullaby their children,[362] and they chant their calls to arms.[363] These are a people who fight,

356 Tolkien, *The Lord of the Rings*, p. 663.

357 *Ibid.*

358 The name of the King's citadel, *Meduseld*, itself means 'meadhall' in Old English.

359 See Shippey, *The Road to Middle-earth*, p. 126 on 'evermind' as emblematic of oral heritage and 'the preservation in memory of ancient deeds and heroes in the expanse of years.'

360 Shippey, *The Road to Middle-earth*, p. 125.

361 'Where now the horse and the rider?' as translated by Aragorn (Tolkien, *The Lord of the Rings*, p. 497), and 'We heard of the horns' (Tolkien, *The Lord of the Rings*, p. 831).

362 Songs which then 'come down among us out of strange places, and walk visible under the Sun.' (Tolkien, *The Lord of the Rings*, p. 537.)

363 'Arise now, arise,' Tolkien, *The Lord of the Rings*, p. 506, 820.

mourn,[364] and even venerate their slain horses[365] in verse and melody. Their national hope is that even in death they may 'make such an end as will be worth a song.'[366]

In this the Rohirric Northmen are quintessentially Germanic, sharing with the historical Saxons, Danes, and Vikings a tradition that is fundamentally oral and poetic. Tom Shippey asserts that 'The King of the Golden Hall' (the chapter in which the Rohirric culture is met) is 'straightforwardly calqued on *Beowulf*,'[367] the greatest of the Anglo-Saxon epic poems, and that Aragorn's recitation of 'Where now the horse and the rider?' is a mirror of *The Wanderer*, part of the Exeter Book from 10th Century England. The Eorlingas see their lives as lyrics.

But this strong tradition of song is very different from the hymn-like singing of the High Elves, whose lyrics remember Elbereth, 'the starlight on the Western seas,'[368] and other 'high' matters. The Rohirrim sing solely about their own people, with staves formed by their experiences and shaped to fit their land. Likewise their proverbs. Even in the royal house there is little high philosophical thought like that of the Elves or Númenóreans (nor even earthy time-worn insight akin to that of rustic Hobbits). Rather, what we see is a younger folk tradition; the practical engagement of the horse-lords' temperament with their new land.

The Wisdom of the Wold

Relocating to Rohan had brought with it an array of new neighbours. Gondor, Saruman the Wizard, and the Galadhrim of Lothlórien on the one hand, the 'dreams and legends' of Fangorn, the Pukel-men, and the Paths of the Dead on the other (along with the ever-present threat of invasion from Orcs and Wainriders to the east or Dunlendings to the west). Resultantly, the proverbs of Rohan tend to cover two principal topics: the peril of other peoples, and the craft of war.

When one of the Rohirrim's armed *Éored* is first encountered, riding back down the Orc-trail to Aragorn, Legolas, and Gimli, its leader Éomer uses proverbs to challenge the incomers and to introduce his people:

364 'Out of doubt, out of dark,' Tolkien, *The Lord of the Rings*, p. 954.
365 Tolkien, *The Lord of the Rings*, p. 827.
366 Tolkien, *The Lord of the Rings*, p. 527.
367 Shippey, *The Road to Middle-earth*, p. 124.
368 Tolkien, *The Lord of the Rings*, p. 1005.

The stranger should declare himself first, he says, and *The Men of the Mark do not lie, and therefore they are not easily deceived.*

This natural distrust of outsiders, amplified by being in a state of war, is similarly shown when Gandalf and the Three Hunters arrive at Edoras. The sayings used by Háma (*The staff in the hand of a wizard may be more than a prop for age*), Gríma (*Ill news is an ill guest*), and Théoden (*News from afar is seldom sooth*) make it clear that, in Rohan's wisdom tradition, wariness and judgement of character is paramount. Yet when Théoden is moved away from fear and into action, his proverbs also shift gear—speaking of courage, hope, and 'great heart'—showing that this national wariness is not motivated by fear.

The inherited stories through which the Eorlingas tell their history to themselves reinforce a national identity based in indomitable courage—what Shippey calls the 'grim and ruthless streak of ancient Northern heroism.'[369] Fram killed the dragon Scatha and made a necklace from his teeth; the gallant Eorl, though under no obligation, rode the length of Wilderland to the aid of Gondor; Eorl's grandson Baldor dared to enter the Paths of the Dead; and Helm Hammerhand, under siege in the Hornburg, crept out by night weaponless to grapple by hand with the enemy.[370]

The Rohirrim are therefore at their best looking fear in the face, regardless of the consequences. Théoden, arising from premature decrepitude, may humbly call himself 'a lesser son of great sires'[371] but in death he knows that he has emulated the greatest of them, and that songs will soon be made of him.

> *'I go to my fathers. And even in their mighty company I shall not now be ashamed.'*[372]

Limited By Language

In addition to a closely-held affection for their forebears enshrined in song, the Rohirrim are equipped with a strong proverbial tradition. The proverbs of the Mark do not appear to cover a wide range of subjects—

369 Shippey, *Roots and Branches*, p. 279.

370 Tolkien, *The Lord of the Rings*, pp. 1039-1042.

371 Tolkien, *The Lord of the Rings*, p. 566.

372 Tolkien, *The Lord of the Rings*, p. 824.

tending instead to stick to the immediate concerns of a martial people—though it is possible that we see no greater variety of subject matter because only the speakers of Westron are heard.

Rohan's leaders, such as Théoden and the House of Eorl, are bilingual—indeed, Éomer's accent is 'in manner and tone like to that of Boromir'[373]—and therefore the proverbs that are heard by members of the Fellowship (who cannot speak Rohirric) almost exclusively belong to this high strata of society, its world and wisdom; people whose lives revolve around authority, not agriculture. The common people, those of fortified towns like Edoras and Aldburg as well as the rural farming communities, probably did not speak much of the Common Tongue. As a result, their voice is silent, along with any distinct proverbial wisdom they might have to share.

To the educated bilingual strata also belong senior members of the royal household, nobles like Háma the Doorward and Gríma the King's counsellor. That these two are conversant in the Common Tongue is shown by the ease of their speech with the visitors, and it is also clear that the proverbs they use are in that language. Háma's *In doubt a man of worth will trust to his own wisdom*, and Gríma's *Webs of deceit were ever woven in Dwimordene* both employ alliteration, a poetic feature would not have been retained were the sayings simple translations. Similarly, the unnamed rider who says *Time does not stand still, though the Sun be lost* is speaking to Merry in the Common Tongue, and again his proverb's alliterative structure shows that it must have been coined in that language. That Rohan has native proverbs in a foreign tongue is testament to the encroaching of the wider world by which the Mark is surrounded, and may also be due to the mixed marriage of Théoden's father Thengel, when 'the speech of Gondor was used in [the royal] house.'[374]

The only proverbial interjections from outside the bilingual sphere of Rohan are from a scout and from Wídfara, members of the common soldiery. Since both are speaking directly to Théoden, and would have had no reason to do so in a foreign language, it is likely that they are speaking Rohirric (though this is not signalled in the text). If so, *He that flies counts every foeman twice* and *The morning will bring new things* represent the only recorded proverbs of the common-folk of Rohan, too

373 Tolkien, *The Lord of the Rings*, p. 421.

374 Tolkien, *The Lord of the Rings*, p. 1044.

meagre a number for nuanced assessment.[375] But the very fact that, of these two sayings, one speaks directly of the need of courage in war and the other of hope, indicates that Rohan's high-hearted warrior-spirit is just as present in the echelons of society as at its royal height.

Théoden

> *'He was a gentle heart and a great king and kept his oaths; and he rose out of the shadows to a last fair morning.'*[376]

King Théoden is a rarity in Rohan—a child of a mixed-marriage. Although he is of the line of kings stretching back to Eorl, he has a unique cross-cultural advantage over his forebears due to a different kind of upbringing and parentage.

The Rohirrim are a proud people, rarely mixing with other nations, but Théoden's father Thengel left the Riddermark as a young adult[377] to live in Gondor. There he met and married Morwen of Lossarnach, a high Númenórean related to the Princes of Dol Amroth. As a result, Théoden was born not in Rohan but in Gondor, and, though he was still a child when his father became King and the family removed to Edoras, Théoden was ethnically mixed, had a foreign language as his mother tongue, and would have been surrounded by foreign perspectives throughout his childhood.

In light of this, the fact that in the latter part of his own reign Théoden restored use of Rohirric as the language of court shows that he did not consider himself as an outsider or an interloper, but rather as the custodian of the heritage and traditions of the Mark. Indeed, in old age few signs remain of his alien birth and upbringing, and Meduseld has no similarity to the White Tower of Minas Tirith. In spite of being conversant in two worldviews and wisdom traditions, Théoden has made no attempt to 'Gondorize' Rohan, preferring rather to re-establish the uniqueness of the people he rules.

---

375 Had the remainder of the Rohirrim spoken the Common Tongue, it is likely that more of their proverbs would have been coined in or translated into it, and a wider, more accurate, range of their wisdom traditions become known.

376 Tolkien, *The Lord of the Rings*, p. 851.

377 Possibly due to a broken relationship with his father, King Fengel, as is implied by Tolkien, *The Lord of the Rings*, p. 1043.

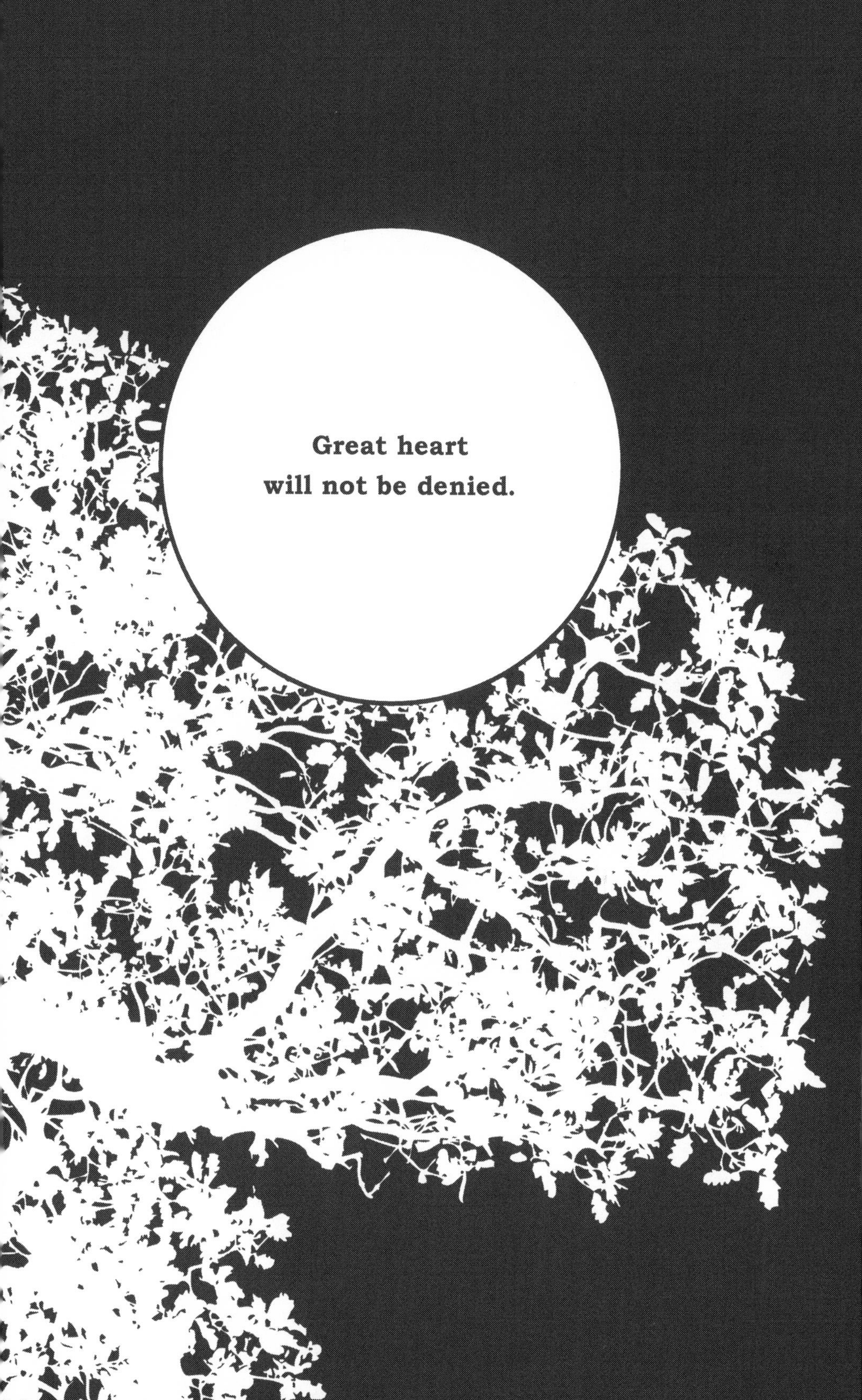
Great heart
will not be denied.

The international, cross-cultural heritage in which he was raised would have given Théoden an advantage unavailable to his forbears: not only would he have had a more objective perspective on his own people than any who had lived solely amongst the Rohirrim, but also he could see the world from an additional viewpoint—that of Gondor. Recognising and comprehending the perspective of Rohan's closest ally and nearest friend (as well as learning from their high Númenórean heritage) would have allowed Théoden a deeper understanding of the Stewards' priorities, and given him the opportunity to align his own policies with their wisdom.

It is possible that a number of Théoden's proverbs are of Gondorian origin, though it is hard to discern. Some, particularly *The world changes, and all that once was strong now proves unsure*, reflect a perspective that would certainly be at home in Minas Tirith; a relic of the greatness of former ages. But elsewhere, the sayings of the King display the direct and courageous pragmatism that is the hallmark of the Rohirrim.

Hope, Fear, and the Urgency of Obligation

Théoden is seen in a range of physical and mental dispositions, and his use of proverbs changes as he changes. In the midst of his Wormtongue-contrived darkness, the despondency of *The young perish and the old linger*, and the cynicism of *News from afar is seldom sooth* reflect the pessimistic poison of his erstwhile counsellor. Later, arising from his decline, we see him in different roles. *In the morning counsels are best, and night changes many thoughts* showcases Théoden-as-politician and the 'wait and see' school of pragmatic statesmanship. Whereas heading into battle, *What we shall achieve only tomorrow will show* is the warrior-king using the sort of axiom of which a Kantian ethicist would approve.

Immanuel Kant taught that results are immaterial to moral worth, which 'only exists when man acts from a sense of duty.'[378] The Rohirrim know all about duty, since their realm was founded and maintained on a promise: the Oath of Eorl, pledging perpetual friendship and alliance between themselves and Gondor. The fruit of the Oath is a national ethic of duty, an absolute determination to corporately fulfil their forefather's promise, whatever the cost. Like a good Kantian ethicist, Théoden

378 Russell, *Op. Cit.*, p. 644.

does not appear to weigh up the likelihood of success, only the urgency of obligation.

Under the influence of Gandalf, the King casts aside regret and fear, and chooses to do the deed at hand. Just as Eorl once rode out of the North, the dutiful Théoden determines to ride to war, even though in doing so he foresees his own demise. No matter. The only success he seeks is 'to make such an end as will be worth a song.'[379] That he is still capable of comprehending childlike wonder (*The days are fated to be filled with marvels*, and *Songs have come down among us out of strange places, and walk visible under the Sun*) alongside the nuances and paradoxes of the malevolent (*Oft evil will shall evil mar*) makes Théoden's rejuvenation into shackle-free warrior king, racing to the aid of Gondor, all the more triumphant.

Arise now, arise, Riders of Théoden!
Dire deeds awake, dark is it eastward.
Let horse be bridled, horn be sounded!
Forth Eorlingas![380]

Éomer

Faithful heart may have froward tongue.

Charging into the fray with the horsetail on his helm flying in the wind, Éomer is emblematic of the Rohirrim's fearless dynamism. Primarily a fighter, not a thinker, he takes after his father, Éomund of Eastfold, who met his death in rashly pursuing a band of Orcs to the Emyn Muil. This event, coupled with the tragic sickening and death of Éomund's wife Théodwyn, left the child Éomer as the elder of two orphans.[381] When he emerged into adulthood and was given his father's charge in the east of the Mark, the same fierce hatred of Orcs that was his father's downfall caused Éomer to disobey orders, and in doing so to save Merry and Pippin from imprisonment, torture, and death.

Éomer is not only fearless in fighting but also in decision-making. In choosing to pursue the Orcs of Saruman, and then aiding Aragorn, Legolas, and Gimli (rather than arresting them as the law demands), he puts

379 Tolkien, *The Lord of the Rings*, p. 527.

380 Tolkien, *The Lord of the Rings*, p. 506.

381 Tolkien, *The Lord of the Rings*, p. 1044.

himself at risk of imprisonment. But does so knowingly: 'In this I place myself, and maybe my very life, in the keeping of your good faith,[382] he explains to Aragorn. Éomer recognises that doing the right thing may be to his own cost—indeed, he is immediately incarcerated on returning to Edoras—but he does not flinch. He has the courage of his convictions.

'Ever near shall be at need nephew to uncle'[383]

Highest amongst Éomer's convictions is fealty to his King. 'I serve only the Lord of the Mark'[384] he declares on meeting Aragorn. This is more than patriotic allegiance or militaristic fealty; it is family and more. As the child of Théoden's sister, Éomer is the King's *sister-son*, a nephew of special importance. Gilliver, Marshall, and Weaver explain that 'in Anglo-Saxon and ancient Germanic custom... the relationship between a man and his sister's son was held to be especially close and binding' and that, amongst other duties, 'It was the sister-son's duty to champion his uncle.'[385] As the child of the King's favourite sister, and as the adopted son of his uncle, Éomer fulfils this role gladly, even when marginalised and unjustly imprisoned. But the deep and tender affection for an aged uncle contrasts strongly with the brash and dynamic young man in full warrior mode.

Furious Wisdom

'Without taking counsel... he spurred headlong back to the front of the great host, and blew a horn, and cried aloud for the onset. Over the field rang his clear voice calling: "Death! Ride, ride to ruin and the world's ending!"'[386]

In battle, Éomer is a terrifying prospect, though even then his fury can betray him. His courage is such that he sees no value in retreat or personal escape when a glorious death can be achieved. On the Pelennor, surrounded with foes and deserted by hope, he laughs at despair and prepares a final shield-wall, only to find that the newly-arrived ships of the Corsairs are filled not with enemies but with friends. Joined by their

382 Tolkien, *The Lord of the Rings*, p. 428.

383 A proverb from Tolkien's 'The Homecoming of Beorhtnoth Beorhthelm's Son,' as cited in Gilliver, Marshall, & Weiner, *Op. Cit.*, p. 190.

384 Tolkien, *The Lord of the Rings*, p. 423.

385 Gilliver, Marshall, & Weiner, *Op. Cit.*, p. 189.

386 Tolkien, *The Lord of the Rings*, p. 826.

leader, Aragorn, he reflects axiomatically: *Hope oft deceives... yet twice blessed is help unlooked for.*

This kind of twin-formulae epigram, with an initial statement undercut or expanded upon by its follow-up, is Éomer's favourite style of proverb, reflecting an enjoyment of paradox and irony more often seen in Gandalf. Sayings of this type[387]—also including *Need brooks no delay, yet late is better than never, Oft the unbidden guest proves the best company*, and *Our Enemy's devices oft serve us in his despite*—show a wry sense of humour, not to mention an understanding that events often confound prediction.

Sardonic proverbs of this sort send the message that life does not always make sense, that reasoned arguments and logical equations are not always reliable. It is perhaps for this reason that, when in counsel with the other Captains of the West, Éomer offers no advice or clever answers, only unwavering service. When he says, 'I have little knowledge of these deep matters; but I need it not,'[388] Éomer is not abdicating his decision-making responsibility, but humbly recognising his own limits.

In being aware of and admitting the bounds of his capabilities in this way, Éomer finds himself in good company, and not only in Middle-earth. Socrates, the father of Western philosophy, is believed to have said that 'true wisdom lies in knowing that you know nothing'—that false assumptions of knowledge are more dangerous than plain ignorance, since such claims are both erroneous and arrogant. Éomer makes no claims for himself, great or small; his wisdom tradition shrewdly teaches to make no pretences. He knows he is a master of arms, not of counsels, and does not need to understand the decisions of his superiors in order to carry them out wholeheartedly.

It is this ego-averse, arrogance-free ethic that makes Éomer such a good soldier. Although willing to disobey orders when circumstances require it, all his duties are performed with a complete lack of self-centredness, a lesson that his sister would have done well to learn.

387 Which may have been learned from King Théoden, who also employs them (eg. *Faithful heart may have froward tongue, Oft evil will shall evil mar*).

388 Tolkien, *The Lord of the Rings*, p. 862.

Éowyn

'I am a shieldmaiden and my hand is ungentle.'[389]

When first seen in her guise as Dernhelm, Merry shivers, perceiving in Éowyn 'the face of one without hope who goes in search of death.'[390] Having disobeyed orders and ridden to war, rather than remain in Rohan as the King's regent, her resolve is validated as she achieves what no man could: the killing of the Lord of the Nazgûl. In doing so she rises higher than any woman, at any time, in any kingdom of Men, and yet her emptiness remains utter.

Recovering in the Houses of Healing, Éowyn feels like a prisoner: she is jealous of the dead, jealous of the now-departed host of the West, even jealous of those with a better view from their windows. She thrashes and flails, desperate to fight but meeting nothing but compassion in return, which only makes it worse. Completely unprovoked, she picks a fight with the Warden (and in doing so proves true her proverb *It needs but one foe to breed a war, not two*), even going as far as to issue a veiled threat to him, *Those who have not swords can still die upon them*. But it is the last of the proverbs she uses that evokes her mood precisely: *It is not always good to be healed in body. Nor is it always evil to die in battle, even in bitter pain.* The Lady of Rohan wishes she was dead.

Duty and Despair

Éowyn grew up as an orphan, adopted into the King's household but with neither mother nor adopted mother. Her lack of female role-models, and the restrictions that barred her from emulating the nation's heroes (virtually all of whom, according to the Appendices, were male), left Éowyn powerless: unable to give vent to the determination, steely character, and latent greatness within her.[391] With a spirit and courage at least the match of Éomer's,[392] but without the opportunity to fight for the fields of Rohan with a company of riders, Éowyn lacks comradeship and is left isolated and alone. She is reduced to 'dry-nursing' the

---

389 Tolkien, *The Lord of the Rings*, p. 939.

390 Tolkien, *The Lord of the Rings*, p. 785.

391 Reminiscent of her grandmother, whom the Rohirrim had named 'Steelsheen' (Tolkien, *The Lord of the Rings*, p. 1044).

392 Tolkien, *The Lord of the Rings*, p. 849.

declining King, a role she deems 'more ignoble than that of the staff he leaned on.'[393]

The arrival of a ragged Ranger to Edoras sparks Éowyn back to life. As Faramir correctly diagnoses, 'You desired to have the love of the Lord Aragorn... but when he gave you only understanding and pity, then you desired to have nothing, unless a brave death in battle.'[394] Having had her love for Aragorn exposed as vain, Éowyn despairs. She seeks no hope even in military victory, only the honour of a valiant end: she goes 'in search of death.' Knowing that none has ever returned from the Paths of the Dead, she begs Aragorn to take her there with him, but is refused, and is instead forced into disguise in order to ride to Minas Tirith with the host of the Eorlingas.

Where will wants not, a way opens, Éowyn declares as Dernhelm, *Good will should not be denied*. Although these words are spoken to and for Merry, a double meaning is also plain: Éowyn is using them to justify her own disobedience. While, by quoting such proverbs, Éowyn shows that she is still in touch with Rohan's philosophical tradition, she is actually being unfaithful to its wisdom. In place of the Rohirric devotion to duty is a different fearless determination: that of self-destruction. Had Éomer employed these same axioms, they would have been an encouragement toward 'great heart' in selfless service, but in Éowyn's mouth they reinforce her own desperate desire to die.

> *'I looked for death in battle... to ride to war like my brother Éomer, or better like Théoden the king, for he died.'*[395]

The Rohirrim do not lie, and Éowyn is no different—her honesty is stunning—but in this mood she becomes quite unlike her people. While Théoden and Éomer embody a Kantian, Deontological ethic—that doing your duty is fundamental to moral goodness—Éowyn scorns such a perspective. 'Too often have I heard of duty,' she says. 'May I not now spend my life as I will?'[396] A self-destructive streak emerges, a nihilism arguing that life carries no intrinsic value or moral purpose, and therefore can be used (or disposed of) at the individual's whim. Éowyn sees no value in her own continued existence, whatever her king or culture might command. Having deserted her post (as *de facto*

---

393 *Ibid.*

394 Tolkien, *The Lord of the Rings*, p. 943.

395 Tolkien, *The Lord of the Rings*, p. 938-9.

396 Tolkien, *The Lord of the Rings*, p. 767.

head of state in the King's absence), she is left to be ruled by her own dark motivations. 'I do not desire healing... and I do not desire the speech of living men'[397] she says.

Disguised as Dernhelm, Éowyn becomes free, but the freedom she gains is the liberty to self-harm. She can ride with the host of the Rohirrim at last, but her motives are not theirs. Surrounded by courageous, faithful men, riding bravely against hopeless odds, she embodies a wisdom of self-dependence and willpower, not of courage or compassion or any of the great virtues. It is therefore fitting that, having failed in her quest for death, she meets her match in the dutiful Faramir, in whom these traits are so prevalent.

Éowyn emerges from her nihilistic darkness not through being argued into submission, but by being loved. Perhaps because she recognises that Faramir is a man 'whom no Rider of the Mark would outmatch in battle,'[398] she is able to listen to him and he to command her respect. Faramir draws her out of despair with his company and kindness, saying *Do not scorn pity that is the gift of a gentle heart,* referring both to Aragorn's reaction to her and to his own love. And it is as he willingly exposes his vulnerable core, that 'the heart of Éowyn changed, or else at last she understood it.'[399] The darkness departs, and she determines to marry, to become a healer, and to 'love all things that grow.'[400] Éowyn remains unconquered in battle, but stops fighting, and Faramir is able to declare to the Warden:

> *'Here is the Lady Éowyn of Rohan, and now she is healed.'*[401]

Rohan: up eorlingas!

Tolkien loved Old English, to the point that (as John Garth observes) he felt that Anglo-Saxon was his true culture and language, denied to him 'crushed and forgotten'[402] in the catastrophe of the Norman Conquest. He devoted much of his working life to it, 'could turn a lecture room

397 Tolkien, *The Lord of the Rings*, p. 939.
398 Tolkien, *The Lord of the Rings*, p. 938.
399 Tolkien, *The Lord of the Rings*, p. 943.
400 *Ibid*.
401 Tolkien, *The Lord of the Rings*, p. 944.
402 Garth, *Op. Cit.*, p. 52.

into a mead hall,'[403] and, in the Mark of Rohan,[404] rehabilitated that lost culture with which he so closely identified. This people were birthed from very near his heart.

The Rohirrim do not merely speak Old English, but a particular Mercian dialect of the language[405] which, as a West-midlander, 'was remote, but at the same time intensely personal' to Tolkien.[406] While the Saxons had seen their language disregarded by the French- and Latin-speaking Normans, at Meduseld Tolkien restores it as a language of court—replacing a foreign *lingua franca*—and to defend it gives its speakers the dynamic equine culture that King Harold lacked at the Battle of Hastings. Even years after its writing, Tolkien singled out the horns of the Rohirrim at cockcrow as a moment in the story that moved him most as he read it.[407]

'Up Eorlingas! Fear no darkness!'[408]

Only days after the death of the King's son had forced the Rohirrim to contemplate the possibility of their kingdom's destruction, the last host of the Eorlingas arrives on the Fields of the Pelennor at dawn. Having been a declining decrepit dotard, fretting in the darkness of Meduseld and leaning on the crooked words of a corrupt counsellor, Théoden now leads his people in joyfully risking everything in order to fulfil their national oath. The joy of battle is upon them and their transformation is complete. Théoden is the resplendent warrior-in-chief, bombastic and inspiring. In all his company, glimmering in the morning light, only the death-wishing Dernhelm appears still to be overwhelmed by darkness. But her light will come.

Out of doubt, out of dark to the day's rising
I came singing in the sun, sword unsheathing.[409]

The lords of the Rohirrim do not stand back and direct their battles from a distance. Denethor of Gondor believes that all great lords use others as their weapons, but the high-hearted wisdom of Rohan disagrees. In

403 Carpenter, *Biography*, p. 133.

404 For Tolkien's use of 'Mark' as a contemporary version of 'Mercia' see Shippey, *The Road to Middle-earth*, p. 123 footnote.

405 Including such names as Saruman, Hasufel, and Herugrim, while Éomer (as noted in Gilliver, Marshall, and Weiner, *Op. Cit.*, p. 122) was an ancestor of the Mercian royal house.

406 Carpenter, *Biography*, p. 132.

407 Carpenter, *Letters*, p. 376.

408 Tolkien, *The Lord of the Rings*, p. 823.

409 Tolkien, *The Lord of the Rings*, p. 829.

their tradition, the King leads from the front, and Théoden does so with such fury of onslaught that it is as much as his *Éored* can do to keep up with his 'hoofs of wrath'[410] as they thunder into the fray. Likewise, the lust of battle is on Éomer to such an extent that he and his riders take their cavalry charge too far and become surrounded. Fearless, he laughs and breaks into song.

For other peoples, war may not be considered the natural or appropriate time for poetry and proverb, but the fighting songs of the Rohirrim and their leaders' axiomatic truths of warcraft (such as *Strike wherever the enemy gathers*) ring across the battlefield nevertheless.

> *'And then all the host of Rohan burst into song, and they sang as they slew'*[411]

Théoden may have a mixed-heritage, but he crowns his life with an undivided heart. He dies, as he was born, in Gondor, but accompanied by the horns and the singing of the Rohirrim. Even his death is triumphant; something like the Nordic hero-figures whose complete refusal to be intimidated Tolkien so loved.[412]

Like the pre-Christian Anglo-Saxons, Théoden's philosophy offers him 'no heaven, no salvation, no reward for virtue except the sombre satisfaction of having done what is right.'[413] This heroic warrior ethic has 'the awareness that death may come, but focuses doggedly on achieving the most with what strength remains.'[414] The Last Host of the Eorlingas does not ride to Minas Tirith because a Happy Ending or reward awaits them, but because it is their duty: the right thing to do. Théoden fulfils his obligations, conquers fear and doubt, and dies in satisfaction. 'Grieve not,' he says with his last breath. 'Great heart will not be denied.'[415]

---

410 Tolkien, *The Lord of the Rings*, p. 820.

411 *Ibid.*

412 Shippey, *The Road to Middle-earth*, p. 256.

413 Shippey, *The Road to Middle-earth*, p. 156.

414 Garth, *Op. Cit.*, p. 71.

415 Tolkien, *The Lord of the Rings*, p. 824.

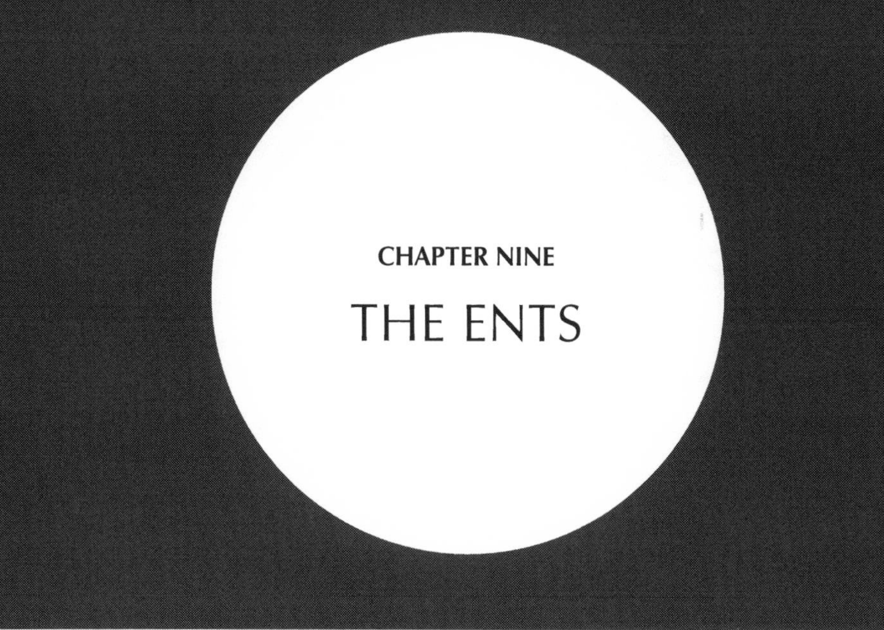

CHAPTER NINE

THE ENTS

'I am not altogether on anybody's side, because nobody is altogether on my side, if you understand me: nobody cares for the woods as I care for them'[416]

Tolkien delighted in trees—looking at them, touching them, drawing them—and his love of the arboreal breathes through all his work. From Doriath to Fangorn, the Old Forest to Mirkwood, Lothlórien to the Woody End, each of his many forests is given a distinct personality, while individual trees (including the White Tree of Minas Tirith, Old Man Willow, and the Party Tree in Hobbiton) are characters in themselves, participants in the tale. Michael Stanton points out that in Middle-earth, 'to be morally sound is to be attuned to the natural world,'[417] while in *The Scouring of the Shire* it is the wanton destruction of the trees that most cuts Frodo and Sam to the heart, and the planting of Galadriel's mallorn that provides consolation.

It is telling that Tolkien's love for trees was such that he portrayed his own vocation in arboreal terms. He described his legendarium—the various histories, languages, peoples, and proverbs of Valinor and Middle-earth—as grown from 'the leaf-mould of the mind,'[418] and in *Leaf By Niggle*, his eponymous hero's lifework is not a tale or a mythology, but

416 Tolkien, *The Lord of the Rings*, p. 461.

417 Stanton, *Op. Cit.*, p. 340.

418 Carpenter, *Biography*, p. 126.

a tree (or a painting of a tree at any rate). Arda itself is therefore both part of a Great Tree and grown from the decomposing compost of leaves from the Tree of Tales. And within it, trees come to life.

The Roots of the Ents

> *'They are but herdsmen. They are not enemies, indeed they are not concerned with us at all.'*[419]

The Ents (or *Onodrim*) are a race apart: a shepherd people whose flocks are not animals but the trees of the forest. Originally partnered by the female Ent-wives, by the time of the War of the Ring they were alone; cloistered in Fangorn Forest and isolated from other races to the point that even their nearest neighbours in Rohan considered them to be no more than a bedside story for children.

The origins of the Onodrim, as recorded in *The Silmarillion*, are ancient. Before Elves, Dwarves, or Men had awakened, the Maia Yavanna feared that they would rule and misrule her creations—the birds, beasts, trees, and plants. 'Shall nothing that I have devised be free from the dominion of others?'[420] she cried to Manwë. He asked her what in her realm she held dearest, and Yavanna named the trees.

> *'Would that the trees might speak on behalf of all things that have roots, and punish those that wrong them!'*[421]

Had Tolkien been asked the same question, his answer doubtless would have been the similar. Humphrey Carpenter describes the Ents as 'the ultimate expression of Tolkien's love and respect for trees.'[422]

The longing that trees might have the ability to defend themselves had weighed heavily on Tolkien since his schooldays. His childhood disappointment, on reaching the climax of Macbeth, that 'Great Birnam wood to high Dunsinane Hill' was only a play on words, disappointed him deeply. He longed to create a means by which the trees might really march into battle.[423] And that is what he did.

419 Tolkien, *The Lord of the Rings*, p. 536.

420 Tolkien, *The Silmarillion*, p. 45.

421 *Ibid.*

422 Carpenter, *Biography*, p. 194. Carpenter also adds the delightful detail that Tolkien admitted modelling Treebeard's *Hoom, Hum* on CS Lewis's booming voice.

423 Carpenter, *Letters*, p. 212, footnote.

Additionally, Tolkien was inspired by a word from the Old English epic *Beowulf*. That word was *ent*, used to describe a giant or mighty person.[424] And so, a single Anglo-Saxon word gave birth to a people (although initially he contemplated making Ents a race of malevolent giants!). The irony of using such a tiny word—a hasty word, even—to describe a large, longevous being would not have been lost on Tolkien.[425]

> *'An Ent?' said Merry. 'What's that?'*[426]

Ents are not trees, but tree-shepherds: they have no other purpose than to tend and defend the forests. Their concerns are therefore narrow and entirely tree-centric. While it is undeniable that, as Treebeard says, 'nobody cares for the woods as I care for them,'[427] it could equally be argued that Ents care for very little else. They do not fight in wars, since nobody is altogether on their side, and they maintain an inward-looking ambivalence to the Wide World that estranges them from other peoples and perspectives.

> *'I do not like worrying about the future... I used to be anxious when the shadow lay on Mirkwood, but when it removed to Mordor, I did not trouble for a while: Mordor is a long way away.'*[428]

Instead of battling, building and buying—the concerns of more hasty people—Ents' delight is given to things easily unnoticed or passed over. Treebeard says that he 'used to spend a week just breathing'[429] and will often 'stand and... think about the Sun, and the grass beyond the wood, and the horses, and the clouds, and the unfolding of the world.'[430] These unhurried, thoughtful cogitations on the world reflect the Ents' long, slow lives in which *Never is too long a word*.

Apart from being taught the gift of language early in the First Age, Ents appear to change little: they live simply, age slowly, and gradually dwindle. This reflective, contemplative, almost Zen-like manner of being

---

424 Carpenter, *Letters*, p. 208.

425 A point made by Gilliver, Marshall, and Weiner, who also point out that 'the entirely unrelated Latin form *ent-* is the present participle stem of the verb 'to be'... suggesting the idea of essential being.' (Gilliver, Marshall, and Weiner, *Op. Cit.*, p. 119). The twin brevity and longevity of 'ent' could therefore be one of Tolkien's philological jokes.

426 Tolkien, *The Lord of the Rings*, p. 453.

427 Tolkien, *The Lord of the Rings*, p. 461.

428 Tolkien, *The Lord of the Rings*, p. 461

429 Tolkien, *The Lord of the Rings*, p. 458.

430 Tolkien, *The Lord of the Rings*, p. 454.

seems delightful; and yet the Ents' existence remains overshadowed by the unstoppable passage of time (what Galadriel called 'the long defeat') in which all that was once unstained is doomed to fade.

The Fate of Fangorn

There is naught that an old Ent can do to hold back [a] storm: he must weather it or crack.

Like a tree caught in a gale, Ents seek to endure their circumstances, not to control them. Peter Kreeft explains that this is an example of Fatalism: the ancient belief that 'History is a set of unending and unchangeable cycles of doom.'[431] Because, to a holder of this view, the future has already somehow been determined, the ethical focus turns to process, not achievements—to do things in the right way, regardless of the effects. These are the focuses of the Ents' philosophy and wisdom tradition.

For Stoics like those of ancient Greece and Rome, 'there is no such thing as chance, and the course of nature is rigidly determined.'[432] The Stoics came to the conclusion that, since whatever happens is inevitable—for who can fight Fate?—what matters and is of real worth is when one stops attempting to control circumstances and instead controls the self (and particularly the will and emotions). The Entish instinct for self-restraint—to hold emotional passion and all other 'hastiness' at arm's length—grows from this Stoic soil, compounded by the process of their becoming 'tree-ish.' The Ents have come to believe that, for better or worse, *Things will go as they will; and there is no need to hurry to meet them.* As they dwindle—as *Sheep get like shepherd, and shepherds like sheep*—the tree-herds increasingly resemble their trees: moving less and becoming increasingly fatalistic and less proactive, in thought and in act.

The wisdom of Fangorn is therefore found in the manner in which Fate (or Doom, to use Tolkien's preferred term) is faced—preferably with an attitude of patient endurance and fortitude. The proverbs and worldview of the Ents are bathed in this upright, noble, but ultimately pessimistic perspective.

431 Kreeft, *Op. Cit.*, p. 137.

432 Russell, *Op. Cit.*, p. 242.

TREEBEARD

'I am an Ent... The Ent, I am, you might say'[433]

Gandalf calls Treebeard 'the oldest living thing that still walks beneath the Sun upon this Middle-earth,'[434] and Celeborn calls him 'Eldest.' When being looked at by The Ent, it is as if 'something that grew in the ground... had suddenly waked up, and was considering you with the same slow care that it had given to its own inside affairs for endless years.'[435] Gandalf recites a riddling rhyme of lore that records the origins of Treebeard and his people:

'Ere elf sang or hammer rang,
Ere iron was found or tree was hewn,
When young was mountain under moon;
Ere ring was made, or wrought was woe,
It walked the forests long ago.'[436]

Treebeard's is a deliberate, measured, unhurried existence; very much like the Ents' language itself, which rolls and lilts in waves of sound, the rumbling rhythmic patterns oblivious to sentences or other grammatical norms. This absence of haste in Entish is a necessary facet of the long, slow life of its speakers, as they remain in rhythm with the things for which they have responsibility. And yet they do use proverbs—Treebeard employs them frequently in his interactions with Merry and Pippin, and with other non-Ents—however surprising this might be.

Do not be hasty.

If the whole purpose of a proverb is to concisely express the wisdom of one's ancestors in a few quick words, using them would seem anathema to the Onodrim, who have few forebears and do not enjoy brevity. Treebeard doesn't approve of the term 'hill' since it is 'a hasty word for a thing that has stood here ever since the part of the world was shaped,'[437] and yet he apparently has no issue with abbreviating long heritage into short, snappy sayings.

433 Tolkien, *The Lord of the Rings*, p. 453.
434 Tolkien, *The Lord of the Rings*, p. 488.
435 Tolkien, *The Lord of the Rings*, p. 452.
436 Tolkien, *The Lord of the Rings*, p. 531.
437 Tolkien, *The Lord of the Rings*, p. 455.

Had the Ents invented this proverbial tradition, or appropriated it from other peoples? Treebeard's idiomatic nature proverbs—like *A snake without fangs may crawl where he will* or *Sheep get like shepherd, and shepherds like sheep*—may conceivably be Elvish imports,[438] whilst a shared perspective on the passing of time could have led to the borrowing of *Bad memories are handed down* and *Never is too long a word* from either Elves or Wizards. But elsewhere, the obvious 'Entishness' of the proverbs used by Treebeard (such as *Fangorn, where the roots are long, and the years lie thicker than the leaves*) suggests that Ents must have been the inventors of at least some of their own sayings.

Another potential explanation for the appearance of thoroughly Entish-sounding proverbs in the Common Speech is a linguistic one. When first created, the Ents were not speaking creatures—before the Elves taught them to talk, the organic acts of living and growing were their only language. Though they subsequently delighted in speech and song, all languages—even their own—might therefore be considered equally 'foreign' to them: each tongue a translation tool used to communicate a non-verbal tree-ish 'inner speech.' In this way, it would be feasible for the Ents to be so conversant in multilingualism[439] that they use multiple translations their own proverbs as a matter of course.

Entish sayings are not distinct by dint of their structure or length so much as their subject matter: as with all wisdom traditions, the Ents' philosophy and wisdom reflects their history and consequent emphases. When Treebeard quotes proverbs, themes such as nature, caution, and the passing of time all intermingle, mixed with a melancholic air.

'It is rather a strange and sad story'[440]

This prevailing Entish sadness comes from the story of their people, wherein a realm that once covered Beleriand, Eriador, and Wilderland is reduced to what was once its east end, and the beautiful Ent-wives (and all hopes of new Entings and new beginnings) are lost. When Treebeard says *Songs like trees bear fruit only in their own time and in their own way: and sometimes they are withered untimely* he is both teaching

438 And if so, most likely from a Silvan culture like that of Lórien, which places a high emphasis on the natural world and, like the Ents, esteems Yavanna highly.

439 Treebeard himself habitually sings and speaks to himself in the languages of other peoples—all five of the recorded songs of the Ents are in Westron, while Tolkien wrote that Ents actually prefer to speak Quenya (Carpenter, *Letters*, p. 224).

440 Tolkien, *The Lord of the Rings*, p. 464.

a lesson learned from tree-herding, and expounding Ents' fatalistic view of their own history. As a people, they have 'withered untimely.'

Leaving Fatalism Behind

> *'They seem slow, queer, and patient, almost sad; and yet I believe they could be roused. If that happened, I would rather not be on the other side.'*[441]

As a tender of trees, submissive to the Doom of history, Treebeard is neither goal-oriented nor proactive by instinct, yet he is shaken out of this torpor by the tree-felling of Isengard. The work of Saruman has been injurious to the Men of Rohan, and very nearly disastrous to the Quest of the Ring as well, but it is not these acts but the wanton destruction of trees—the herds of which the Ents were created to be shepherds—that finally motivates Treebeard to act.

Convening the Entmoot that decides to attack Isengard is in many ways a last resort, but even then, Treebeard shows his immense discomfort at allowing himself to 'become too hot' and to make a decision based on emotion. He stops himself, self-consciously: 'I spoke hastily. We must not be hasty... for it is easier to shout *stop!* than to do it.'[442]

As well as a good example of how Treebeard uses proverbs (*Do not be hasty*, in altered form, and *It is easier to shout stop! than to do it*), this brief passage reveals the debate that is going on below the surface. Treebeard is Stoically seeking to back away from his anger and not be led by sentiment, but he cannot deny the righteousness of his indignation. He is facing an existential crisis. 'His long slow wrath is brimming over,'[443] says Gandalf.

> *'A thing is about to happen which has not happened since the Elder Days: the Ents are going to wake up and find that they are strong.'*[444]

Merry and Pippin's arrival in Fangorn is like 'the falling of small stones that starts an avalanche in the mountains.'[445] The avalanche itself—the

441 Tolkien, *The Lord of the Rings*, p. 470.
442 Tolkien, *The Lord of the Rings*, p. 463.
443 Tolkien, *The Lord of the Rings*, p. 488.
444 *Ibid.*
445 Tolkien, *The Lord of the Rings*, p. 485.

Last March of the Ents—is the result of a philosophical conversion, from the Fatalistic creed of amending the will to fit with the world, to a proactive desire to instead amend the world.

Although the Entmoot takes nearly three days in its deliberations, what is achieved in that time is an incredibly swift turnaround in the praxis of the Entish culture. No longer will they hide in their final stronghold, weathering the storm, holding out for as long as possible; they will engage in the world, even if in doing so they meet their downfall. The March is begun in the knowledge that *If we stayed at home and did nothing, doom would find us anyway, sooner or later.*

And so, just as Tolkien had always longed, the trees finally march to war. In the event, having their isolation and inactivity broken results in a more proactive period for the Onodrim, as they follow the successful assault on Isengard by mustering a forest of Huorns to the Battle of Helm's Deep, then attacking and destroying the remnant of an Orc army on the Wold of Rohan.[446]

But this phase of fruitful activity seems doomed not to last. In giving the Vale of Isengard into the Ents' keeping, Aragorn attempts to cast new vision, reminding Treebeard that wide lands now lie open to the establishment of new forests, and that even the search for the Ent-wives can be restarted. But the Ent shakes his head. In spite of rising up to defeat Saruman, to aid Théoden, and to establish the Watchwood and the Treegarth of Orthanc, it is clear that has no great hope for the future. Treebeard feels Doom approaching once more.

> *Forests may grow. Woods may spread. But not Ents.*

446 Tolkien, *The Lord of the Rings*, p. 597.

CHAPTER TEN

THE PEOPLES OF GONDOR

'We are a failing people, a springless autumn.'[447]

When the boats of the Fellowship first enter the ancient bounds of Gondor, they do so by passing the Argonath: the vast Ozymandias-like figures of Isildur and Anárion, carved in rock, between which Anduin flows. The impression intended, and given, by the epic scale and grandeur of these forbidding pillars is one of phenomenal craft and indomitable strength; the might of the Men of the West.

After the Downfall of Númenor and the establishment of the Dúnedain as the mightiest lords of Middle-earth, similar feats of splendour were scattered throughout their territory: the Dome of the Stars on the great bridge at Osgiliath; the White Pillar overlooking Umbar, the havens of Pelargir and Lond Daer; the fortresses of Minas Ithil and Minas Anor; the unearthly Stone of Erech; the tower of Amon Súl at Weathertop; the citadel of Orthanc at the centre of the ring of Isengard; and Elostirion amid the White Towers of Emyn Beraid. In the days of their flourishing, when the Númenóreans flexed their muscles, astounding feats abounded.

'There is some good stone-work here... but also some that is less good... doubtless the good stone-work is the older... It is ever so

447 Tolkien, *The Lord of the Rings*, p. 662.

> *with the things that Men begin: there is a frost in Spring, or a blight in Summer, and they fail of their promise.'*[448]

But as Gimli infers, through inspecting the walls of Minas Tirith, the days of incalculable Númenórean might are long gone. Elendil's realm of Arnor has dwindled into grass-grown mounds, and Gondor's pride is primarily placed in what it can preserve rather than what it produces anew. The descendents of Númenor still look backwards with fondness and pride, but they now look forward with trepidation. *What was is less dark than what is to come*, says Denethor, in reference both to contemporary events and to the meta-narrative of Gondor.

Exceptional Gondor

> *'The old wisdom and beauty brought out of the West remained long in the realm of the sons of Elendil the Fair, and they linger there still.'*[449]

Upon settling in Middle-earth, the Númenóreans would initially have been entirely distinct from their Mannish subjects. By dint of ethnicity, language, technological ability, physical size, and culture, they were different: the remnant of a highly-developed civilisation, far in advance of the lesser Men amongst whom they settled. From the founding days of Gondor, the Dúnedain would therefore have constituted an upper caste or aristocracy, dominant in influence though not numbers. And while, over the centuries, their bloodlines became increasingly intermingled with those of lesser races,[450] the Men of the West never forgot or regretted their high heritage, nor the responsibilities it gave them. They remained exceptional.

> *'There is no purpose higher in the world as is now stands than the good of Gondor'*[451]

So says Denethor the Steward. Due to Gondor's undeniable political significance, a philosophy has developed in Minas Tirith that ethically justifies this high national self-view. For those like Denethor, 'the good of

448 Tolkien, *The Lord of the Rings*, p. 854-5.

449 Tolkien, *The Lord of the Rings*, p. 662.

450 As is seen by the civil-war of the Kin-strife, and the marriage of Thengel of Rohan to Morwen of Lossarnach (Tolkien, *The Lord of the Rings*, p. 1044).

451 Tolkien, *The Lord of the Rings*, p. 741.

Gondor' has become synonymous with moral goodness itself, meaning that all other ethical decisions are, in their eyes, subject to it.

This school of moral philosophy is called Exceptionalism. It teaches that a country, institution, or person can literally be peerless, a unique case, and therefore should not be subject to the ethical norms that would otherwise govern them. In the contemporary context, examples of Exceptionalism tend to be political (eg. Richard Nixon's assertion that 'When the President does it, that means that it is not illegal'[452]) or based in ethnicity (eg. Aryanism) or nationalism (eg. Nuclear Non-Proliferation Treaty members' argument that, while their own nuclear status is morally unproblematic, it would be 'wrong' for other countries to develop the same capabilities). Such ethics declare that there is one rule for the Exceptional nation or person, and another for the rest. This appears to have been the prevailing view among the leaders of Gondor.

And with good reason. 'Where will other men look for help, if Gondor fails?'[453] asks Denethor, when accused by Gandalf of thinking 'as is your wont... of Gondor only.'[454] Beregond says the same, but in the form of a proverb: *If we fall, who will stand?* Such statements, while occasionally grandiose and self-centred, reflect the historical reality of Gondor's role: bastion of the West against the wild East and South. Mordor, Easterlings, Haradrim, Wainriders, and Corsairs have all been restrained because of the strength and valour of Minas Tirith. Without Gondor's freedom to prioritise itself, the West would not have endured. Exceptionalism appears justified.

The Exceptionalist strand of Gondor's wisdom tradition turns declarations of the nation's unique greatness into proverbs. Assertions—such as *The Men of Minas Tirith are true to their word,* and *It is not the way of the Men of Minas Tirith to desert their friends at need*—appear to have been adopted as axioms, though it is not clear whether these are true proverbs, passed down by oral tradition, or mere nationalistic slogans. But the perspective they exemplify—that whatever the weaknesses elsewhere *The Men of Minas Tirith will never be overcome*—clearly suggests that a stream of Gondorian lore is devoted to the belief that their country is a special case.

---

452 www.streetlaw.org/en/Page/722/Nixons_Views_on_Presidential_Power_Excerpts_from_a_1977_Interview_with_David_Frost (retrieved March 30, 2014).

453 Tolkien, *The Lord of the Rings*, p. 796.

454 Tolkien, *The Lord of the Rings*, p. 795.

Even in the days of its fading, Gondor's exceptional nature is multifaceted. In its might and inherited greatness it is easy to forget that it is also a large and diverse nation. The Men of Minas Tirith may be proverbial, but they contrast strongly with other inhabitants of Gondor: the hillmen of Morthond and Lamedon; the princes and harpers of Dol Amroth; the fishing communities of the Ethir; the singers of Lebennin; the mariners of Pelargir; and the Rangers of Ithilien. Each strand of Gondorian culture would have had their own distinct wisdom tradition, though none quite so distinct as the inhabitants of Drúadan Forest.

A fascinating range of peoples live in Gondor, but the country's most peculiar anthropological study do not consider themselves part of the country at all. Hidden from view, only a short distance from Minas Tirith, lives a small isolated nation. These are the Drúedain.[455]

The Drúedain

> *'Remnants of an older time they be, living few and secretly, wild and wary as beasts.'*[456]

By the time of their encounter with the host of the Rohirrim, the Drúedain appear to have been reduced to one final stronghold: Drúadan Forest in Anórien.[457] As a society that is both ancient and hidden, they may be spoken of in the same breath as other isolated woodland communities, such as the Ents of Fangorn, the Elves of Lothlórien, and Bombadil and Goldberry in the Old Forest—comparisons the Drûgs perhaps would have enjoyed.

The forests of Middle-earth—'the wilderness outside the boundaries set by civilization'[458]—each appear to harbour a different strain of the same 'Wild Man' tendency, with threatening shadowy figures abounding. However, while each conforms to Verlyn Flieger's characterisation of 'the archetypal outsider, the prowler on the borderlands between

455 Other names for this people include *Drughu, Drûgs, Woses, Púkel-men, and Wild Men of the Woods.*

456 Tolkien, *The Lord of the Rings*, p. 813.

457 However, *Unfinished Tales* relates an unpublished 'jotting' suggesting that during the War of the Ring 'many Drúedain… came forth out of the caves where they dwelt [in Drúwaith Iaur] to attack remnants of Saruman's forces that had been driven southwards.' (Tolkien, *Unfinished Tales*, p. 387, note.)

458 Verlyn Flieger, 'Tolkien's Wild Men,' from *Tolkien the Medievalist*, Jane Chance, Editor (Routledge, 2003), p. 95.

the wild and tame,'[459] they all prove to be benevolent to the cause and trenchant in their rejection of the Enemy.

Each of these 'wild' cultures combines a longevous perspective and a close affinity with nature, and although the Drúedain are the exception, in that as Men they are mortal, they too appear to change as slowly as the ground beneath their feet. Loren Wilkinson speaks about the special value in Middle-earth of those living 'in an ancient, unchanging relationship with their place,'[460] a category which he extends to the bee-keeping, animal-loving Beorn and the hobbit gardener Sam. The stewardly relationship—so strong and so ageless—is, Wilkinson asserts, what the War of the Ring is really fought for: so that life-as-it-has-always-been can continue.

Wild Wisdom

There is little doubt that the Drúedain would be as indifferent to the Ring and its promises of power as was Bombadil, since they have no desire other than to be who they are and to continue as they always have. As a wild folk of the woods, they have no technology and little or no practical literacy, relying instead on oral tradition for all their inherited learning. The Rohirrim hear little or none of their language, only 'great headman' Ghân-buri-Ghân speaking haltingly in the Common Tongue. But however limited his language, there are still proverbs—of a sort[461]—and as they are used we glimpse the particular priorities of his people.

The most obviously axiomatic of Ghân's statements, *Dead men are not friends to living men, and give them no gifts*, reveals a blunt non-euphemistic willingness to embrace harsh reality. The Drúedain are a primitive people and don't beat about the bush; they know their own strengths and do not play them down. *Wild Men are wild, free, but not children* says Ghân, *Wild Men have long ears and long eyes; know all paths*.

Although it is by no means a perfect match, there is much in the Drúedain's makeup and thought to make them kindred spirits of the Cynics, those ancient Greeks who rejected (what Bertrand Russell calls) 'the

459 *Ibid.*

460 Loren Wilkinson, 'Tolkien and the Surrendering of Power,' *Tree of Tales: Tolkien, Literature, and Theology, Trevor* Hart and Ivan Khovacs, Editors (Baylor University Press, 2007), p. 79.

461 If they are true proverbs, they would be translations of Drúedain sayings into the Westron.

amenities of civilisation'[462]—manners, dress, ownership of property *et al.*—in order to pursue a universal brotherhood with all creation. The word 'cynic' means 'canine,' reflecting a determination to live an unaffected 'natural' life, like a dog. The Drúedain aren't obliged to be wild—their forest is within sight of the settlements of Tall Men, and at times in their history have even lived in shared communities with them[463]—but they refuse to give up their wildness and freedom for the city whose inhabitants 'eat stone for food.'[464]

As prehistoric figures surviving beyond their time, living on into the 'modern' world of Denethor's Gondor but not belonging to it, the Drúedain are in some ways akin to Tolkien, CS Lewis, and the other Inklings: a group of pre-modern reactionaries born out of their time, rejecting urbanism and industrialism, and cynical of 'progress.'[465] While the Inklings were forced to continue living and working in mainstream society (their only haven being an intellectual and imaginative one, shared with like minds), the Drúedain were able to separate themselves physically; hidden in the forest and safe from intrusion. The resulting Drúedain worldview—a philosophical mix allied to 'aboriginal' cynics, isolationists, and anachronistic curios—is in sharp relief to all other Men of Middle-earth.

While the Drúedain are not tempted by the 'bright lights' of the stone city, they do not feel in competition with either Gondor or Rohan either. They may have no desire for the convolutions of 'civilisation,' but they do recognise that the freedom to remain wild and to continue their ancient relationship with the forest depends on the success of the War; hence their help for Théoden and repeated demands that the Rohirrim *Drive away bad air and darkness with bright iron.*

462 Russell, *Op. Cit.*, p. 222.

463 Many generations had passed since the Drúedain had normative relationships with other races, but at one time they had lived in mixed settlements with other Men: with the Folk of Haleth in Beleriand, and even for a time in Númenor (see Tolkien, *Unfinished Tales*, p. 385, note). The majority, however, always dwelt in the lands later occupied by Gondor, as is shown by the Púkel-men statues of Dunharrow and by the name *Drúwaith Iaur*, 'Old Pukel-land' in the remote Andrath.

464 Tolkien, *The Lord of the Rings*, p. 814.

465 CS Lewis, in his inaugural lecture upon becoming Professor of Mediaeval and Renaissance Literature at Cambridge, spoke of himself as one of the few remaining members of (what he called) Old Western Culture; the pre-mechanised, pre-industrial West. 'I may yet be useful as a specimen,' he remarked. 'There are not going to be many more dinosaurs.' (Carpenter, *The Inklings*, p. 238).

> *'We fight not. Hunt only. Kill gorgûn in woods, hate orc-folk. You hate gorgûn too. We help as we can.'*[466]

The Drúedain have not been treated well by other Men—they appear at times to have even been hunted 'like beasts'[467]—but their hatred for Orcs is absolute and ancient, passed down from generation to generation. In 'The Faithful Stone,'[468] a tale from the First Age, the source of this unbreakable enmity is revealed. In that era, Orcs had hunted, captured, and tortured Drúedain for sport, and thanks to unbroken oral tradition it was never forgotten. When the Rohirrim raise the question of reward for the Drûgs' help, the veracity of Ghân's response shows how little his people care for the things that other men treasure, and that the passing of several millennia had not dulled their bitter desire for retribution.

> *Kill gorgûn! Kill orc-folk! No other words please Wild Men.*[469]

The Trained Professionals

Alone amongst the civilisations of Men, Gondor is recognised as a learned society. It is recorded as having lore-masters,[470] scribes,[471] and vast treasuries of historical records documenting not only great matters like the inscription on the One Ring, but also minor events such as the settlement of the Shire.[472]

The presence of the hospital-like Houses of Healing, and of a professional herb-master—a man who 'knows all the old names'—therein, shows that Gondor also held botanical and medical science in high esteem. Additionally, the herb-master's slightly-derogatory assumption that Aragorn is 'merely a captain of war'[473] implies that his own learning may traditionally be accorded a higher status in Gondor than that of those engaged in fighting. It is the loss of this kind of attitude that is lamented by Faramir:

466 Tolkien, *The Lord of the Rings*, p. 814.
467 Tolkien, *The Lord of the Rings*, p. 815.
468 Tolkien, *Unfinished Tales*, p. 380-2.
469 Tolkien, *The Lord of the Rings*, p. 816.
470 Tolkien, *The Lord of the Rings*, p. 946.
471 Tolkien, *The Lord of the Rings*, p. 14-15.
472 Tolkien, *The Lord of the Rings*, p. 4.
473 Tolkien, *The Lord of the Rings*, p. 847.

> *'We... now love war and valour as things good in themselves, both a sport and an end; and though we still hold that a warrior should have more skills and knowledge than only the craft of weapons and slaying, we esteem a warrior, nonetheless, above men of other crafts. Such is the need of our days.'*[474]

Whatever the degree of decline, it is plain that when engulfed by the War of the Ring, the city of Minas Tirith still maintained a trained class of scholars and scientists, and that these were respected people, exalted to high rank—a practice unknown in other Mannish realms. As a result of this literate, learned echelon, the nation's high heritage could be remembered and preserved in a manner unavailable to other mortal races, who instead rely primarily on oral tradition—on stories, sayings, and songs. Gondor has these things, but in addition to its book-learning, not instead of it. And while the degree to which Gondor had a single unified philosophy is debatable, due to the varying cultures of its fiefs and ethnic groups, there is no doubt of its strong proverbial tradition.

Unlike other Mannish realms, in Gondor we have access to proverbs used both by civic leaders and by those in the strata of society below them: Beregond of the Guard (and his son Bergil); Ingold of the Rammas; Hirgon the errand-rider; the 'old wife' Ioreth; the Herb-master; and the Warden of the Houses of Healing. Merry and Pippin hear axioms in the mouths of all the above, and through those sayings the wisdom of the trained rank-and-file is displayed.

THE MILITARY

> *'The Men of Minas Tirith will never be overcome!'*[475]

Gondor's form of government is aristocratic, with an oligarchic centralisation of power based around the highest Númenórean houses.[476] For such a system to work, absolute submission to authority is indispensable, and the nation's military men are emblematic of the sort of citizen their society requires.

474 Tolkien, *The Lord of the Rings*, p. 663

475 Tolkien, *The Lord of the Rings*, p. 866.

476 However, regional leaderships—such as the Princes of Dol Amroth and the Lords of Lossarnach and Ringlo Vale—do also exist. These lords were very probably present at the Council summoned by Denethor. (See Tolkien, *The Lord of the Rings*, p. 798.)

Soldiers should be expected to follow the orders of their captains, but what is noticeable is the absolute deference shown by all the Men of Gondor towards the nation's leaders. Whether the shrewd, astute, but burdened politician Denethor, the bombastic and imperious Boromir, or the tender-hearted warrior-philosopher Faramir, each is revered to the point of awe. This in turn plays into a nationalistic impulse, as the state becomes as unarguably good and true as its faultless figureheads. 'The Lord Denethor is unlike other men'[477] says Beregond, expressing the people's almost messianic view of the Steward.

Beregond is a well-trained soldier and a respected man due to his status as a Guard. But, on meeting Pippin, it is clear that he is also inexperienced and untravelled, and therefore an inquisitive listener and an asker of frank, friendly questions. The proverbs he uses are mostly typical of men-at-arms: useful but carrying no deep insight or philosophical weight. With focuses specific to the military and a well-worn authenticity to them, they feel like they have developed over multiple centuries of Gondorian warcraft. *It is over-late to send for aid when you are already besieged*, he says, and *Men who go warring afield look ever to the next hope of food and of drink*.

These statements are presented with little ego. Indeed, when Beregond uses proverbs that sound worldly-wise—like *Strange accents do not mar fair speech* and *At the table small men may do the greater deeds*—he is quick to make it clear that they are generally known insights and not his own, introducing them with 'they say' and 'we say.' He knows his place

Hirgon and Ingold represent soldiery of a different sort: they are met 'in the field,' on active duty, and appear to have more practical experience (as well as more responsibility) than Beregond. Though only met in passing, and in haste, their speech is both graceful and axiomatic, employing proverbs as an aid to brevity and as a rhetorical tool.

When Ingold bars Gandalf's path at the Rammas, citing the proverb *Wish for no strangers in the land* as his justification, he is not being rude, only professional. And when Gandalf does him the courtesy of arguing his case—that Pippin, though a 'stranger,' should be admitted—with a proverb that would appeal to the military mind (*Valour... cannot be computed by stature*), Ingold acquiesces and then honours Pippin's humility, saying *Many a doer of great deeds might say no more*.

477 Tolkien, *The Lord of the Rings*, p. 748.

Hirgon appears to be from a higher Númenórean house, since he bears a striking resemblance to Boromir and is entrusted with the Red Arrow, summoning Théoden and the Rohirrim to fulfil the ancient Oath of Eorl. He speaks to the King with elegance and authority, adding weight to Denethor's already weighty summons by mingling proverbs with his message. *Remember old friendship and oaths long spoken*, he says, and *For your own good... do all that you may*. It appears likely that Hirgon is no mere soldier or message-carrier but a trained diplomat: Denethor's voice to foreign dignitaries. When Théoden explains that the Rohirrim could not prudently reach Minas Tirith in less than a week, Hirgon is distraught but responds with the dignity of his office. He does not seek to argue, but sighs a resigned (and diplomatic) *If it must be so, it must*.

It is to be expected that each of these figures should identify with the prevailing Exceptionalist view of Gondor, and the nation's centrality to whatever hope is left in Middle-earth. Beregond may tell Pippin that, 'we are but one piece in it, whatever pride may say,'[478] but a few seconds later, he is left wondering, *If we fall, who shall stand?* This Gondor-centric ethic, in a time of national decline and the waxing strength of Mordor, inevitably leads to deathly pessimism. Beregond's conclusion, that *All things must come utterly to an end in time*, reflects both the pride and despair of the city and its Lord: equating the demise of Gondor with that of all good things. Ironically, he is partly right—the War does bring an end to Gondor as he knows it, though not to be replaced with ignominy and darkness, but with the returned King, whose hands are the hands of a healer.

The Healers

> *'Though all lore was in these latter days fallen from its fullness of old, the leechcraft of Gondor was still wise.'*[479]

While Pippin forges an easy connection with a plain-speaking soldier and his son, Merry sees Minas Tirith from a different vantage point; not the Guards' mess but the Houses of Healing, where a coterie of wise men and women minister to the dying and the recovering. This distinct group are notable for their trained knowledge and being 'skilled in the

478 Tolkien, *The Lord of the Rings*, p. 748.
479 Tolkien, *The Lord of the Rings*, p. 842.

The hands
of the king
are the hands
of a healer.

healing of wound and hurt, and all such sickness as east of the Sea mortal men were subject to.'[480]

But the Houses of Healing appear to be staffed by those whose trained cleverness has outstripped their insight. They have technical knowledge but fail to utilise the more traditional tools at their disposal; having memorised ancient proverb-prophecies, they fail to recognise the applicability of their message. As Ioreth sighs, helpless against the Black Shadow under which Faramir and Éowyn have fallen:

> *'Would that there were kings in Gondor, as there were once upon a time, they say! For it is said in old lore:* The hands of the king are the hands of a healer. *And so the rightful king could ever be known.'*[481]

There are rumours throughout the city that, perhaps, a king has returned, but Ioreth, busy 'with this and that,' has ignored them. Had she not, and then put two and two together, this old saying would have led her immediately to the dreadful malady's solution. Happily, Gandalf overhears her proverb and immediately takes it at face value, calling Aragorn from the Pelennor into the city.

Similarly, the Healers have memorised such lines as *When the black breath blows and death's shadow grows and all lights pass, come athelas!* but these they repeat without understanding. Such words have been passed down the generations for practical reasons, but the Healers, for all their training, are oblivious to the fact. The King has returned—as Faramir immediately recognises as he returns to consciousness—yet until the Herb-master sees it with his own eyes, *Life to the dying in the king's hand lying* is of as much practical use as *the cow jumped over the Moon*. As an academic exercise the Herb-master recites the names of Kingsfoil in various languages, but, unaware of the plant's true worth and value, is content that no more is required of him. 'He shows…' (as Shippey explains) 'how genuine knowledge can dwindle down to ancient lore, which is remembered but no longer felt to have any practical value.'[482]

Gandalf's diagnosis for the Houses of Healing is that it needs 'less lore and more wisdom,'[483] putting his finger on the issue at hand: the Healers

480 *Ibid.*

481 *Ibid.*

482 Shippey, *Roots and Branches,* p. 163.

483 Tolkien, *The Lord of the Rings*, p. 847.

may be well educated in medical knowledge, but the only member of the Houses' staff sufficiently wise to use and apply traditional sayings correctly is not a Healer at all *per se* but the Warden, an administrative overseer. His two proverbs (deployed in discussion with the recuperating, argumentative Éowyn) are a perfect fit for his context: the interplay between hurting and healing. He laments to that *The world is full enough of hurts and mischances without wars to multiply them,* but also knows that—in contrast, perhaps, to the city's present specialisation of tasks—*the healing hand should also wield the sword*. The middle manager's perspicacity dwarfs that of his specialists.

The Healers know their stuff, but are shown to lack the wherewithal and pragmatic instinct to see it applied. Their faithful learning of proverbs and rhymes of lore has served a real purpose—without it, the lives of Faramir and others would not have been saved—but only because they happen to be overheard by other, wiser ears.

The Númenórean Houses

> *'That is a fair lord and a great captain of men,' said Legolas. 'If Gondor has such men still in these days of fading, great must have been its glory in the days of its rising'*[484]

'What has your social origin got to do with your political judgement and wisdom?'[485] asks ethicist Piers Benn. From the philosopher-kings of Plato's *Republic* to the absolutist tsars of imperial Russia, the idea that 'the best people to run a country are those with a certain privileged social background'[486] has a long heritage. And for the entire three thousand year history of Gondor, the nation is exclusively ruled by a privileged echelon: an ethnic minority descended from the Faithful of Númenor. Gondor is no democracy.

The high houses of Gondor are a remnant of the greatest and most technically-advanced civilisation of Men that had ever existed, and although they became backward-looking rather than forward-thinking, they revered and preserved the great and the good that was their inheritance. In the early days of Gondor, the Númenóreans' monopoly of power was entirely logical and pragmatic: in comparison to their wealth

484 Tolkien, *The Lord of the Rings*, p. 855.
485 Piers Benn, *Ethics* (UCL Press, 1998) p. 27.
486 *Ibid.*

of knowledge, other Men of Middle-earth were simple to the point of savagery. The Númenóreans led because they were the ones best qualified to do so.

However, the best that Gondor could offer in education, in opportunity, and in positions of authority continued to be given solely to this ruling minority, meaning that even after three millennia close relatives such as Denethor, Boromir, Faramir, and Prince Imrahil continued to be pre-eminent in matters of skill and knowledge as well as birth.

> *'We in the house of Denethor know much ancient lore by long tradition, and there are moreover in our treasuries many things preserved: books and tablets writ on withered parchments, yea, and on stone, and on leaves of silver and of gold, in divers characters. Some none can now read; and for the rest, few ever unlock them.'*[487]

This 'long tradition' is the oral heritage of Númenórean Gondor, augmented by commemorative flourishes like the Standing Silence before meals.[488] Proverbs and rhymes of lore had passed down the centuries, and even as Gondor inevitably declined, its wisdom endured.

DENETHOR

> *'He is not as other men of this time... whatever be his descent from father to son, by some chance the blood of Westernesse runs nearly true in him'*[489]

So says Gandalf, and Beregond reiterates: 'The Lord Denethor is unlike other men.'[490] Even to Pippin's inexperienced eye, he looks 'much more like a great wizard than Gandalf... more kingly, beautiful, and powerful'[491]—a fitting leader for a great nation at the time of its greatest test.

Posterity could have awarded Denethor a place among the greatest of the Edain—heroic chieftains like Hador and Húrin, glorious kings like Elros, Aldarion, and Elendil, and far-sighted stewards like Mardil and

487 Tolkien, *The Lord of the Rings*, p. 655.

488 When men pause in an act of remembrance 'towards Númenor that was, and beyond to Elvenhome that is, and to that which is beyond Elvenhome and will ever be.' (Tolkien, *The Lord of the Rings*, p. 661.)

489 Tolkien, *The Lord of the Rings*, p. 742.

490 Tolkien, *The Lord of the Rings*, p. 748.

491 Tolkien, *The Lord of the Rings*, p. 740.

Cirion—but when the test comes, he falls short. When Gandalf tells him that 'your part is to go out to the battle of your City, where maybe death awaits you'[492] the Steward refuses the role, believing that his actions no longer have any value since 'battle is vain.'[493] He sees far, but in the end is defeated by what he has seen.

Denethor's lost hopes had not been arrogant or even particularly power-hungry, he had simply wanted things to be as they had in the past: 'to be the Lord of this City in peace, and leave my chair to a son after me.'[494] But in the final stages of his crooked despair, to be supplanted by Sauron or Aragorn appear as twin evils, since each would rob him of his desire. He would rather die than be subject to either.

Twisted Sight

'Didst thou think that the eyes of the White Tower were blind?'[495]

Denethor fails through the corruption of his greatest strength: his far-sightedness. As Gandalf observes, 'He can perceive, if he bends his will thither, much of what is passing in the minds of men, even of those that dwell far off.'[496] *Though the Stones be lost,* says the proverb, *still the lords of Gondor have keener sight than lesser men.* Such deep perception makes Denethor a masterful leader in all areas of policy that are founded on knowledge. Unsurprisingly, the esteem in which he is held by his people is complete and universal; he is held in reverence and absolutely obeyed. But it is in his greatness that he falls.

In Minas Tirith, it has long been speculated of Denethor that 'as he sits alone in his high chamber in the Tower at night, and bends his thought this way and that, he can read somewhat of the future; and that he will at times search even the mind of the Enemy, wrestling with him.'[497] This is surprisingly close to the truth. The Appendices record that 'needing knowledge, but being proud, and trusting in his own strength of will, he dared to look in the palantír.'[498]

492 Tolkien, *The Lord of the Rings*, p. 834.
493 Tolkien, *The Lord of the Rings*, p. 835.
494 Tolkien, *The Lord of the Rings*, p. 836.
495 Tolkien, *The Lord of the Rings*, p. 835.
496 Tolkien, *The Lord of the Rings*, p. 742-3.
497 Tolkien, *The Lord of the Rings*, p. 748.
498 Tolkien, *The Lord of the Rings*, p. 1030-31.

The palantír—'that which looks far off'—is too tempting a tool to refuse, and though Denethor proves less corruptible than Saruman, who is mastered by desire for power, the deceptions of Sauron still enter his mind. 'In the days of his wisdom,' says Gandalf, 'Denethor did not presume to use it… knowing the limits of his own strength. But his wisdom failed.'[499]

Denethor sees much, but *seeing is both good and perilous*, as Galadriel's proverb affirms. The Steward's pursuit of knowledge, outstripping his judgement, brings him into peril. Holding another palantír, Sauron can directly influence the Steward's perception. Denethor begins to see wrongly, or to misinterpret what he sees. The palantír shows him a fleet sail up Anduin and the unconquerable waxing of Sauron's strength, leading him to presume—just as Saruman had—that its victory was certain. His far sight fails.

The Wisdom of the White Tower

Denethor's proverbs are hard-edged, like their master. His great Númenórean lineage has equipped him with sayings designed to aid the figurehead leader who has to listen to and weigh up different counselling voices. *Pride would be folly that disdained help and counsel at need*, he quotes, but also *Counsels may be found that are neither the webs of wizards nor the haste of fools*. On the eve of battle he summons a Council of military leaders—an opportunity to listen and be advised—yet when they met he 'was in no mood that day to bow to others.'[500] By this point in his life there are few, if any, by whom Denethor would allow himself to be advised.

As battle approaches, the hard edges become harder—*Much must be risked in war*, he declares, and *Ifs are vain*—while a suggestion of Ethnocentrism and nationalistic self-preservation is shown in *The Lord of Gondor is not to be made the tool of other men's purposes*. Yet even in desperate times, a remnant of balance is still to be found: *Let all who fight the Enemy in their fashion be at one,* he says.

What is noticeable is that, regardless of subject matter, all Denethor's proverbs are practical to the point of expediency—no moral absolutes are ever declared. Denethor's ethics (and the proverbs he uses to justify them) are consequentialist and results-oriented; the chief result in

499 Tolkien, *The Lord of the Rings*, p. 838.
500 Tolkien, *The Lord of the Rings*, p. 798.

question being the national interest of Gondor. From this perspective, actions are not seen as right or wrong in themselves; they are only beneficial to Gondor or not.

> *'You think, as is your wont, of Gondor only,' said Gandalf. Yet there are other men...'*
> *'And where will other men look for help, if Gondor falls?' answered Denethor.*[501]

Denethor's position (and that of his country) in the vanguard of resistance to Sauron has given him an ethical justification for seeking the good of Gondor above all other things. He believes that Gondor is the rock on which all the good of Middle-earth is founded, and without it, all would crumble. In order for good to endure at all, Gondor must endure. Hence his desire for the Ring: not to serve or promote himself, but to save Gondor.

In many ways, Denethor had actually gone further than Gondor-is-exceptional Ethnocentricism. His pride—twisted by Sauron, via the palantír—had turned into suspicion of others, and by the end he had begun to believe lies about those who should have been his friends: that Gandalf wished to rule in his stead; that his son's love and loyalty had been stolen; and that Pippin had been placed as a spy. By this time, he is no longer seeking to save Gondor in order to preserve the future of its allies, he is saving Gondor from its allies. *Looks may belie the man*, he says to Pippin, but it is a proverb with a sly double meaning: half a compliment to the honour of the hobbit, and half suspicious of his motives. Trapped in such a mindset, Denethor is left isolated, mistrusting 'all others who resisted Sauron, unless they served him alone.'[502]

Desperate and Demoralised

Tolkien wrote that, in his greatness, Denethor despised lesser men[503] like the Rohirrim. Yet when the pinch comes, a lesser man is what he is shown to be. Having heard Faramir's report about Frodo being led to Cirith Ungol, and faced with the vast armies of Mordor, Denethor receives the stricken body of his remaining son. Retreating to his tower and the palantír, he sees that 'against the Power that now rises there

501 Tolkien, *The Lord of the Rings*, p. 795-796.

502 Tolkien, *The Lord of the Rings*, p. 1031.

503 Carpenter, *Letters*, p. 241.

is no victory.'[504] When he returns, his face is 'more deathlike than his son's.'[505] Faced with the failure of his polity and his philosophy, his courage deserts him. He gives up.

But Denethor does not only despair of victory, but also of goodness, virtue, and courage. Unable to face defeat, he abandons the people who revere him and whom he commands, turning to filicide and self-destruction. He is *demoralised*, not only in the sense of losing hope, but also in the more archaic sense of having his morals corrupted.

The contrast between his choices and those of King Théoden could not be starker. Whilst neither sees much hope ahead, for their countries, their families, or themselves, their responses are diametrically opposed: Denethor despairs and self-destructs; Théoden emerges from the depression of losing his son Théodred to become the model of a heroic warrior-king. 'Out of doubt, out of dark,'[506] as he sings on the Pelennor, the battlefield Denethor refuses to enter.

As Denethor's principles disintegrate into despair, he dismisses all other attitudes as 'a fool's hope.' Gandalf nearly joins him—'my heart almost failed me,'[507] he tells Pippin—but he refuses to be cowed and instead chooses to follow the wisdom of his own proverbs, such as *Despair is only for those who see the end beyond all doubt*. Gandalf's proverbs offer the antidote to the demoralisation of Denethor, providing both morale and moral motivation. All along he has said to others that *Even the very wise cannot see all ends*, and *All we have to decide is what to do with the time that is given us,* and now he needs such wisdom himself to prevent him from giving in to hopelessness.

Gandalf perseveres, and hindsight proves him right. Likewise, Théoden persists and his choice is rewarded. The King's willingness to ride without hope saves Minas Tirith from being entered, and buys sufficient time for Aragorn's fleet to sail up Anduin from Pelargir. In choosing courage over despair, neither Gandalf nor Théoden knew (or even expected) a happy result to automatically follow, but they persisted nonetheless. As Shippey says, 'While persistence offers no guarantees, it does give 'luck'

504 Tolkien, *The Lord of the Rings*, p. 835.
505 Tolkien, *The Lord of the Rings*, p. 803.
506 Tolkien, *The Lord of the Rings*, p. 829.
507 Tolkien, *The Lord of the Rings*, p. 797.

a chance to operate, through unknown allies or unknown weaknesses in the opposition.'[508]

Denethor has no expectation of 'luck' and turns down persistence. The great weakness of a results-oriented polity such as his is that when hope fails and disaster looms, there is no solace in having done 'the right thing,' nor motive to act virtuously. Denethor 'will not fight to the last, but turns like a heathen to suicide and the sacrifice of his kin.'[509] Had he stepped forward to fight, however hopelessly, Gandalf would not have been sidetracked in Rath Dínen, rescuing Faramir, meaning that Théoden (amongst others) would probably not have died. Having put his faith in consequences, the consequences of Denethor's actions prove grievous. He destroys other lives than just his own.

Boromir

> *'No heir of Minas Tirith has for long years been so hardy in toil, so onward into battle, or blown a mightier note on the Great Horn.'*[510]

An exceptional son of an exceptional nation, Boromir is the standard bearer for Gondorian Exceptionalism. From his perspective, all things of value, importance, or goodness by definition relate directly to Gondor.

When his dream tells him 'Doom is near at hand,' Boromir assumes that it means the doom of Minas Tirith.[511] When he rides to Rivendell and sees that the lands between are primarily at peace, he presumes that the price of their freedom has been paid solely by his people.[512] When he is told that the Ring must be destroyed because all that is done with it turns to evil, he suggests that this would not be the case for 'true-hearted men' like those of Minas Tirith, who would not be corrupted.[513] He argues persuasively:

> *'Believe not that in the land of Gondor the blood of Númenor is spent, nor all its pride and dignity forgotten. By our valour... alone*

508 Shippey, *The Road to Middle-earth*, p. 165.
509 Shippey, *The Road to Middle-earth*, p. 158.
510 Tolkien, *The Lord of the Rings*, p. 664.
511 Tolkien, *The Lord of the Rings*, p. 240-1.
512 Tolkien, *The Lord of the Rings*, p. 239.
513 Tolkien, *The Lord of the Rings*, p. 389.

> *are peace and freedom maintained in the lands behind us, bulwark of the West.'*[514]

In this Boromir is at least partly mistaken, but correcting him does not work; he cannot help but remain sceptical of any who are not formally in league with the White Tower. In this, he is clearly his father's son: *Let all the foes of Gondor flee!* he cries, sounding his horn—not 'the foes of the West' or 'all servants of the Enemy,' but 'the foes of Gondor.' To Boromir there is no good but the good of Gondor.

The Greatest Good

Declarations of Gondorian greatness litter Boromir's speech, including assertions that he seems to have adopted as axioms, like *The Men of Minas Tirith are true to their word,* and *It is not the way of the Men of Minas Tirith to desert their friends at need.* While it is not clear whether or not these are true proverbs, received from oral tradition, the use of similar sayings by compatriots such as Beregond and Bergil[515] suggests that a stream of Gondorian lore is indeed devoted to nationalistic sloganeering. If this is so, such a tradition would find a natural home in a military context, and of all places it is the military context in which Boromir is most at home.

As a man of valour and captain of war, Boromir is virtually without peer. But while the traditional Númenórean view seems to have been that *A warrior should have more skills and knowledge than only the craft of weapons and slaying,* Boromir has not his brother's aptitude for learning, 'caring little for lore, save the tales of old battles.'[516] Indeed, as Shippey observes, both Faramir and Éomer perceive that Boromir is more akin to the fearless, high-hearted Rohirrim than to the far-sighted and learned Númenóreans from whom he is descended.[517]

Of the eleven proverbs used by Boromir, nearly all are directly applicable to warcraft or his station as Captain of Gondor, including:

> *Valour needs first strength, and then a weapon.*
> *The wolf that one hears is worse than the orc that one fears.*
> *When heads are at a loss bodies must serve.*

514 Tolkien, *The Lord of the Rings*, p. 239.

515 Such as *The Men of Minas Tirith will never be overcome!* and *If we fall, who shall stand?*

516 Tolkien, *The Lord of the Rings*, p. 1031.

517 Shippey, *The Road to Middle-earth*, p. 130.

It is by our own folly that the Enemy will defeat us.

It is clear from these sayings that Boromir is no unschooled ignoramus, relying on brute force to achieve his ends: these are all insightful lessons from a hard-won heritage. Being expert in this martial tradition has helped Boromir's development into a courageous commander and an inspirational leader of men, but that is where his ambitions cease—seeking to widen his range would feel beneath him.

Had any other character used the proverb *The might of Elrond is in wisdom, not in weapons,* they would have been honouring Elrond and affirming his status as counsellor nonpareil, as well as drawing attention to the indispensably foundational role that wise counsel plays in all war-waging. However, when employed by Boromir, the proverb sounds almost derogatory, as if to him wisdom is something to fall back on when weapons fail. In this we see that Boromir, like the Rohirrim, has come to 'love war and valour as things good in themselves.'[518]

> *'The fearless, the ruthless, these alone will achieve victory. What could not a warrior do in this hour, a great leader? ... The Ring would give me power of Command. How I would drive the hosts of Mordor, and all men would flock to my banner!'*[519]

Had he succeeded his father as Steward, Boromir would likely have become something like the dictatorial figure of his Ring-inspired fantasy: a general to be obeyed, hosts flocking to his banner. While Denethor 'listened to counsel, and then followed his own mind,'[520] Boromir is frustrated by discussion, finding that *Where there are so many, all speech becomes a debate without end*. To that end, he tells Frodo that *Two together may perhaps find wisdom*, though the context—of a powerful man trying to impose his will on a frightened, isolated hobbit—makes it clear that, for Boromir, 'finding wisdom' occurs when others accede to his wishes and obey his commands.

'Alas for Boromir! It was too sore a trial!'[521] says Faramir, who knew better than anyone the undoubted strengths and near-disastrous weaknesses of his brother. Frodo is right not to 'trust in the strength and truth of Men'[522]

518 Tolkien, *The Lord of the Rings*, p. 663.
519 Tolkien, *The Lord of the Rings*, p. 389.
520 Tolkien, *The Lord of the Rings*, p. 1031.
521 Tolkien, *The Lord of the Rings*, p. 665.
522 Tolkien, *The Lord of the Rings*, p. 388.

and to escape the clutches of the Ring-crazed warrior. Denethor claims that, had Boromir taken the Ring, his son 'would have brought me a mighty gift,' but Gandalf knows better: 'He would have kept it for his own, and when he returned you would not have known your son.'[523]

> *'They will look for him from the White Tower... but he will not return'*[524]

Knowing how close Boromir came to taking the Ring and, with it, destroying both the City he loved and all the remaining legacy of high Númenor, it is a relief that he fails and dies. And he dies well—as Faramir could tell from the beatific look on his face—like the great warrior he always was. His life ends in the arms of the future King of Gondor, who reassures him that Minas Tirith shall not fall. Boromir smiles. Nothing in his life became him like the leaving it.

Faramir

> *'Ah well, sir,' said Sam, 'you said my master had an elvish air; and that was good and true. But I can say this: you have an air too, sir, that reminds me of, of—well, Gandalf, of wizards.'*
> *'Maybe,' said Faramir. 'Maybe you discern from far away the air of Númenor.'*[525]

For many years, Tolkien experienced a terrible recurrent dream: a huge tsunami-like wave, unstoppable, breaking over trees and green fields.[526] That vision became the *Akallabêth,* the Downfall of Númenor; the story of how the greatest civilisation of Men was lost beneath the waves. But it was not only the dream that became part of Arda; the dreamer himself entered the story.

> *'It reminds me of Númenor... of the great dark wave climbing over the green lands... darkness inescapable. I often dream of it.'*[527]

So says Faramir, having been bequeathed the vision by its original recipient. While many fans and critics have attempted to portray Tolkien as one of his characters—to some he is the wise old sage Gandalf, to others

523 Tolkien, *The Lord of the Rings*, p. 795.
524 Tolkien, *The Lord of the Rings*, p. 407.
525 Tolkien, *The Lord of the Rings*, p. 667.
526 Carpenter, *Letters*, p. 213.
527 Tolkien, *The Lord of the Rings*, p. 931.

a stay-at-home hobbit—he himself said that as far as any character is like him it is Faramir.[528] The two share many practical similarities: both served (and were wounded) as army officers, both are scholars by inclination, and both maintain a reverence for ancient truths in spite of (or perhaps because of) present darkness.[529] Although one should not go as far as to say that Faramir *is* Tolkien, perhaps it might be fair to assert that Faramir is Tolkien as he would have liked himself to be.

Tolkien's claim to be like Faramir concludes with him adding, with typical bathos, 'except that I lack... Courage.'[530] Faramir, one might say, is Tolkien-plus-courage. All the things that Tolkien might have aspired to be—the warrior, the wooer, the leader, the scholar, the tender heart—Faramir was able to be, because he had both the inclination towards them and the courage not to fall short under trial.

The Wizard's Pupil

> *'Here was... one of the Kings of Men born into a later time, but touched with the wisdom and sadness of the Elder Race.'*[531]

The younger brother of the great-but-flawed Boromir, and son of the greater-but-more-flawed Denethor, Faramir represents all that is, or could be, good about Gondor. The great testing point for Faramir comes at the refuge of Henneth Annûn in Ithilien when he has Frodo and Sam, and therefore the Ring, at his mercy. 'Now's a chance to show your quality,'[532] challenges Sam, recognising the gravity of the moment. But faced with the same temptation that corrupted Boromir—supreme dominance within arms' reach, and with it the ability to accomplish any and every feasible desire—Faramir is moved not to ambition and assault but to pity and sorrow. 'I am not such a man,' he says.[533]

> *'He read the hearts of men as shrewdly as his father, but what he read moved him sooner to pity than to scorn. He was gentle in bearing, and a lover of lore and... welcomed Gandalf at such times as*

528 Carpenter, *Letters*, p. 232, footnote.

529 These are parallels noted by Garth, *Op. Cit.*, p. 310.

530 Courage, as CS Lewis said in a book dedicated to Tolkien, is 'not simply *one* of the virtues, but the form of every virtue at the testing point.' (CS Lewis, *The Screwtape Letters*, (Zondervan, 1996) p. 161.)

531 Tolkien, *The Lord of the Rings*, p. 792.

532 Tolkien, *The Lord of the Rings*, p. 665.

533 Tolkien, *The Lord of the Rings*, p. 666.

> *he came to the City, and he learned what he could from his wisdom; and in this as in many other matters he displeased his father.'*[534]

When Sam remarks that Faramir reminds him of Gandalf he is very perceptive: Faramir is indeed a 'wizard's pupil.'[535] This title, as received from Denethor, is intended as little more than petty name-calling, though in truth there could be few greater compliments. In the disturbed mind of the Steward, Gandalf is a competitor; a schemer seeking to supplant him with an upstart king and 'to stand behind every throne, north, south, or west.'[536] That Faramir should, from childhood, have sought out and learned from this wizard must have been devastating to Denethor, feeding the fiction that Gandalf had 'stolen half my son's love.'[537]

Since Gandalf was not a regular visitor to Minas Tirith, Faramir must have been a supremely keen student to be so profoundly affected by his influence. Not only do the two share a common skill-set—both being rather in the mould of Plato's ideal ruler, the Philosopher King[538]—but also their speech patterns are noticeably alike. In the same way that Gandalf is 'proverbious,' coining his own aphorisms and reshaping existing sayings to fit his own purposes, the flow of Faramir's speech is constantly interwoven with proverbial wisdom. While other people quote traditional sayings clearly, often in standalone sentences, Faramir's proverbs are barely discernible; rich but subtle ingredients contributing to the wider flavour. They play so natural a part of Faramir's speech that they can pass by, unnoticed.

> *'War must be, while we defend our lives against a destroyer who would devour all; but I do not love the bright sword for its sharpness, nor the arrow for its swiftness, nor the warrior for his glory. I love only that which they defend'*[539]

The above speech begins with a clear proverb, conspicuous because of its alliterative structure, but then slips proverbiously straight into a second—*Do not love the bright sword for its sharpness, nor the arrow*

---

534 Tolkien, *The Lord of the Rings*, p. 1031.

535 Tolkien, *The Lord of the Rings*, p. 836.

536 Tolkien, *The Lord of the Rings*, p. 835.

537 Tolkien, *The Lord of the Rings*, p. 836.

538 In Plato's *The Republic*, Socrates is recorded discussing the ideal form of government, in which the 'ship of state' is steered by philosophers, whose role is to promote virtue and facilitate the harmonious co-operation of all.

539 Tolkien, *The Lord of the Rings*, p. 656.

for its swiftness, nor the warrior for his glory—before the addendum *love only that which they defend*. Faramir's ability to leap from one saying to another shows the understanding of the proverbious mind: that all true wisdom is interconnected and overlapping, while the melding of three elements creates a sentence with the richness of proverbial wisdom without any of the condescension that a listener might perceive by feeling quoted at.

Faramir rarely prefaces a saying with an obvious 'it is said…' marker (he only does so twice, with *Night oft brings news to near kindred* and *Murder will out*). In addition to avoiding patronising his listener, this suggests that, like a true proverbious person, Faramir engages with his wisdom tradition subconsciously. Many hear and recite proverbs, but he embodies them—he goes beyond memorisation into incarnation. When explaining to the hobbits that 'We are truth-speakers, we men of Gondor. We *boast seldom, and then perform, or die in the attempt*'[540] it is significant that Faramir defines 'truth-speakers' as a matter not merely of honesty in speech, but of having the integrity to put words into action. This is the Wizard's Pupil at his most Gandalfian.

The Inheritor of Númenor

As an incarnation—a words-in-action enfleshment—of the Númenórean wisdom tradition, Faramir's qualities and abilities are as multifaceted and admirable as his heritage. Not for nothing does the message of his fathers tell him that *A warrior should have more skills and knowledge than only the craft of weapons and slaying*. According to Beregond, Faramir's life manifests this:

> *'Men are slow to believe that a captain can be wise and learned in the scrolls of lore and song, as he is, and yet a man of hardihood and swift judgement in the field. But such is Faramir.'*[541]

The large number of proverbs that Faramir uses reflects the breadth of his learning. From the moral value of honesty (*Do not snare even an orc with a falsehood*) and the etiquette of social hierarchy (*Do not speak before your master*), to compassion (*Do not scorn pity that is the gift of a gentle heart*), honour (*The praise of the praiseworthy is above all rewards*), and staying power (*Endure with patience the hours of waiting*),

540 Tolkien, *The Lord of the Rings*, p. 665.

541 Tolkien, *The Lord of the Rings*, p. 750.

the sheer range of subject matter is impressive, especially when contrasted with the narrow militaristic focus of his brother Boromir. And in the mouth of Faramir, this is not merely a collection of useful advice to help men choose well in difficulty; it is a holistic recipe for good living. The richness and breadth of the high heritage of Númenórean Gondor is evident throughout.

Living in the shadow of the Shadow has given Faramir ample opportunity to prove the strength of his wisdom tradition, but—unlike his brother, who had the same opportunities—it has also made him aware of his own weakness (Boromir, you can be sure, would never have said *There are some perils from which a man must flee.)* Faramir is no coward or weakling, but his proverbs have helped him recognise that physical strength is not the only strength.

The Great Wave covered and destroyed Númenor because of a failing similar to that exhibited by Boromir: the Kings of Men believed too strongly in their own valour and greatness. Ar-Pharazôn the Golden, the last and greatest king of Westernesse, was so mighty that he captured Sauron himself, only to start listening to the deceiver's words. *Great kings take what is their right* he was told, and so fell, seeking to conquer the Valar and to win unending life by force.

> *'And here in the wild I have you: two halflings, and a host of men at my call, and the Ring of Rings. A pretty stroke of fortune! A chance for Faramir, Captain of Gondor, to show his quality! Ha!'*[542]

At the refuge of Henneth Annûn, Faramir's response to the Ring is remarkable. Boromir had slavered over it, Gandalf backed away, and even Galadriel endured its allure as her greatest test. But Faramir does not appear even to be tempted. Instead of being provoked to desire, he sits down and laughs quietly to himself.

Faramir doesn't only reject the Ring; he rejects the desire for dominating strength—the desire that destroyed Númenor. In doing so, he also determines the kind of strength Gondor would come to embody after the war under its new king. Fortitude, not force, would be the way; a wisdom courageous enough not to hide behind physical might, and strong enough to want more than power.

542 Tolkien, *The Lord of the Rings*, p. 665.

Gondor: the exceptional past and future

> *'Pippin gazed in growing wonder at the great stone city, vaster and more splendid than anything that he had dreamed of… Yet it was in truth falling year by year into decay'*[543]

From its peak of power (when it held sway over Harondor, Umbar, near Harad, Calenardhon, Isengard, Enedwaith, Ithilien, Dagorlad, and the passes of Mordor), Gondor has faded. In its decayed Middle Age, Tolkien compared it to Mediaeval Byzantium, the proud, venerable, but increasingly impotent relic of Greco-Roman glory.[544] These latter-day Númenóreans of Gondor are a withering people, despite their strong roots. 'We are become Middle Men, of the Twilight,' reflects Faramir, 'but with memory of other things.'[545] The great days have passed.

> *'For myself,' said Faramir, 'I would see the White Tree in flower again in the courts of the kings, and the Silver Crown return, and Minas Tirith in peace: Minas Anor again as of old, full of light, high and fair, beautiful as a queen'*[546]

The Dúnedain of Gondor reverence the past and yearn for good things to endure deathlessly, as embodied in the hallows of Rath Dínen, where the nation's kings and stewards lay gloriously entombed. The Men of Gondor live surrounded by the crumbling remnants of their former glory, craving (but not expecting) their return.

Yet this nation is also a living remnant of ancient goodness. Two millennia of gradual decline had seen the loss of territory, the failing of the Royal line, and the waning of its founding wisdom, yet Denethor's Gondor is still the greatest of the kingdoms of Men, the bastion of resistance to Sauron, and the guardian of the heritage of Númenor. 'Gondor wanes,' admits Boromir, 'but Gondor stands, and even at the end of its strength is still very strong.'[547] In all the realms of Middle-earth, Gondor is still clearly a special case.

The problem with special cases is that when there is no greater good than self-preservation, all policies and tactics, however apparently immoral,

543 Tolkien, *The Lord of the Rings*, p. 736.

544 Carpenter, *Letters*, p. 157.

545 Tolkien, *The Lord of the Rings*, p. 663.

546 Tolkien, *The Lord of the Rings*, p. 656.

547 Tolkien, *The Lord of the Rings*, p. 260.

become justifiable options. Neither Boromir nor Denethor have moral qualms about using the Ring against Sauron—not because doing so would have been in itself morally good, but because by doing so, the good of Gondor could have been achieved. It is this ethical expediency that undermines Denethor's moral authority. He castigates the returning Faramir for his generous support of Frodo and Sam—for releasing, guiding, and encouraging them rather than taking them (and the Ring) captive. Faramir has acted rightly according to all the great virtues, but to Denethor, virtue is only valid subject to the needs of the state. He seeks to justify this abandonment of nobility by using the proverb *In desperate hours gentleness may be repaid with death*. 'So be it,'[548] replies Faramir, preferring death.

The hands of the king are the hands of a healer.

Just as Faramir emerges from death—the Ranger of Ithilien fittingly healed by the Ranger of the North—the nation of Gondor itself receives healing through its returning King. Not only does Aragorn on arrival in Minas Tirith immediately use and fulfil old proverbs—bringing a fresh vitality to Gondor's traditions in doing so—but also he brings new life and a new era, an era more in keeping with the wisdom of Faramir than that of Denethor.

With the Reunited Kingdom comes expansion where there had only been decay and decline, new life where there had only been embalming, and international friendship where there had only been ethnocentrism and self-centredness. Gondor is still a special case, but for a different reason: its role in embodying all that is still great, noble, and wise in Middle-earth.

The gates of Minas Tirith are rebuilt by Dwarves of Erebor; an Elven colony is established in Ithilien under Legolas; and the Oath of Eorl is renewed with Rohan. In these acts, Gondor shows that it now welcomes and values all nations. It also starts to understand that there are things of greater value than the greatness of Gondor, as Aragorn demonstrates by giving away land: the region around Núrnen to the released slaves of Mordor; Drúadan Forest to Ghân-buri-Ghân and his people; Isengard to Treebeard and the Ents; and the Shire to the Hobbits.

After long, slow decline, the embalmed kingdom of the Númenóreans is once more bright under its new leaders. With the coming of King

548 Tolkien, *The Lord of the Rings*, p. 794.

Elessar and Queen Arwen,[549] the White Tree is in flower again, the Silver Crown has returned, and Minas Tirith is at peace: Minas Anor of old, just as its new Steward Faramir had dreamed. The heroic work of Frodo and Sam might have won the war, but the renewed wisdom of Gondor wins the peace.

549 Arwen, it should be noted, is the niece of Númenor's first king, Elrond's brother Elros.

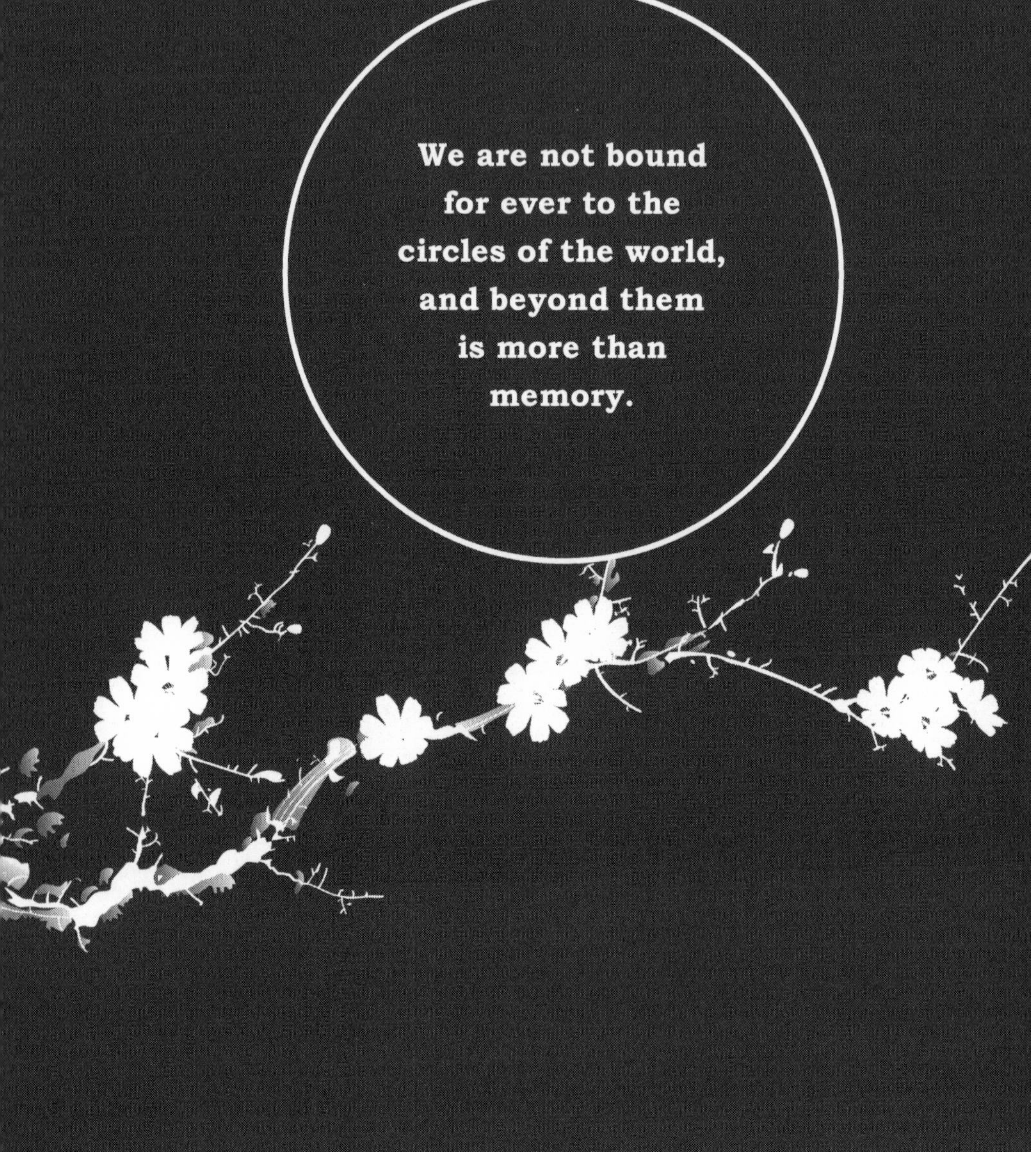
We are not bound
for ever to the
circles of the world,
and beyond them
is more than
memory.

CHAPTER ELEVEN

ARAGORN

Not all those who wander are lost

The mysterious Strider, huddled in the corner of an inn in a small provincial town, far from Middle-earth's seats of power and scenes of action, does not promise much. At least, not at first glance. 'I look foul and feel fair. Is that it?'[550] he laughs. But *handsome is as handsome does*.

> *'Do you really mean that Strider is one of the people of the old Kings?' said Frodo in wonder. 'I thought they had all vanished long ago. I thought he was only a Ranger.'*
> *'Only a Ranger!' cried Gandalf. 'My dear Frodo, that is just what the Rangers are: the last remnant in the North of the great people, the Men of the West.'*[551]

A man of many names, talents and predecessors, Aragorn is royalty wrapped in a rough-and-ready wardrobe. In Rivendell, where he is most truly known, the Dúnadan is recognised as the living emblem of the blood of High Númenor run true, but in terms of wisdom tradition, he represents a greater heritage than that of his ethnic forebears alone. For while Aragorn does indeed become 'the most hardy of living Men, skilled in their crafts and lore,' it is also clear that he is more than a lord of the Edain, 'for he was elven-wise.'[552]

550 Tolkien, *The Lord of the Rings*, p. 168.
551 Tolkien, *The Lord of the Rings*, p. 215.
552 Tolkien, *The Lord of the Rings*, p. 1035.

From the poetic to the pragmatic, Aragorn's proverbs are numerous and wide-ranging. They tend to be spoken quietly, submitted with humility, and clothed in thoughtfulness, as if each saying encapsulates a lesson that has been learned personally, even painfully. When, for example, Aragorn affirms Frodo's desire to return to the Shire with *The tree grows best in the land of its sires*, we hear within his words the long ache of the homeless wanderer; and likewise *A hunted man sometimes wearies of distrust and longs for friendship* reflects the angst to which his role and calling has often condemned him.

The message is in each case straightforward, but these sayings appear weightier because of the grim Ranger, stained by many travels, from whom they come. There is a solemn soulfulness behind Strider's sayings, as if he and they are rooted in a deeper unseen well of wisdom.

The Wisdom Repository

> *'Here is Aragorn son of Arathorn, chieftain of the Dúnedain of Arnor, Captain of the Host of the West, bearer of the Star of the North, wielder of the Sword Reforged, victorious in battle, whose hands bring healing'*[553]

Raised in Rivendell as the foster-son of Elrond, and known throughout his youth as *Estel* ('hope'), Aragorn did not learn his true name or his lineage until the age of twenty. At that time, having met Arwen and discovered his love for her, he left Imladris and went into the Wild alone, spending sixty years in multiple labours for the enemies of the Enemy. The last descendent and heir of the Kings became a familiar feature at Bree (as Strider), fought in wars with Rohan and Gondor (as the mysterious Thorongil), and travelled into the far South and East 'exploring the hearts of Men, both evil and good.'[554]

> *'What do you know?'*
> *'Too much; too many dark things'*[555]

Through the labours of many hard and dangerous years, the last of the Númenóreans learns much, and learns to apply what he learns: to lead

553 Tolkien, *The Lord of the Rings*, p. 946.

554 Tolkien, *The Lord of the Rings*, p. 1035.

555 Tolkien, *The Lord of the Rings*, p. 160.

without domineering, serve without demanding honour, and wander without being lost.

Aragorn's wide-ranging experiences are informed and supplemented by friendships both with the Wise and the lowly, the powerful and the meek. There is something touching about his choice to adopt 'Strider' (albeit in its Quenya form) as the name of his royal house, displaying as it does his ability to be at ease both with the 'wine out of a golden cup' of Butterbur's imagination, and the innkeeper's own mugs of ale. Wherever his wandering has taken him, Aragorn appears able to be at home.

In Bree, when the hobbits first meet the Ranger, he speaks in the idiom of the locals, adopting their accent and quoting two of their proverbs. And while *Drink, fire, and chance-meeting are pleasant enough,* this is not an accurate representation of the Dúnadan. As the Quest develops and the contexts change, Aragorn's knowledge and use of proverbs reveals his mastery of Middle-earth's traditions.

En route for Rivendell with the hobbits, he speaks as a resourceful Ranger:

> *Fire is our friend in the wilderness.*

Attacked by the Nazgûl on Weathertop, he is the remnant of those who repelled ancient Angmar:

> *All blades perish that pierce [the] dreadful King.*

And explaining the downfall of Rhudaur, he is the descendent of the Kings of Arnor:

> *The heirs of Elendil do not forget.*

In Rivendell, Elessar exhibits the wisdom of the Eldar:

> *We are not bound for ever to the circles of the world,*
> *and beyond them is more than memory*

But, on leaving it, he is wary of the dangers of the Dwarf-kingdom:

> *If you pass the doors of Moria, beware!*

And he knows the lore of Galadhrim:

> *Not idly do the leaves of Lórien fall.*

In company with Elf and Dwarf, he addresses a Man accordingly:

> *Good and ill have not changed since yesteryear; nor are they one thing among Elves and Dwarves and another among Men.*

And his wisdom even accounts for the Entwood:

> *It is perilous to cut bough or twig from a living tree in Fangorn.*

With the horse-lords of Rohan, he speaks with appropriately equine proverbs:

> *Seldom does thief ride home to the stable.*

In Minas Tirith, his sayings extend to the defending of great cities:

> *Men are better than gates.*

And He even knows the lore of Mordor:

> *If man must needs walk in sight of the Black Gate, or tread the deadly flowers of Morgul Vale, then perils he will have.*

These examples illustrate the range and wealth of wisdom Aragorn has absorbed. He has not simply visited various countries, he has taken on board their traditions and perspectives, as embodied in proverbs. Enriched to this degree, Aragorn is not only *au fait* with the various philosophical worldviews of the many peoples amongst whom he has lived, but he is also equipped to speak to each in a way which would not be heard by them as alien or foreign.[556]

Because of this ability to act as a cultural bridge, speaking in the heart-language of his listeners, Aragorn is able to make all peoples feel honoured and respected in a way they might not expect from a man of his high lineage. He has authority to lead by virtue of birth and experience, but he prefers to commend his views, not command them. Proverbs provide him with a neutral, non-confrontational means of doing so. There is no patronising condescension in Aragorn, and as he honours Middle-earth's wisdom traditions he receives his listeners' esteem in return.

If, as Peter Kreeft says, '*The Lord of the Rings* is a deep mine with many precious gems,'[557] then Aragorn is a metaphorical miner, unearthing the precious and the beautiful from each kingdom and people of Mid-

556 The only accessible wisdom tradition with which he does not appear familiar is that of the Shire-hobbits, whose land the Rangers guard but do not enter.

557 Kreeft, p. 20.

dle-earth. He is both homeless and at home everywhere, an anthropological anomaly and a wisdom repository.

All That's Gold...

Aragorn's knowledge of oral tradition is not limited to proverbs: according to Butterbur 'he can tell a rare tale when he has the mind';[558] under Weathertop he sings a selection from the Lay Of Leithian (which he clearly knows in multiple languages); faced with the Paths of the Dead he recalls the prophetic-poetic words of Malbeth the Seer; and in the Houses of Healing he recites a Rhyme of Lore:

'When the black breath blows
and death's shadow grows
and all lights pass,
come athelas! come athelas!
Life to the dying
In the king's hand lying![559]

In the same way that Gandalf would have recited and repeated such lines and verses in his wanderings as an aid to memory, Aragorn has taken the three strands of oral tradition—songs, stories, and sayings—and made them his companions on his long road.

It is apt, then, that in seeking to find fitting words to describe the Dúnadan, Bilbo settles on proverbs and poetry as the best medium. His poem, first encountered in Gandalf's letter and later recited at the Council of Elrond, contains some of Middle-earth's most enduring wisdom:

'All that is gold does not glitter,
Not all those who wander are lost;
The old that is strong does not wither,
Deep roots are not reached by the frost.

From the ashes a fire shall be woken,
A light from the shadows shall spring;
Renewed shall be blade that was broken:
The crownless again shall be king.'[560]

558 *LOTR*, p. 153.

559 Tolkien, *The Lord of the Rings*, p. 847.

560 Tolkien, *The Lord of the Rings*, p. 241.

'I believe my looks are against me'[561] says Strider in Bree. And though Pippin agrees, the Shire principle that *Folk are not always what they seem* and *Handsome is as handsome does* makes seeing past the surface easier for a hobbit than for a proud, impressive figure like Boromir. Appearances may be to the contrary, but Bilbo had perceived that underneath the 'strange-looking weather-beaten' exterior lies a vast wealth.

Strider does not glitter but he is golden; he perpetually wanders but is not lost; he has endured much but is unwithered; and his roots—leading back through the Númenórean kings and beyond to Eärendil and Beren One-hand—are deep and enduring. The mysterious figure leaning against the wall of *the Prancing Pony*'s common-room may not promise much, but with Aragorn what you see is most emphatically not what you get, and what you get is the combined wisdom of Middle-earth.

561 Tolkien, *The Lord of the Rings*, p. 167.

AFTERWORD

ON GOOD AND EVIL

While *The Lord Of The Rings* in particular, and Tolkien's legendarium in general, are often caricatured as a straightforward battle between good and evil, the reality is far less simplistic. As Tom Shippey observes, Tolkien 'thought more deeply than his critics have ever recognised about just those issues he is commonly alleged to ignore: the processes of temptation, the complex nature of good and evil, the relationship between reality and our fallible perception of it.'[562]

Since wisdom traditions are the primary means within the story by which virtue and nobility are promoted, we would expect that those who use them are ethically sound, but the truth is not so clear-cut: the proverbs of Middle-earth are found in the mouths of the immoral and corrupt as well as the noble and upright.[563] Seeing this should lead us to question the very nature of good and evil as it is presented in Tolkien's world. Far from a black and white face-off between the forces of darkness and of light, Middle-earth contains a complex, nuanced view of what goodness and evil actually are, and how they come to exist.

562 Shippey, *The Road to Middle-earth,* p. 140.

563 Examples abound, including Boromir quoting proverbs while assaulting Frodo, and Saruman citing sayings from the rail of Orthanc. Even Orcs use proverbs, with the Uruk-hai of Isengard saying *Rest while you can* and *Little people should not meddle in affairs that are too big for them*, while *Where there's a whip there's a will* is the refrain of the Orcs of Mordor.

Goodness

In *The Silmarillion*, we read of the origins of Arda, and specifically of its original goodness. The Ainulindalë describes how the world was brought into being by the singing of a great and harmonious music—a task delegated by Ilúvatar to the many diverse voices of his angelic beings, the Ainur. This Great Music was 'deep and wide and beautiful,' it was sung 'in unison and harmony,' and each of the created beings involved had the freedom to adorn the Theme 'each with his own thoughts and devices.'[564]

At this point in time—in fact, a point *before* time—there was as yet no such thing as evil; there were no malevolent acts, and no immoral motives. The Great Music shows us the original goodness of Arda: diverse, harmonious, collaborative, and creative. And just as the divine goodness of the Creator could not be expressed without multiple voices, multiple harmonies, and a level of individual creativity,[565] all the subsequent goodnesses within Tolkien's world—the virtues towards which the proverbs of Middle-earth attempt to point—are also diverse, harmonious, collaborative, and creative.

The diversity of goodness is shown in the sheer variety of virtuous people and acts on view in Middle-earth. For example, Gandalf is good, and so is the Gaffer, but when it comes to the art of living they are markedly different: Gandalf's goodness is world-aware, wandering, tender-spirited, and learnéd, while the Gaffer's is parochial, pragmatic, and defiantly illiterate. In theory, such contrasting philosophies should be hopelessly at odds with one another, but in practice they are not in competition at all; they are in harmony. Because goodness itself is diverse and multifaceted, no single stance or person can encompass it; multiple approaches are required. If there were only one type of virtue, it would no longer be virtue.

The heroes of Middle-earth—from Galadriel and Gil-galad to Gimli and Ghân-buri-Ghân—are all strongly distinct from one another; their goodnesses differ because that is the nature of goodness. One could even go as far as to say that they are distinct *because* they are good. This great range of goodnesses is a testimony to the virtue of creative liberty and freewill. Just as there were multiple harmonious voices in the Great

564 Tolkien, *The Silmarillion*, p. 15-16.

565 Tolkien's term *Sub-creator*, used to describe the creative activity of humans as an appropriate reflection of being made in the image of the creator God, is also applicable to the angelic Ainur.

Music—with each singer empowered to embellish the Theme as they saw fit—there are multiple ways to live well, and none of them is necessarily contradictory or in conflict with each other. As a result, the proverbs of Middle-earth offer a range of perspectives that is as diverse as goodness itself. They offer not wisdom, but *wisdoms*—multiple philosophies, not one ethos to rule them all.

This scope for freewill and creative liberty does not imply that right and wrong are purely relative terms amongst Tolkien's peoples, or that 'anything goes.' As Aragorn says, *Good and ill have not changed since yesteryear; nor are they one thing among Elves and Dwarves and another among Men.* Evil undeniably exists, but it is good and appropriate for each culture and each individual to have a distinct perspective on what it is to avoid it, and in so doing live a full and virtuous life.

With each wisdom tradition modelling a differing approach, moral living is portrayed not as a single puritanical straight-and-narrow path of obedience and rule-abiding, but as a broad meadow full of possibility and variety. This is in sharp contrast to the monotonous conformity of evil.

Evil

The Music of the Ainur not only describes the origin and nature of goodness in Arda, but also the root from which all evil originated. This moment of primordial rebellion, for which Tolkien uses the loaded theological term 'Fall,'[566] occurs during the singing of the Music, when one of the created beings, Melkor, starts 'to increase the power and glory of the part assigned to himself.'[567]

Not satisfied with merely being one contributor among many, Melkor wants to be in charge, setting up his own musical Theme to be in competition with that of Ilúvatar. This theme, joined with by some of the other Ainur, has 'little harmony, but rather a clamorous unison' and is 'loud, and vain, and endlessly repeated.'[568]

Though this prehistoric rebellion is described in ornate musical terms, evil is nonetheless shown to originate as a selfish discord, rooted in a desire to dominate, and resulting in ugly, drab uniformity. Diversity,

566 Tolkien, *The Silmarillion*, p. vx.
567 Tolkien, *The Silmarillion*, p. 16.
568 Tolkien, *The Silmarillion*, p. 17.

harmony, collaboration, and creativity—the marks of original goodness—are each comprehensively rejected. In doing so, Melkor becomes Morgoth, the 'Black Enemy,' and sets the tone for all who emulate him.

Nothing is evil in the beginning, as Elrond tells the Council, and none of Middle-earth's corrupt were anything other than good to begin with—as Peter Kreeft points out, 'Morgoth was one of the Ainur, Sauron was a Maia, Saruman was the head of Gandalf's order of Wizards, the Orcs were Elves, the Ringwraiths were great Men, and Gollum was a Hobbit.'[569] All evil in Middle-earth is therefore tainted goodness, and differs from it in one key way: while each approach to goodness is distinct, allowing a range of expression, evil is monotonous—as endlessly repetitive as Melkor's theme of clamorous unison. All the malice of Middle-earth conforms to the same shape, and walks the same path: self-sufficiency turns into arrogance and gives birth to the will to power. Melkor wanted 'to be called Lord,'[570] Sauron made the One Ring 'so that he could rule all,'[571] and Saruman desired 'power, power to order all things.'[572]

The history of Arda repeatedly shows that it is the *libido dominandi*—the lust for power—that corrupts. The virtue of creative liberty, inherent in the Great Music, is twisted by the tyrannical desire to direct and dictate.[573] In Tolkien's world, power—when it dominates or seeks to dominate other wills and minds—is evil, but that doesn't make it any less tempting, even to good people. In fact, those who fall into immorality and expediency usually do so believing that, in some way, their motives are sound. Melkor himself originally sought to 'order all things for the good,'[574] just as, in later ages, Sauron began with fair motives: reorganising and rehabilitation the ruined lands of Middle-earth,[575] and Saruman was willing to subjugate others because of his 'high and

569 Kreeft, *Op. Cit.*, p. 178.

570 Tolkien, *The Silmarillion*, p. 18.

571 Tolkien, *The Lord of the Rings*, p. 50.

572 Tolkien, *The Lord of the Rings*, p. 252.

573 Even Orcs, no more than miserable fear-driven slaves, compulsively attempt to assert their dominance: defacing the statue of the old King at the Cross-roads, fighting among themselves, and delighting to 'slash and beat down growing things.' Orcs only submit under threat of pain or death, leaving the large and powerful to cow the smaller into obedience by means of physical domination and violence. This is illustrated by the overheard conversation between a large warrior *Uruk* and a small *Snaga* (tracker-orc) in the Morgai, in the squabbling between the groups from Moria, Isengard, and Mordor on the Wold, and in the deadly quarrelling of the Orcs of Cirith Ungol.

574 Tolkien, *The Silmarillion*, p. 18.

575 Carpenter, *Letters*, p. 151.

ultimate purpose: Knowledge, Rule, Order.'[576] Power is tempting because it provides the means to achieve ostensibly noble ends, only working its corruption in the process.

The fact that evil in Arda is both repulsive and recognisably logical is one of the triumphs of Tolkien's work: the adversaries of his heroes all have reasons for their actions, reasons by which they are presumably convinced. We, outside the story, are exactly the same: the greatest tyrants and scoundrels of history have felt justified in their twisted, power-hungry actions. The only difference between our choices and those in Middle-earth is that we do not have the temptation of the Ring.

The Ring

One Ring to rule them all, One Ring to find them,
One Ring to bring them all and in the Darkness bind them.

So chanted Sauron—one of the singing Ainur who originally joined with Melkor's discordant theme—as he made the Ring, intending in this mirror-image act of sung creation to set himself up as God-king over Middle-earth. The sole rhyme of lore originating from a malevolent source deals with the ultimate purpose of evil—to rule everything, everywhere. The One Ring, while beautiful, is the epitome of evil and the antithesis of the great goodness of creation: the power it offers inspires no collaboration or harmony, only tyranny and domination. In it, the deep-and-wide-and-beautiful has been rejected in favour of the shallow, the narrow, and the ugly.

Because, in Middle-earth, all evil originates in goodness, there are no wholly good or bad people, only shades of corruption. Therefore, the line between good and evil 'is not just external, between the white chess pieces and the black, but within every single piece on the board.'[577] The corrupting process of power is potentially at work in every person, and the Ring magnifies and accelerates it—proving too great a test for Boromir, who aches for 'power of Command'[578] and is overcome by visions of great alliances and glorious victories under his banner. Even Hobbits, who are generally protected from the *libido dominandi* by their native lack of strength and ambition, can be twisted: Sam sees visions

576 Tolkien, *The Lord of the Rings*, p. 253.

577 Kreeft, *Op. Cit.*, p. 178.

578 Tolkien, *The Lord of the Rings*, p. 389.

of Gorgoroth turned into a garden; and Sméagol drools over his puny fantasies of Gollum the Great eating fish 'every day, three times a day, fresh from the sea.'[579]

When within reach of the potency and capacity of the Ring to achieve virtually any goal, even the most trustworthy and wholesome are tempted—it is with good reason that Gandalf and Elrond refuse to even contemplate taking it themselves. Power corrupts, and absolute power—the power than the Ring affords—corrupts absolutely. To use the Ring is to become another Dark Lord, and 'the only measure he knows is desire,' says Gandalf, 'desire for power.'[580]

The Ring therefore encapsulates Middle-earth's understanding of good and evil. Goodness—like the Elven Rings and their bearers—is collaborative, harmonious, and diverse, but there is only one Ring to rule them all. Lust for power can never be satisfied in a fraternity of tyrants; it exists entirely to dominate; to drown out all music but its own. [581]

With no room for diversity or creative nuance—only tyranny, submitted to with absolute obedience—evil leads to the ultimate conformity: darkness. It is notable that the most completely 'unfallen' figures in Middle-earth, Bombadil and Goldberry, are resplendent in vivacious colour; a defiant contrast to the Dark Lord of the Black Land, for whom—commanding his Black Riders from the Dark Tower with the Ring on his Black Hand—even the harmonious diversity of colour is destroyed by his descent into corruption.[582]

Another aspect of this utter conformity is that evil cannot befriend or engage in mutual collaboration—it appears to be in a perpetual state of rebellion against all things, including itself. Aragorn sees this, saying *It is difficult with evil folk to know when they are in league, and when they are cheating one another.* When Gandalf takes this further, saying *One cannot be both tyrant and counsellor,* he displays an understanding that malice is always seeking complete mastery—Saruman could never have truly joined with Sauron, only challenged or submitted to him.

579 Tolkien, *The Lord of the Rings*, p. 619.

580 Tolkien, *The Lord of the Rings*, p. 262.

581 The only proverb heard in the mouth of Sauron himself—*Great kings take what is their right*—hints at the Dark Lord's underlying motive: sense of entitlement feeding the desire for greatness.

582 Saruman, it should be noted, is told 'You have no colour now' when his fall is confirmed by Gandalf; and Morgoth is thrown into the 'outer darkness.'

'Strange powers have our enemies, and strange weaknesses!'[583]

Evil's greatest weakness is therefore its capacity for self-harm and self-defeat—the right hand cutting off the left in its desire to rule—as recorded with obvious relish by several wisdom traditions. *Often does hatred hurt itself*, says Gandalf, after the precious palantír of Orthanc is thrown at him (Théoden's adds the similar *Oft evil will shall evil mar*), while *Our Enemy's devices oft serve us in his despite*, is the observation of Éomer, as Sauron's masking clouds of gloom serve to protect the Rohirrim from being easily observed. It is Boromir's attack that protects Frodo from potential capture at the hands of Saruman's orcs; it is the treachery of Gollum, leading Frodo and Sam to Shelob's Lair, that gives the hobbits an unlikely entrance to Mordor; and it is Gollum's unending lust for the Ring that enables it to finally reach the Fire and be destroyed, when Frodo could not give it up.

Every worm has his weak spot, as a wise hobbit once said, and Sauron is no exception. By forging the One Ring in order to have sufficient power to completely dominate all others, he inadvertently created the only means by which Middle-earth could defeat him. Had he known a proverb like *A treacherous weapon is ever a danger to the hand*, he might have been wiser. It is Sauron's malice and desire for domination that provide not only a focal point around which all the Free Peoples could unite, but also an Achilles' heel of weakness to direct their efforts towards. Often indeed does hatred hurt itself.

And The Moral of the Story is...

'The beginning of wisdom is this: Get wisdom.'[584]

As this volume has demonstrated, Middle-earth is full of wise words, thoughtful sayings, and pragmatic proverbs, while its narratives engage us in great subjects like courage, hope, and the nature of good and evil. It therefore appears to be an ideal place for us in (what Tolkien would call) the Primary World to 'get wisdom.' But how ought we to apply the truths of a fictional realm? Should we even try?

When pressed, as he often was, on the matter of what the Ring 'means,' or what his 'message' might be, Tolkien was affronted. He derided and

583 Tolkien, *The Lord of the Rings*, p. 581.

584 Proverbs 4:7, *Holy Bible, New International Version.*

disdained morality stories and ethical allegories, and hated it when well-meaning people included his works in that genre.[585] When accused by a critic of being 'a believer in moral didacticism'—someone who hides a moral message behind the veneer of a story—he responded by saying that the very opposite was true, and that he sought neither to teach nor preach.[586]

'The book... is not about anything but itself.'[587]

The tales of Middle-earth are not lectures. Like most storytellers in most societies throughout history, Tolkien was not writing (what Orson Scott Card calls) 'essays in disguise' to be decoded by thoughtful critics.[588] He hated the idea. While Middle-earth describes and displays great virtues and vices, Tolkien did not create his languages, invent his peoples, or write his tales as a means of gaining a pulpit or convincing others of his philosophical or theological convictions. His goal was not to instruct, but to enchant: to create a secondary reality so comprehensive in its scope and so thrilling in its content that readers would be under its spell, immersed.

There is therefore no point at which the reader of *The Lord of the Rings* or *The Hobbit* is supposed to lean back and ask, in the grand Victorian manner, what 'the moral of the story' is. There is no 'secret message' to be uncovered, and to look for one is to become Saruman, breaking a thing to find out what it is. That is not the path of wisdom. And yet, as his 1939 lecture *On Fairy Stories* explains, Tolkien believed that fanciful tales of the Perilous Realm should be taken seriously: not relegated to the nursery but treasured as vessels of transcendent truth. When Celeborn says, *Do not despise the lore that has come down from distant years*, it is as much for our ears as for Boromir's.

In the well-feigned history of Middle-earth, what is offered to us is wisdom and truth: not a simple lesson to learn, but over seven thousand years' worth of learned lessons to apply. Each one of these lessons may be considered a leaf on Tolkien's Great Tree—not an end in and of itself,

585 'I cordially dislike allegory... I much prefer history, true or feigned, with its varied applicability to the thought and experience of readers.' (Tolkien, *The Lord of the Rings*, p. xv).

586 Carpenter, *Letters*, p. 414.

587 Tolkien as quoted by *The Daily Telegraph*, March 22, 1968, (http://www.telegraph.co.uk/culture/film/film-news/11261158/JRR-Tolkien-Film-my-books-Its-easier-to-film-The-Odyssey.html retrieved on 20/12/2014).

588 Orson Scott Card, 'How Tolkien Means,' *Meditations on Middle-Earth*, p. 156.

but adding depth of detail to the whole. The enduring genius of Tolkien's Tree is that its beauty works on multiple levels: we can prioritise the Big Picture—of goodness corrupted by evil but ultimately triumphing—or we can emphasise the minutiae; the leaves of language or lore upon which Tolkien lovingly dwelt. Either way, without self-consciously looking for the author's 'secret message' we get wisdom anyway, discovering that both in the broad brush-strokes and in the fine detail Arda is truth-filled, enriching, and applicable.

Myths, folk-tales, and works of fantasy may be fictional, but they are not lies. They tell us about what is authentic and real, revealing truths that mundane reality obscures. We need such stories as those of Arda, since they allow a new setting for the stale and moth-eaten, which suddenly seem brighter and clearer than they ever did when encumbered by the plain factual existence of our daily grind. Tolkien believed that the writer of Fantasy, the Sub-creator, may 'actually assist in the effoliation and multiple enrichment of creation.'[589] And he proved it in his creation of Middle-earth. The moral of his story, it might be said, is that the story itself is moral—as we delve deeper into Tolkien's world, we enrich our own.

589 JRR Tolkien, 'On Fairy Stories,' *Tree and Leaf* (Unwin Hyman, 1964), p. 73.

All we have
to decide is
what to do
with the time
that is given us.

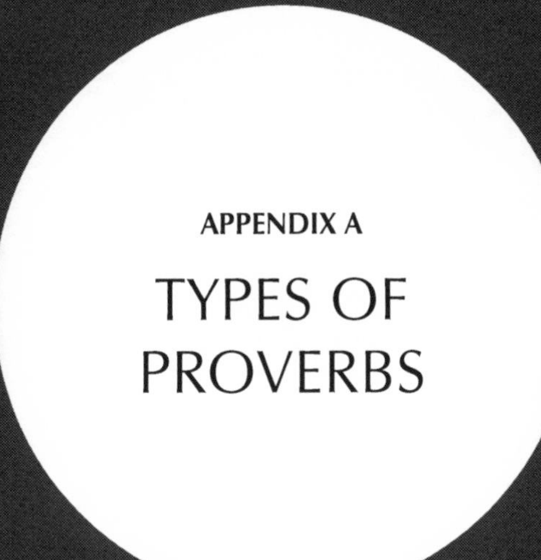

APPENDIX A

TYPES OF PROVERBS

Proverb (n.)
A short, well-known, pithy saying, stating a general truth or piece of advice.

Oxford English Dictionary

As previously stated, there is no way of definitively telling what is or isn't a proverb of Middle-earth. However, while 'proverb' has no easily defined boundaries, it also functions as an umbrella term, encompassing multiple genres of sayings that do have more precise definitions, due to their identifiable features and uses. Some of the most common are listed below, illustrated with examples of Tolkien's invention.

Adage

A memorably-worded saying containing a fact of experience held to be true by many, usually gaining credibility by long use.

Handsome is as handsome does. **Sam** and **Pippin**.
One thing drives out another. **Butterbur**.
At the table small men may do the greater deeds. **Beregond**.

Aphorism

A concise definition or assertion, memorable for insight, wit, or poetic nature.

The might of Elrond is in wisdom not in weapons. **Boromir**.
Ill news is an ill guest. **Wormtongue**.

The skill of the Dwarves is in their hands rather than in their tongues. **Galadriel**.

Axiom

An accepted premise, asserted to provide a starting point for further reasoning.

All that is gold does not glitter. **Bilbo**.
Nothing is evil in the beginning. **Elrond**.
All things must come utterly to an end in time. **Beregond**.

Ellipsis

A statement that omits unnecessary elements in order to be brief.

More haste, less speed. **Gollum**.
Sheep get like shepherd, and shepherds like sheep. **Treebeard**.
If it must be so, it must. **Hirgon**.

Epigram

A brief, witty statement, often satirical or paradoxical, usually found as a couplet or a statement in two halves.

Short cuts make delays, but inns make longer ones. **Frodo**.
Where there's a whip there's a will. **Mordor Orc**.
Those who have not swords can still die upon them. **Éowyn**.

Idiom

A figurative phrase, whose meaning cannot be derived simply by its content, due to the use of imagery not presented in context.

Proper fourteen-twenty! **Hobbit Ale-Drinker**.
Surer of finding the way home in a blind night than the cats of Queen Berúthiel. **Aragorn**.
Strange as news from Bree. **Eastfarthing Hobbits**.

Maxim

A fundamental rule or principle of behaviour, able to be given as advice or adopted as a motto.

Do not be hasty. **Treebeard**.
Do not meddle in the affairs of Wizards. **Gildor**.
Don't let your heads get too big for your hats. **Bilbo**.

Truism

A factual phrase, usually lacking metaphorical or poetic embellishment yet entering common use through wider application.

Anduin the Great flows past many shores. **Elrond**.
Night must follow noon. **Galadriel**.
Tomorrow is unknown. **Legolas**.

Twin Formulae

A phrase in two halves, gaining credit through the contrast or compatibility between the two elements.

Live and learn. **Gaffer**.

Be bold, but wary! **Bombadil**.

A tight belt and a light tooth. **Sam**.

APPENDIX B

THE PROVERBS OF MIDDLE-EARTH

In Chronological Order

The Hobbit

Dark for dark business. **Dwarves.**
Don't be precise, and don't worry. **Dwalin.**
If you sit on the door-step long enough, you will think of something. **Bilbo.**
Adventures are not all pony-rides in May-sunshine. **Narrator** [**Bilbo**'s thoughts].
Elvish singing is not a thing to miss, in June under the stars. **Narrator.**
Valleys have ears, and some elves have over merry tongues. **Gandalf.**
There is nothing like looking, if you want to find something. **Thorin.**
It might be worse, and then again it might be a good deal better. **Thorin.**
The less inquisitive you are... the less trouble you are likely to find. **Dwarves.**
Answers [are] to be guessed not given. **Bilbo.**
Don't bring things that are of no use. **Gandalf.**
Escaping goblins to be caught by wolves. **Bilbo.**
Naughty little boys that play with fire get punished. **Gandalf.**
Near the edge of Mirkwood... take the word of no one that you [do] not know as well as your brother or better. **Beorn.**
Mirkwood is dark, dangerous, & difficult. **Beorn.**
Depend on your luck and your courage. **Beorn.**
There are no safe paths. **Gandalf.**
Don't start grumbling against orders, or something bad will happen. **Thorin.**
There is nothing in the feeling of weight in an idle toss-pot's arms. **Galion.**
If you come in peace lay down your arms. **Captain of the Guard.**
Lock nor bar may hinder the homecoming spoken of old. **Thorin.**

There is no knowing what a dwarf will not dare and do for revenge. **Narrator**.
Third time pays for all. **Bilbo**.
Dwarves are not heroes. **Narrator**.
It does not do to leave a live dragon out of your calculations. **Narrator**.
Every worm has his weak spot. **Bilbo**.
Lucky numbers don't always come off. **Smaug**.
Don't have more to do with dwarves than you can help. **Smaug**.
Never laugh at live dragons. **Bilbo**.
While there's life there's hope. **Bilbo**.
Up the Bowman, and down with Moneybags! **People of Laketown**.
It is an ill wind... that blows no one any good. **Elvenking**.
The wealthy may have pity beyond right on the needy that befriended them when they were in want. **Bard**.
Gather your wisdom. **Bard**.
Winter and snow will bite both men and elves, and they may find their dwelling in the waste grievous to bear. **Thorin**.
Your own wisdom must decide your course. **Roac**.
Dwarves are sometimes politer in word than in deed. **Bilbo**.
A fool deserves to starve. **Bard**.
Goblins are the foes of all, and at their coming all other quarrels are forgotten. **Narrator**.
Defeat may be glorious. **Bilbo**.
If more of us valued food and cheer and song above hoarded gold, it would be a merrier world. **Thorin**.
Appear where you are most needed. **Elvenking**.
Even dragons have their ending. **Bilbo**.
A little sleep does a great cure. **Bilbo**.
Merry is May-time! **Bilbo**.
Share and share alike. **Gandalf**.
All things come to an end. **Narrator**.
Roads go ever ever on. **Bilbo**.

The Lord of the Rings

It will have to be paid for. **Shire Hobbits.**
Boats are quite tricky enough for those that sit still. **Gaffer**.
You shouldn't listen to all you hear. **Gaffer**.
Don't go getting mixed up in the business of your betters, or you'll land in trouble too big for you. **Gaffer**.
You can say what you like. **Sandyman**.
Bag End's a queer place, and its folk are queerer. **Sandyman**.
The Road goes ever on and on. **Bilbo**.
Some folk have all the luck. **Shire Hobbits**.
Always after a defeat and a respite, the Shadow takes another shape and grows again. **Gandalf**.

All we have to decide is what to do with the time that is given us. **Gandalf**.
Mordor draws all wicked things. **Gandalf**.
Many that live deserve death. And some that die deserve life. **Gandalf**.
Do not be too eager to deal out death in judgement. **Gandalf**.
Even the very wise cannot see all ends. **Gandalf**.
Rings have a way of being found. **Gandalf**.
One Ring to rule them all, One Ring to find them, One Ring to bring them all and in the darkness bind them. In the Land of Mordor where the Shadows lie. **Gandalf** [**Sauron**'s words].
Be careful of what you say, even to your closest friends. **Gandalf**.
The Enemy has many spies and many ways of hearing. **Gandalf**.
It's a dangerous business going out of your door. **Bilbo** [quoted by **Frodo**].
You step into the Road, and if you don't keep your feet, there is no knowing where you might be swept off to. **Bilbo** [quoted by **Frodo**].
The wide world is all about you: you can fence yourselves in, but you cannot forever fence it out. **Gildor**.
Do not meddle in the affairs of Wizards, for they are subtle and quick to anger. **Gildor**.
Go not to the Elves for counsel, for they will say both no and yes. **Frodo**.
Seldom give unguarded advice. **Gildor**.
Advice is a dangerous gift, even from the wise to the wise, and all courses may run ill. **Gildor**.
Courage is found in unlikely places. **Gildor**.
Short cuts make long delays. **Pippin**.
Short cuts make delays, but inns make longer ones. **Frodo**.
All's well as ends well. **Maggot**.
A loon is he that will not sing. **Pippin** [**Bilbo**'s words].
Some things are ill to hear when the world's in shadow. **Bombadil**.
Heed no nightly noise. **Goldberry** and **Bombadil**.
Naught wakes hobbit-folk in the early morning. **Bombadil**.
Make haste while the Sun shines. **Goldberry**.
Long tales are thirsty, and long listening is hungry. **Bombadil**.
Clothes are but little loss, if you escape from drowning. **Bombadil**.
Sharp blades are good to have. **Bombadil**.
Be bold, but wary. **Bombadil**.
Strange as news from Bree. **Eastfarthing Hobbits**.
Your business is your own. **Harry**.
It never rains but it pours. **Butterbur**.
One thing drives out another. **Butterbur**.
Make yourselves at home! **Butterbur**.
As you please! **Butterbur**.
Mind your Ps and Qs. **Merry**.
There's no accounting for East and West. **Butterbur**.
Drink, fire, and chance-meeting are pleasant enough. **Aragorn**.
There are queer folk about. **Harry** and **Aragorn**.

What's done can't be undone. **Butterbur**.
Caution is one thing and wavering is another. **Aragorn**.
You know your own business. **Butterbur**.
Every little helps. **Aragorn**.
All that is gold does not glitter. **Gandalf** [**Bilbo**'s words].
Not all those who wander are lost. **Gandalf** [**Bilbo**'s words].
The old that is strong does not wither. **Gandalf** [**Bilbo**'s words].
Deep roots are not reached by a frost. **Gandalf** [**Bilbo**'s words].
A hunted man sometimes wearies of distrust and longs for friendship. **Aragorn**.
Handsome is as handsome does. **Pippin**.
Apples for walking, and a pipe for sitting. **Sam**.
Fire is our friend in the wilderness. **Aragorn**.
All blades perish that pierce [that] dreadful King. **Aragorn**.
The heirs of Elendil do not forget. **Aragorn**.
There are many powers in the world, for good or for evil. **Gandalf**.
Dwarves' tongues run on when speaking of their handiwork. **Gloin**.
To sheep other sheep no doubt appear different. **Lindir**.
Come and go as you like, as long as you don't make a noise. **Bilbo**.
The might of Elrond is in wisdom, not in weapons. **Boromir**.
The spies of the Enemy are many. **Legolas**.
What roads would any dare to tread... if the Dunedain were asleep? **Aragorn**.
If simple folk are free from care and fear, simple they will be. **Aragorn**.
If man must needs walk in sight of the Black Gate, or tread the deadly flowers of Morgul Vale, then perils he will have. **Aragorn**.
What was is less dark than what is to come. **Denethor**.
What was lost may yet be found. **Saruman**.
Treason has ever been our greatest foe. **Gandalf**.
White cloth may be dyed. The white page can be overwritten; and the white light can be broken. **Saruman**.
He that breaks a thing to find out what it is has left the path of wisdom. **Gandalf**.
Even the most subtle spiders may leave a weak thread. **Gandalf**.
It is perilous to study too deeply the arts of the Enemy, for good or for ill. **Elrond**.
Oft in lies truth is hidden. **Glorfindel**.
Nothing is evil in the beginning. **Elrond**.
None can foretell what will come to pass, if we take this road or that. **Elrond**.
Valour needs first strength, and then a weapon. **Boromir**.
Anduin the Great flows past many shores. **Elrond**.
Despair is only for those who see the end beyond all doubt. **Gandalf**.
It is wisdom to recognise necessity. **Gandalf**.
Such is oft the course of deeds that move the wheels of the world: small hands do them because they must, while the eyes of the great are elsewhere. **Elrond**.
Only a small part is played in great deeds by any hero. **Gandalf**.
Hobbits ought to stick together. **Pippin**.
When pools are black and trees are bare 'tis evil in the wild to fare. **Bilbo**.
In every wood in every spring there is a different green. **Bilbo**.

Never mind about looks. **Bilbo**.
You'll want it, if you haven't got it. **Sam**.
Trust rather to... friendship than to great wisdom. **Gandalf**.
Fear the many eyes of the servants of Sauron. **Elrond**.
Let all the foes of Gondor flee! **Boromir**.
Dwarves make light of burdens. **Narrator**.
Faithless is he that says farewell when the road darkens. **Gimli**.
Let him not vow to walk in the dark, who has not seen the nightfall. **Elrond**.
Sworn word may strengthen quaking heart. **Gimli**. *Or break it.* **Elrond**.
Look not far ahead. **Elrond**.
Dark is the water of Kheled-zaram, and cold are the springs of Kibil-nala. **Gimli** [and later, **Galadriel**].
Much evil must befall a country before it wholly forgets the Elves, if once they dwelt there. **Gandalf**.
If you bring a Ranger with you, it is well to pay attention to him. **Gandalf**.
It matters little who is the enemy, if [one] cannot beat off his attack. **Gandalf**.
When heads are at a loss bodies must serve. **Boromir**.
Let a ploughman plough, but choose an otter for swimming. **Legolas**.
Those who pass the gates of Barad-dur do not return. **Gandalf**.
One must tread the path that need chooses. **Gandalf**.
If you pass the doors of Moria, beware! **Aragorn**.
The wolf that one hears is worse than the orc that one fears. **Boromir**.
Where the warg howls, there also the orc prowls. **Aragorn**.
There are older and fouler things than Orcs in the deep places of the world. **Gandalf**.
Surer of finding the way home in a blind night than the cats of Queen Beruthiel. **Aragorn**.
Let the guide go first while you have one. **Aragorn**.
Few come out who once go in [to Lórien]; and of that few none have escaped unscathed. **Boromir**.
Live and learn. **Sam** [quoting the **Gaffer**].
In nothing is the power of the Dark Lord more clearly shown than in the estrangement that divides all those who still oppose him. **Haldir**.
A plague on Dwarves and their stiff necks! **Legolas**.
The world is indeed full of peril, and in it there are many dark places... But still there is much that is fair, and though in all lands love is now mingled with grief, it grows perhaps the stronger. **Haldir**.
The light perceives the very heart of the darkness. **Haldir**.
Though the world is now dark better days are at hand. **Celeborn**.
However it may be with the guide, the followers are blameless. **Galadriel**.
The Men of Minas Tirith are true to their word. **Boromir**.
Seeing is both good and perilous. **Galadriel**.
It's the job that's never started as takes longest to finish. **Sam** [quoting the **Gaffer**].
None can be sure of peace. **Celeborn**.

Never travel far without a rope. **Lórien Elf**.

Maybe the paths that you each shall tread are already laid before your feet, though you do not see them. **Celeborn**.

Do not despise the lore that has come down from distant years. **Celeborn**.

Oft it may chance that old wives keep in memory word of things that once were needful for the wise to know. **Celeborn**.

Night must follow noon. **Galadriel**.

The skill of the Dwarves is in their hands rather than in their tongues. **Galadriel**.

Such is the way of it: to find and to lose, as it seems to those whose boat is on the running stream. **Legolas**.

Memory is not what the heart desires. **Gimli**.

Time does not tarry ever, but change and growth is not in all things and places alike. **Legolas**.

The passing seasons are but ripples ever repeated in the long long stream. **Legolas**.

It is not the way of the Men of Minas Tirith to desert their friends at need. **Boromir**.

The legs of Men will lag on a rough road, while a Dwarf goes on, be the burden twice his own weight. **Gimli**.

Where there are so many, all speech becomes a debate without end. **Boromir**.

Two together may perhaps find wisdom. **Boromir**.

Each to his own kind. **Boromir**.

It is by our own folly that the Enemy will defeat us. **Boromir**.

Let us first do what we must do. **Legolas**.

Maybe there is no right choice. **Gimli**.

Endure the East Wind, but... do not ask it for tidings. **Aragorn**.

Not idly do the leaves of Lorien fall. **Aragorn**.

Stone-hard are the Dwarves in labour or journey. **Narrator**.

Rest a little to run the better. **Gimli**.

Where sight fails the earth may bring us rumour. **Aragorn**.

Keen are the eyes of the Elves. **Aragorn**.

Tomorrow is unknown. **Legolas**.

Rede oft is found at the rising of the Sun. **Legolas**.

The stranger should declare himself first. **Éomer**.

These are indeed strange days. Dreams and legends spring to life out of the grass. **Éomer**.

Not we but those who come after will make the legends of our time. **Aragorn**.

When the great fall, the less must lead. **Aragorn**.

Do we walk in legends or on the green earth in the daylight? **Éothain**.

The Men of the Mark do not lie, and therefore they are not easily deceived. **Éomer**.

Hardy is the race of Elendil. **Éomer**.

Good and ill have not changed since yesteryear; nor are they one thing among Elves and Dwarves and another among Men. **Aragorn**.

May you find what you seek. **Éomer**.

There are some things that it is better to begin than to refuse, even though the end may be dark. **Aragorn**.

It is perilous to cut bough or twig from a living tree in Fangorn. **Aragorn**.

Rest while you can. **Orc Guard**.

Little people should not meddle in affairs that are too big for them. **Grishnákh**.

You know your own business best. **Merry**.

Do not be hasty. **Treebeard**.

Bad memories are handed down. **Treebeard**.

Sheep get like shepherd, and shepherds like sheep. **Treebeard**.

The years lie thicker than the leaves. **Treebeard**.

There is naught that an old Ent can do to hold back [a] storm: he must weather it or crack. **Treebeard**.

It is a mark of evil things that came in the Great Darkness that they cannot abide the Sun. **Treebeard**.

It is easier to shout 'stop!' than to do it. **Treebeard**.

If we stayed at home and did nothing, doom would find us anyway, sooner or later. **Treebeard**.

Songs like trees bear fruit only in their own time and in their own way: and sometimes they are withered untimely. **Treebeard**.

Few can foresee whither their road will lead them, till they come to its end. **Legolas**.

He that strikes the first blow, if he strikes it hard enough, may need to strike no more. **Gandalf**.

A treacherous weapon is ever a danger to the hand. **Gandalf**.

It is a comfort not to be mistaken at all points. **Gandalf**.

Hope is not victory. **Gandalf**.

Go where you must go. **Gandalf**.

Deep is the abyss that is spanned by Durin's Bridge, and none has measured it. **Gimli**.

Draw no weapon, speak no haughty word. **Gandalf**.

A king will have his way in his own hall, be it folly or wisdom. **Gandalf**.

Seldom does thief ride home to the stable. **Aragorn**.

Prudence is one thing, but discourtesy is another. **Gandalf**.

Every man has something too dear to trust to another. **Aragorn**.

The staff in the hand of a wizard may be more than a prop for age. **Háma**.

In doubt a man of worth will trust to his own wisdom. **Háma**.

All friends should gather together, lest each be singly destroyed. **Gandalf**.

News from afar is seldom sooth. **Théoden**.

Ill news is an ill guest. **Wormtongue**.

Webs of deceit were ever woven in Dwimordene. **Wormtongue**.

The wise speak only of what they know. **Gandalf**.

The young perish and the old linger. **Théoden**.

Faithful heart may have froward tongue. **Théoden**.

To crooked eyes truth may wear a wry face. **Gandalf**.

Dwarves are strange folk. **Legolas**.

Men need many words before deeds. **Gimli**.

Oft the unbidden guest proves the best company. **Éomer**.

He that flies counts every foeman twice. **Westfold Scout**.

The world changes, and all that once was strong now proves unsure. **Théoden**.

Dawn is ever the hope of men. **Aragorn**.

None knows what the new day shall bring him. **Aragorn**.

Do not judge the counsel of Gandalf until all is over. **Aragorn**.

Strange are the ways of men. **Gimli**.

Songs have come down among us out of strange places, and walk visible under the Sun. **Théoden**.

The days are fated to be filled with marvels. **Théoden**.

You are not without allies, even though you know them not. **Gandalf**.

The evil of Sauron cannot be wholly cured, nor made as if it had not been. **Gandalf**.

Drink is not enough for content. **Merry**.

Share pipes, as good friends must at a pinch. **Merry**.

One who cannot cast away a treasure at needs is in fetters. **Aragorn**.

It is difficult with evil folk to know when they are in league, and when they are cheating one another. **Aragorn**.

Put all the rats in one trap. **Gandalf** [reported by **Pippin**].

A wild beast cornered is not safe to approach. **Gandalf**.

Does an unarmed man come down to speak to robbers out of doors? **Saruman**.

The guest who has escaped from the roof, will think twice before he comes in by the door. **Gandalf**.

To every man his part. **Saruman**.

Meddle not in policies which you do not understand. **Saruman**.

The treacherous are ever distrustful. **Gandalf**.

One cannot be both tyrant and counsellor. **Gandalf**.

Often does hatred hurt itself. **Gandalf**.

When the plot is ripe it remains no longer secret. **Gandalf**.

Strange are the turns of fortune! **Gandalf**.

Things will go as they will; and there is no need to hurry to meet them. **Treebeard**.

Do not meddle in the affairs of Wizards, for they are subtle and quick to anger. **Merry** [remembering **Sam** quoting **Gildor**].

No Took ever beat a Brandybuck for inquisitiveness. **Merry**.

Peril comes in the night when least expected. **Gandalf**.

There is nothing Sauron cannot turn to evil uses. **Gandalf**.

Oft evil will shall evil mar. **Théoden**.

Perilous to us all are the devices of an art deeper than we possess ourselves. **Gandalf**.

Let not the swift wait for the slow. **Gandalf**.

Hope is in speed. **Gandalf**.

The biter bit, the hawk under the eagle's foot, the spider in a steel web. **Gandalf**.

The burned hand teaches best. After that advice about fire goes to the heart. **Gandalf**.

Every day that passes is a precious day lost. **Frodo**.

More haste less speed. **Gollum**.

A rope may be a help in many needs. **Haldir** [remembered by **Sam**].

Many that live deserve death. And some that die deserve life. **Gandalf** [remembered by **Frodo**].

Do not be too eager to deal out death in the name of justice. [**Gandalf** [remembered by **Frodo**].

Even the wise cannot see all ends. **Gandalf** [remembered by **Frodo**].

Turn and about. **Sam**.

One good turn deserves another. **Frodo**.

Third time pays for all. **Sam**.

A tight belt and a light tooth. **Sam**.

Men can only come to morning through the shadows. **Narrator**.

What comes after must come. **Frodo**.

You'll come to a bad end if you don't watch your step. **Gaffer** [remembered by **Sam**].

Strange as news from Bree. **Sam**.

Not as sure as Shiretalk. **Sam**.

Each to his own fashion. **Sam**.

Turn over a new leaf, and keep it turned. **Sam**.

Wise man trusts not to chance-meeting on the road. **Faramir**.

Do not snare even an orc with a falsehood. **Faramir**.

Do not slay man or beast needlessly, and not gladly even when it is needed. **Faramir**.

Surely there are many perils in the world. **Frodo**.

Do not speak before your master. **Faramir**.

Tidings of death have many wings. **Faramir**.

Night oft brings news to near kindred. **Faramir**.

If Men have dealings with the Mistress of Magic who dwells in the Golden Wood, then they may look for strange things to follow. **Faramir**.

It is perilous for mortal man to walk out of the world of this Sun. **Faramir**.

Such things [as mighty heirlooms] do not breed peace among confederates. **Faramir**.

Murder will out. **Faramir**.

War must be, while we defend our lives against a destroyer who would devour all. **Faramir**.

Do not love the bright sword for its sharpness, nor the arrow for its swiftness, nor the warrior for his glory… Love only that which they defend. **Faramir**.

Better mistrust undeserved than rash words. **Narrator** [**Frodo**'s thoughts].

Fair speech may hide a foul heart. **Sam**.

If you're short of sleep cold water on the neck's like rain on a wilted lettuce. **Sam**.

A warrior should have more skills and knowledge than only the craft of weapons and slaying. **Faramir**.
Boast seldom, and then perform, or die in the attempt. **Faramir**.
There are some perils from which a man must flee. **Faramir**.
Handsome is as handsome does. **Sam**.
The praise of the praiseworthy is above all rewards. **Faramir**.
The servant has a claim on the master for service, even service in fear. **Narrator** [**Frodo**'s thoughts].
There is no open gate into the Nameless Land. **Faramir**.
It seems less evil to counsel another man to break troth than to do so oneself. **Faramir**.
The Sun will soon rise above the shadow. **Faramir**.
If you can only speak ill of those who showed you mercy, keep silent. **Frodo**.
Where there's life there's hope... and need of vittles. **Gaffer** [remembered by **Sam**].
Don't take names to yourself... whether they are true or false. **Frodo**.
Never leave your master. **Sam**.
Wish for no strangers in the land. **Ingold**.
Valour... cannot be computed by stature. **Gandalf**.
Many a doer of great deeds might say no more. **Ingold**.
Leave your trowels and sharpen your swords. **Gandalf**.
Be not unjust in your grief. **Gandalf**.
The mightiest man may be slain by one arrow. **Pippin**.
Looks may belie the man—or the halfling. **Denethor**.
Though the Stones be lost... still the lords of Gondor have keener sight than lesser men. **Denethor**.
When you are a dotard you will die. **Gandalf**.
Pride would be folly that disdained help and counsel at need. **Denethor**.
Deal out gifts according to your own designs. **Denethor**.
The Lord of Gondor is not to be made the tool of other men's purposes. **Denethor**.
Generous deed should not be checked by cold counsel. **Gandalf**.
No need to brood on what tomorrow may bring. **Gandalf**.
Men who go warring afield look ever to the next hope of food and of drink. **Beregond**.
At the table small men may do the greater deeds. **Beregond**.
Strange accents do not mar fair speech. **Beregond**.
It is over-late to send for aid when you are already besieged. **Beregond**.
All things must come utterly to an end in time. **Beregond**.
If we fall, who shall stand? **Beregond**.
We may stand, if only on one leg, or at least be left still upon our knees. **Pippin**.
Folk are not always what they seem. **Pippin**.
Don't believe what strangers say of themselves. **Pippin**.
Every little is a gain. **Men of Minas Tirith**.
Deeds will not be less valiant because they are unpraised. **Aragorn**.

Remember old friendship and oaths long spoken. **Hirgon** [**Denethor**'s message]
For your own good... do all that you may. **Hirgon** [**Denethor**'s message]
Do not spoil the wonder with haste. **Legolas**.
The hasty stroke goes oft astray. **Aragorn**.
If it must be so, it must. **Hirgon**.
Time does not stand still, though the Sun be lost. **Rider of Rohan.**
In the morning counsels are best, and night changes many thoughts. **Théoden**.
Where will wants not, a way opens. **Éowyn**.
Good will should not be denied. **Éowyn**.
In desperate hours gentleness may be repaid with death. **Denethor**.
Counsels may be found that are neither the webs of wizards nor the haste of fools. **Denethor**.
Ifs are vain. **Denethor**.
Much must be risked in war. **Denethor**.
Let all who fight the Enemy in their fashion be at one. **Denethor**.
A traitor may betray himself and do good that he does not intend. **Gandalf**.
Wild Men are wild, free, but not children. **Ghân**.
Wild Men have long ears and long eyes; know all paths. **Ghân**.
Dead men are not friends to living men, and give them no gifts. **Ghân**.
Our Enemy's devices oft serve us in his despite. **Éomer**.
What we shall achieve only tomorrow will show. **Théoden**.
Strike wherever the enemy gathers. **Théoden**.
Need brooks no delay, yet late is better than never. **Éomer**.
The morning will bring new things. **Wídfara**.
Too late is worse than never. **Narrator** [**Merry**'s thoughts].
Great heart will not be denied. **Théoden**.
Hope oft deceives... yet twice blessed is help unlooked for. **Éomer**.
It's not always a misfortune being overlooked. **Merry**.
Even in the heart of our stronghold the Enemy has power to strike us. **Gandalf**.
The hands of the king are the hands of a healer. **Ioreth**.
When the black breath blows and death's shadow grows and all lights pass, come athelas! **Herbmaster**.
Life to the dying in the king's hand lying. **Herbmaster**.
It is best to love first what you are fitted to love. **Merry**.
You must start somewhere and have some roots. **Merry**.
The soil of the Shire is deep. **Merry**.
Deep in the hearts of all [Elves] lies the sea-longing, which it is perilous to stir. **Legolas**.
It is ever so with the things that Men begin: there is a frost in Spring, or a blight in Summer, and they fail of their promise. **Gimli**.
Seldom do [Men] fail of their seed, and that will lie in the dust and rot to spring up again in times and places unlooked-for. **Legolas**.
Oft hope is born, when all is forlorn. **Legolas** [remembered by **Gimli**].
Follow what may, great deeds are not lessened in worth. **Legolas**.

It is not our part to master all the tides of the world, but to do what is in us for the succour of those years wherein we are set. **Gandalf**.

Uproot the evil in the fields that [you] know, so that those who live after may have clean earth to till. **Gandalf**.

To waver is to fall. **Aragorn**.

Prepare against all chances, good as well as evil. **Imrahil**.

Men are better than gates. **Aragorn**.

The Men of Minas Tirith will never be overcome. **Bergil**.

The one small garden of a free gardener... not a garden swollen to a realm. **Narrator** [**Sam**'s thoughts].

The Shadow... can only mock, it cannot make. **Frodo**.

It's no good worrying about tomorrow. It probably won't come. **Frodo**.

Wait and see. **Sam**.

Where there's a whip there's a will. **Durthang Orc**.

Trust to luck. **Sam**.

Talking won't mend nothing. **Sam**.

Pain and delight flow together and tears are the very wine of blessedness. **Narrator**.

Mortals cannot go drinking ent-draughts and expect no more to come of them than of a pot of beer. **Gimli**.

The hands of the King are hands of healing. **Gandalf**.

One can't be everywhere at once. **Sam**.

The healing hand should also wield the sword. **Warden**.

The world is full enough of hurts and mischances without wars to multiply them. **Warden**.

It needs but one foe to breed a war, not two. **Éowyn**.

Those who have not swords can still die upon them. **Éowyn**.

It is not always good to be healed in body. Nor is it always evil to die in battle, even in bitter pain. **Éowyn**.

Do not scorn pity that is the gift of a gentle heart. **Faramir**.

Endure with patience the hours of waiting. **Faramir**.

Many like to know beforehand what is to be set on the table; but those who labour to prepare the feast like to keep their secret. **Gandalf**.

Wonder makes the words of praise louder. **Gandalf**.

The tree grows best in the land of its sires. **Aragorn**.

Forests may grow. Woods may spread. But not Ents. **Treebeard**.

Though the fruit of the Tree comes seldom to ripeness, yet the life within may then lie sleeping through many long years, and none can foretell the time in which it will awake. **Gandalf**.

Never is too long a word. **Treebeard**.

A snake without fangs may crawl where he will. **Treebeard**.

Use well the days. **Galadriel**.

A beggar must be grateful, if a thief returns even a morsel of his own. **Saruman**.

One thief deserves another. **Saruman**.

Don't let your heads get too big for your hats. **Bilbo**.

There is no real going back. **Frodo**.
There are some wounds which cannot be wholly cured. **Gandalf**.
One thing drives out another. **Butterbur**.
Keep your tempers and hold your hands. **Frodo**.
You've got to have grist before you can grind. **Cotton**.
The sooner the better. **Merry**.
One ill turn deserves another. **Saruman**.
It is useless to meet revenge with revenge: it will heal nothing. **Frodo**.
It's an ill wind as blows nobody no good. **Gaffer**.
All's well as ends Better! **Gaffer**.
Make it short, then you won't have to cut it short. **Gaffer**.
Use all the wits and knowledge you have of your own. **Frodo**.
Proper fourteen-twenty! **Hobbit Ale-Drinker**.
It must often be so, when things are in danger: some one has to give them up, lose them, so that others may keep them. **Frodo**.
Better to ride three together than one alone. **Gandalf**.
Not all tears are an evil. **Gandalf**.

Appendices

The hammer will at least keep the arms strong until they can wield sharper tools again. **Thorin**.
It needs gold to breed gold. **Thrór**.
Old kings that refuse a proffered staff may fall on their knees. **Freca**.
We are not bound for ever to the circles of the world, and beyond them is more than memory. **Aragorn**.
Dark is the Shadow. **Arwen**.
The years will bring what they will. **Elrond**.
In dangerous days men hide their chief treasure. **Aragorn**.
Precious stones are pebbles in Gondor for children to play with. '**Lesser Men.**'
Great kings take what is their right. **Sauron**.

APPENDIX C

THE PROVERBS BY PEOPLE GROUP

The Hobbits

If you sit on the door-step long enough, you will think of something. **Bilbo**.
Adventures are not all pony-rides in May-sunshine. **Narrator** [**Bilbo**'s thoughts].
Answers [are] to be guessed not given. **Bilbo**.
Escaping goblins to be caught by wolves. **Bilbo**.
Third time pays for all. **Bilbo**.
Every worm has his weak spot. **Bilbo**.
Never laugh at live dragons. **Bilbo**.
While there's life there's hope. **Bilbo**.
Dwarves are sometimes politer in word than in deed. **Bilbo**.
Defeat may be glorious. **Bilbo**.
Even dragons have their ending. **Bilbo**.
A little sleep does a great cure. **Bilbo**.
Merry is May-time! **Bilbo**.
Roads go ever ever on. **Bilbo**.
It will have to be paid for. **Shire Hobbits.**
Boats are quite tricky enough for those that sit still. **Gaffer**.
You shouldn't listen to all you hear. **Gaffer**.
Don't go getting mixed up in the business of your betters, or you'll land in trouble too big for you. **Gaffer**.
You can say what you like. **Sandyman**.
Bag End's a queer place, and its folk are queerer. **Sandyman**.
The Road goes ever on and on. **Bilbo**.
Some folk have all the luck. **Shire Hobbits**.
It's a dangerous business going out of your door. **Bilbo** [quoted by **Frodo**].

You step into the Road, and if you don't keep your feet, there is no knowing where you might be swept off to. **Bilbo** [quoted by **Frodo**].
Go not to the Elves for counsel, for they will say both no and yes. **Frodo**.
Short cuts make long delays. **Pippin**.
Short cuts make delays, but inns make longer ones. **Frodo**.
All's well as ends well. **Maggot**.
A loon is he that will not sing. **Pippin** [**Bilbo**'s words].
Strange as news from Bree. **Eastfarthing Hobbits**.
Mind your Ps and Qs. **Merry**.
All that is gold does not glitter. **Gandalf** [**Bilbo**'s words].
Not all those who wander are lost. **Gandalf** [**Bilbo**'s words].
The old that is strong does not wither. **Gandalf** [**Bilbo**'s words].
Deep roots are not reached by a frost. **Gandalf** [**Bilbo**'s words].
Handsome is as handsome does. **Pippin**.
Apples for walking, and a pipe for sitting. **Sam**.
Come and go as you like, as long as you don't make a noise. **Bilbo**.
Hobbits ought to stick together. **Pippin**.
When pools are black and trees are bare 'tis evil in the wild to fare. **Bilbo**.
In every wood in every spring there is a different green. **Bilbo**.
Never mind about looks. **Bilbo**.
You'll want it, if you haven't got it. **Sam**.
Live and learn. **Sam** [quoting the **Gaffer**].
It's the job that's never started as takes longest to finish. **Sam** [quoting the **Gaffer**].
You know your own business best. **Merry**.
Drink is not enough for content. **Merry**.
Share pipes, as good friends must at a pinch. **Merry**.
Do not meddle in the affairs of Wizards, for they are subtle and quick to anger. **Merry** [remembering **Sam** quoting **Gildor**].
No Took ever beat a Brandybuck for inquisitiveness. **Merry**.
Every day that passes is a precious day lost. **Frodo**.
A rope may be a help in many needs. **Haldir** [remembered by **Sam**].
Many that live deserve death. And some that die deserve life. **Gandalf** [remembered by **Frodo**].
Do not be too eager to deal out death in the name of justice. [**Gandalf** [remembered by **Frodo**].
Even the wise cannot see all ends. **Gandalf** [remembered by **Frodo**].
Turn and about. **Sam**.
One good turn deserves another. **Frodo**.
Third time pays for all. **Sam**.
A tight belt and a light tooth. **Sam**.
What comes after must come. **Frodo**.
You'll come to a bad end if you don't watch your step. **Gaffer** [remembered by **Sam**].
Strange as news from Bree. **Sam**.

Not as sure as Shiretalk. **Sam**.
Each to his own fashion. **Sam**.
Turn over a new leaf, and keep it turned. **Sam**.
Surely there are many perils in the world. **Frodo**.
Better mistrust undeserved than rash words. **Narrator** [**Frodo**'s thoughts].
Fair speech may hide a foul heart. **Sam**.
If you're short of sleep cold water on the neck's like rain on a wilted lettuce. **Sam**.
Handsome is as handsome does. **Sam**.
The servant has a claim on the master for service, even service in fear. **Narrator** [**Frodo**'s thoughts].
If you can only speak ill of those who showed you mercy, keep silent. **Frodo**.
Where there's life there's hope... and need of vittles. **Gaffer** [remembered by **Sam**].
Don't take names to yourself... whether they are true or false. **Frodo**.
Never leave your master. **Sam**.
The mightiest man may be slain by one arrow. **Pippin**.
We may stand, if only on one leg, or at least be left still upon our knees. **Pippin**.
Folk are not always what they seem. **Pippin**.
Don't believe what strangers say of themselves. **Pippin**.
Too late is worse than never. **Narrator** [**Merry**'s thoughts].
It's not always a misfortune being overlooked. **Merry**.
It is best to love first what you are fitted to love. **Merry**.
You must start somewhere and have some roots. **Merry**.
The soil of the Shire is deep. **Merry**.
The one small garden of a free gardener... not a garden swollen to a realm. **Narrator** [**Sam**'s thoughts].
The Shadow... can only mock, it cannot make. **Frodo**.
It's no good worrying about tomorrow. It probably won't come. **Frodo**.
Wait and see. **Sam**.
Trust to luck. **Sam**.
Talking won't mend nothing. **Sam**.
One can't be everywhere at once. **Sam**.
Don't let your heads get too big for your hats. **Bilbo**.
There is no real going back. **Frodo**.
Keep your tempers and hold your hands. **Frodo**.
You've got to have grist before you can grind. **Cotton**.
The sooner the better. **Merry**.
It is useless to meet revenge with revenge: it will heal nothing. **Frodo**.
It's an ill wind as blows nobody no good. **Gaffer**.
All's well as ends Better! **Gaffer**.
Make it short, then you won't have to cut it short. **Gaffer**.
Use all the wits and knowledge you have of your own. **Frodo**.
Proper fourteen-twenty! **Hobbit Ale-Drinker**.

It must often be so, when things are in danger: some one has to give them up, lose them, so that others may keep them. **Frodo**.

Bombadil and Goldberry

Some things are ill to hear when the world's in shadow. **Bombadil**.
Heed no nightly noise. **Goldberry** and **Bombadil**.
Naught wakes hobbit-folk in the early morning. **Bombadil**.
Make haste while the Sun shines. **Goldberry**.
Long tales are thirsty, and long listening is hungry. **Bombadil**.
Clothes are but little loss, if you escape from drowning. **Bombadil**.
Sharp blades are good to have. **Bombadil**.
Be bold, but wary. **Bombadil**.

The Breelanders

Your business is your own. **Harry**.
It never rains but it pours. **Butterbur**.
One thing drives out another. **Butterbur**.
Make yourselves at home! **Butterbur**.
As you please! **Butterbur**.
There's no accounting for East and West. **Butterbur**.
There are queer folk about. **Harry** and **Aragorn**.
What's done can't be undone. **Butterbur**.
You know your own business. **Butterbur**.
One thing drives out another. **Butterbur**.

The Istari

Valleys have ears, and some elves have over merry tongues. **Gandalf**.
Don't bring things that are of no use. **Gandalf**.
Naughty little boys that play with fire get punished. **Gandalf**.
There are no safe paths. **Gandalf**.
Share and share alike. **Gandalf**.
Always after a defeat and a respite, the Shadow takes another shape and grows again. **Gandalf**.
All we have to decide is what to do with the time that is given us. **Gandalf**.
Mordor draws all wicked things. **Gandalf**.
Many that live deserve death. And some that die deserve life. **Gandalf**.
Do not be too eager to deal out death in judgement. **Gandalf**.
Even the very wise cannot see all ends. **Gandalf**.
Rings have a way of being found. **Gandalf**.

One Ring to rule them all, One Ring to find them, One Ring to bring them all and in the darkness bind them. In the Land of Mordor where the Shadows lie. **Gandalf** [**Sauron**'s words].
Be careful of what you say, even to your closest friends. **Gandalf**.
The Enemy has many spies and many ways of hearing. **Gandalf**.
All that is gold does not glitter. **Gandalf** [**Bilbo**'s words].
Not all those who wander are lost. **Gandalf** [**Bilbo**'s words].
The old that is strong does not wither. **Gandalf** [**Bilbo**'s words].
Deep roots are not reached by a frost. **Gandalf** [**Bilbo**'s words].
There are many powers in the world, for good or for evil. **Gandalf**.
What was lost may yet be found. **Saruman**.
Treason has ever been our greatest foe. **Gandalf**.
White cloth may be dyed. The white page can be overwritten; and the white light can be broken. **Saruman**.
He that breaks a thing to find out what it is has left the path of wisdom. **Gandalf**.
Even the most subtle spiders may leave a weak thread. **Gandalf**.
Despair is only for those who see the end beyond all doubt. **Gandalf**.
It is wisdom to recognise necessity. **Gandalf**.
Only a small part is played in great deeds by any hero. **Gandalf**.
Trust rather to… friendship than to great wisdom. **Gandalf**.
Much evil must befall a country before it wholly forgets the Elves, if once they dwelt there. **Gandalf**.
If you bring a Ranger with you, it is well to pay attention to him. **Gandalf**.
It matters little who is the enemy, if [one] cannot beat off his attack. **Gandalf**.
Those who pass the gates of Barad-dur do not return. **Gandalf**.
One must tread the path that need chooses. **Gandalf**.
There are older and fouler things than Orcs in the deep places of the world. **Gandalf**.
He that strikes the first blow, if he strikes it hard enough, may need to strike no more. **Gandalf**.
A treacherous weapon is ever a danger to the hand. **Gandalf**.
It is a comfort not to be mistaken at all points. **Gandalf**.
Hope is not victory. **Gandalf**.
Go where you must go. **Gandalf**.
Draw no weapon, speak no haughty word. **Gandalf**.
A king will have his way in his own hall, be it folly or wisdom. **Gandalf**.
Prudence is one thing, but discourtesy is another. **Gandalf**.
All friends should gather together, lest each be singly destroyed. **Gandalf**.
The wise speak only of what they know. **Gandalf**.
To crooked eyes truth may wear a wry face. **Gandalf**.
You are not without allies, even though you know them not. **Gandalf**.
The evil of Sauron cannot be wholly cured, nor made as if it had not been. **Gandalf**.
Put all the rats in one trap. **Gandalf** [reported by **Pippin**].
A wild beast cornered is not safe to approach. **Gandalf**.

Does an unarmed man come down to speak to robbers out of doors? **Saruman**.
The guest who has escaped from the roof, will think twice before he comes in by the door. **Gandalf**.
To every man his part. **Saruman**.
Meddle not in policies which you do not understand. **Saruman**.
The treacherous are ever distrustful. **Gandalf**.
One cannot be both tyrant and counsellor. **Gandalf**.
Often does hatred hurt itself. **Gandalf**.
When the plot is ripe it remains no longer secret. **Gandalf**.
Strange are the turns of fortune! **Gandalf**.
Peril comes in the night when least expected. **Gandalf**.
There is nothing Sauron cannot turn to evil uses. **Gandalf**.
Perilous to us all are the devices of an art deeper than we possess ourselves. **Gandalf**.
Let not the swift wait for the slow. **Gandalf**.
Hope is in speed. **Gandalf**.
The biter bit, the hawk under the eagle's foot, the spider in a steel web. **Gandalf**.
The burned hand teaches best. After that advice about fire goes to the heart. **Gandalf**.
Many that live deserve death. And some that die deserve life. **Gandalf** [remembered by **Frodo**].
Do not be too eager to deal out death in the name of justice. [**Gandalf** [remembered by **Frodo**].
Even the wise cannot see all ends. **Gandalf** [remembered by **Frodo**].
Valour... cannot be computed by stature. **Gandalf**.
Leave your trowels and sharpen your swords. **Gandalf**.
Be not unjust in your grief. **Gandalf**.
When you are a dotard you will die. **Gandalf**.
Generous deed should not be checked by cold counsel. **Gandalf**.
No need to brood on what tomorrow may bring. **Gandalf**.
A traitor may betray himself and do good that he does not intend. **Gandalf**.
Even in the heart of our stronghold the Enemy has power to strike us. **Gandalf**.
It is not our part to master all the tides of the world, but to do what is in us for the succour of those years wherein we are set. **Gandalf**.
Uproot the evil in the fields that [you] know, so that those who live after may have clean earth to till. **Gandalf**.
The hands of the King are hands of healing. **Gandalf**.
Many like to know beforehand what is to be set on the table; but those who labour to prepare the feast like to keep their secret. **Gandalf**.
Wonder makes the words of praise louder. **Gandalf**.
Though the fruit of the Tree comes seldom to ripeness, yet the life within may then lie sleeping through many long years, and none can foretell the time in which it will awake. **Gandalf**.
A beggar must be grateful, if a thief returns even a morsel of his own. **Saruman**.
One thief deserves another. **Saruman**.

There are some wounds which cannot be wholly cured. **Gandalf**.
One ill turn deserves another. **Saruman**.
Better to ride three together than one alone. **Gandalf**.
Not all tears are an evil. **Gandalf**.

The Half-Elven

It is perilous to study too deeply the arts of the Enemy, for good or for ill. **Elrond**.
Nothing is evil in the beginning. **Elrond**.
None can foretell what will come to pass, if we take this road or that. **Elrond**.
Anduin the Great flows past many shores. **Elrond**.
Such is oft the course of deeds that move the wheels of the world: small hands do them because they must, while the eyes of the great are elsewhere. **Elrond**.
Fear the many eyes of the servants of Sauron. **Elrond**.
Let him not vow to walk in the dark, who has not seen the nightfall. **Elrond**.
Sworn word may strengthen quaking heart. **Gimli**. *Or break it.* **Elrond**.
Look not far ahead. **Elrond**.
Dark is the Shadow. **Arwen**.
The years will bring what they will. **Elrond**.

The Elves

There is nothing in the feeling of weight in an idle toss-pot's arms. **Galion**.
It is an ill wind... that blows no one any good. **Elvenking**.
Appear where you are most needed. **Elvenking**.
The wide world is all about you: you can fence yourselves in, but you cannot forever fence it out. **Gildor**.
Do not meddle in the affairs of Wizards, for they are subtle and quick to anger. **Gildor**.
Seldom give unguarded advice. **Gildor**.
Advice is a dangerous gift, even from the wise to the wise, and all courses may run ill. **Gildor**.
Courage is found in unlikely places. **Gildor**.
To sheep other sheep no doubt appear different. **Lindir**.
The spies of the Enemy are many. **Legolas**.
Oft in lies truth is hidden. **Glorfindel**.
Dark is the water of Kheled-zaram, and cold are the springs of Kibil-nala. **Gimli** [and later, **Galadriel**].
Let a ploughman plough, but choose an otter for swimming. **Legolas**.
In nothing is the power of the Dark Lord more clearly shown than in the estrangement that divides all those who still oppose him. **Haldir**.
A plague on Dwarves and their stiff necks! **Legolas**.

The world is indeed full of peril, and in it there are many dark places... But still there is much that is fair, and though in all lands love is now mingled with grief, it grows perhaps the stronger. **Haldir**.
The light perceives the very heart of the darkness. **Haldir**.
Though the world is now dark better days are at hand. **Celeborn**.
However it may be with the guide, the followers are blameless. **Galadriel**.
Seeing is both good and perilous. **Galadriel**.
None can be sure of peace. **Celeborn**.
Never travel far without a rope. **Lórien Elf**.
Maybe the paths that you each shall tread are already laid before your feet, though you do not see them. **Celeborn**.
Do not despise the lore that has come down from distant years. **Celeborn**.
Oft it may chance that old wives keep in memory word of things that once were needful for the wise to know. **Celeborn**.
Night must follow noon. **Galadriel**.
The skill of the Dwarves is in their hands rather than in their tongues. **Galadriel**.
Such is the way of it: to find and to lose, as it seems to those whose boat is on the running stream. **Legolas**.
Time does not tarry ever, but change and growth is not in all things and places alike. **Legolas**.
The passing seasons are but ripples ever repeated in the long long stream. **Legolas**.
Let us first do what we must do. **Legolas**.
Tomorrow is unknown. **Legolas**.
Rede oft is found at the rising of the Sun. **Legolas**.
Few can foresee whither their road will lead them, till they come to its end. **Legolas**.
Dwarves are strange folk. **Legolas**.
A rope may be a help in many needs. **Haldir** [remembered by **Sam**].
Do not spoil the wonder with haste. **Legolas**.
Deep in the hearts of all [Elves] lies the sea-longing, which it is perilous to stir. **Legolas**.
Seldom do [Men] fail of their seed, and that will lie in the dust and rot to spring up again in times and places unlooked-for. **Legolas**.
Oft hope is born, when all is forlorn. **Legolas** [remembered by **Gimli**].
Follow what may, great deeds are not lessened in worth. **Legolas**.
Use well the days. **Galadriel**.

The Dwarves

Dark for dark business. **Dwarves**.
Don't be precise, and don't worry. **Dwalin**.
There is nothing like looking, if you want to find something. **Thorin**.

It might be worse, and then again it might be a good deal better. **Thorin**.
The less inquisitive you are... the less trouble you are likely to find. **Dwarves**.
Don't start grumbling against orders, or something bad will happen. **Thorin**.
Lock nor bar may hinder the homecoming spoken of old. **Thorin**.
Winter and snow will bite both men and elves, and they may find their dwelling in the waste grievous to bear. **Thorin**.
If more of us valued food and cheer and song above hoarded gold, it would be a merrier world. **Thorin**.
Dwarves' tongues run on when speaking of their handiwork. **Gloin**.
Faithless is he that says farewell when the road darkens. **Gimli**.
Sworn word may strengthen quaking heart. **Gimli**. *Or break it.* **Elrond**.
Dark is the water of Kheled-zaram, and cold are the springs of Kibil-nala. **Gimli** [and later, **Galadriel**].
Memory is not what the heart desires. **Gimli**.
The legs of Men will lag on a rough road, while a Dwarf goes on, be the burden twice his own weight. **Gimli**.
Maybe there is no right choice. **Gimli**.
Rest a little to run the better. **Gimli**.
Deep is the abyss that is spanned by Durin's Bridge, and none has measured it. **Gimli**.
Men need many words before deeds. **Gimli**.
Strange are the ways of men. **Gimli**.
It is ever so with the things that Men begin: there is a frost in Spring, or a blight in Summer, and they fail of their promise. **Gimli**.
Mortals cannot go drinking ent-draughts and expect no more to come of them than of a pot of beer. **Gimli**.
The hammer will at least keep the arms strong until they can wield sharper tools again. **Thorin**.
It needs gold to breed gold. **Thrór**.

The Rohirrim

The stranger should declare himself first. **Éomer**.
These are indeed strange days. Dreams and legends spring to life out of the grass. **Éomer**.
Do we walk in legends or on the green earth in the daylight? **Éothain**.
The Men of the Mark do not lie, and therefore they are not easily deceived. **Éomer**.
Hardy is the race of Elendil. **Éomer**.
May you find what you seek. **Éomer**.
The staff in the hand of a wizard may be more than a prop for age. **Háma**.
In doubt a man of worth will trust to his own wisdom. **Háma**.
News from afar is seldom sooth. **Théoden**.
Ill news is an ill guest. **Wormtongue**.

Webs of deceit were ever woven in Dwimordene. **Wormtongue**.

The young perish and the old linger. **Théoden**.

Faithful heart may have froward tongue. **Théoden**.

Oft the unbidden guest proves the best company. **Éomer**.

He that flies counts every foeman twice. **Westfold Scout**.

The world changes, and all that once was strong now proves unsure. **Théoden**.

Songs have come down among us out of strange places, and walk visible under the Sun. **Théoden**.

The days are fated to be filled with marvels. **Théoden**.

Oft evil will shall evil mar. **Théoden**.

Time does not stand still, though the Sun be lost. **Rider of Rohan.**

In the morning counsels are best, and night changes many thoughts. **Théoden**.

Where will wants not, a way opens. **Éowyn**.

Good will should not be denied. **Éowyn**.

Our Enemy's devices oft serve us in his despite. **Éomer**.

What we shall achieve only tomorrow will show. **Théoden**.

Strike wherever the enemy gathers. **Théoden**.

Need brooks no delay, yet late is better than never. **Éomer**.

The morning will bring new things. **Wídfara**.

Great heart will not be denied. **Théoden**.

Hope oft deceives... yet twice blessed is help unlooked for. **Éomer**.

It needs but one foe to breed a war, not two. **Éowyn**.

Those who have not swords can still die upon them. **Éowyn**.

It is not always good to be healed in body. Nor is it always evil to die in battle, even in bitter pain. **Éowyn**.

Old kings that refuse a proffered staff may fall on their knees. **Freca**.

The Ents

Do not be hasty. **Treebeard**.

Bad memories are handed down. **Treebeard**.

Sheep get like shepherd, and shepherds like sheep. **Treebeard**.

The years lie thicker than the leaves. **Treebeard**.

There is naught that an old Ent can do to hold back [a] storm: he must weather it or crack. **Treebeard**.

It is a mark of evil things that came in the Great Darkness that they cannot abide the Sun. **Treebeard**.

It is easier to shout 'stop!' than to do it. **Treebeard**.

If we stayed at home and did nothing, doom would find us anyway, sooner or later. **Treebeard**.

Songs like trees bear fruit only in their own time and in their own way: and sometimes they are withered untimely. **Treebeard**.

Things will go as they will; and there is no need to hurry to meet them. **Treebeard**.

Forests may grow. Woods may spread. But not Ents. **Treebeard**.

Never is too long a word. **Treebeard**.

A snake without fangs may crawl where he will. **Treebeard**.

The Peoples of Gondor

The might of Elrond is in wisdom, not in weapons. **Boromir**.

What was is less dark than what is to come. **Denethor**.

Valour needs first strength, and then a weapon. **Boromir**.

Let all the foes of Gondor flee! **Boromir**.

When heads are at a loss bodies must serve. **Boromir**.

The wolf that one hears is worse than the orc that one fears. **Boromir**.

Few come out who once go in [to Lórien]; and of that few none have escaped unscathed. **Boromir**.

The Men of Minas Tirith are true to their word. **Boromir**.

It is not the way of the Men of Minas Tirith to desert their friends at need. **Boromir**.

Where there are so many, all speech becomes a debate without end. **Boromir**.

Two together may perhaps find wisdom. **Boromir**.

Each to his own kind. **Boromir**.

It is by our own folly that the Enemy will defeat us. **Boromir**.

Wise man trusts not to chance-meeting on the road. **Faramir**.

Do not snare even an orc with a falsehood. **Faramir**.

Do not slay man or beast needlessly, and not gladly even when it is needed. **Faramir**.

Do not speak before your master. **Faramir**.

Tidings of death have many wings. **Faramir**.

Night oft brings news to near kindred. **Faramir**.

If Men have dealings with the Mistress of Magic who dwells in the Golden Wood, then they may look for strange things to follow. **Faramir**.

It is perilous for mortal man to walk out of the world of this Sun. **Faramir**.

Such things [as mighty heirlooms] do not breed peace among confederates. **Faramir**.

Murder will out. **Faramir**.

War must be, while we defend our lives against a destroyer who would devour all. **Faramir**.

Do not love the bright sword for its sharpness, nor the arrow for its swiftness, nor the warrior for his glory... Love only that which they defend. **Faramir**.

A warrior should have more skills and knowledge than only the craft of weapons and slaying. **Faramir**.

Boast seldom, and then perform, or die in the attempt. **Faramir**.

There are some perils from which a man must flee. **Faramir**.

The praise of the praiseworthy is above all rewards. **Faramir**.

There is no open gate into the Nameless Land. **Faramir**.

It seems less evil to counsel another man to break troth than to do so oneself. **Faramir**.

The Sun will soon rise above the shadow. **Faramir**.

Wish for no strangers in the land. **Ingold**.

Many a doer of great deeds might say no more. **Ingold**.

Looks may belie the man—or the halfling. **Denethor**.

Though the Stones be lost... still the lords of Gondor have keener sight than lesser men. **Denethor**.

Pride would be folly that disdained help and counsel at need. **Denethor**.

Deal out gifts according to your own designs. **Denethor**.

The Lord of Gondor is not to be made the tool of other men's purposes. **Denethor**.

Men who go warring afield look ever to the next hope of food and of drink. **Beregond**.

At the table small men may do the greater deeds. **Beregond**.

Strange accents do not mar fair speech. **Beregond**.

It is over-late to send for aid when you are already besieged. **Beregond**.

All things must come utterly to an end in time. **Beregond**.

If we fall, who shall stand? **Beregond**.

Every little is a gain. **Men of Minas Tirith**.

Remember old friendship and oaths long spoken. **Hirgon** [**Denethor**'s message]

For your own good... do all that you may. **Hirgon** [**Denethor**'s message]

If it must be so, it must. **Hirgon**.

In desperate hours gentleness may be repaid with death. **Denethor**.

Counsels may be found that are neither the webs of wizards nor the haste of fools. **Denethor**.

Ifs are vain. **Denethor**.

Much must be risked in war. **Denethor**.

Let all who fight the Enemy in their fashion be at one. **Denethor**.

Wild Men are wild, free, but not children. **Ghân**.

Wild Men have long ears and long eyes; know all paths. **Ghân**.

Dead men are not friends to living men, and give them no gifts. **Ghân**.

The hands of the king are the hands of a healer. **Ioreth**.

When the black breath blows and death's shadow grows and all lights pass, come athelas! **Herbmaster**.

Life to the dying in the king's hand lying. **Herbmaster**.

Prepare against all chances, good as well as evil. **Imrahil**.

The Men of Minas Tirith will never be overcome. **Bergil**.

The healing hand should also wield the sword. **Warden**.

The world is full enough of hurts and mischances without wars to multiply them. **Warden**.

Do not scorn pity that is the gift of a gentle heart. **Faramir**.

Endure with patience the hours of waiting. **Faramir**.

Aragorn

Drink, fire, and chance-meeting are pleasant enough. **Aragorn**.

There are queer folk about. **Harry** and **Aragorn**.

Caution is one thing and wavering is another. **Aragorn**.

Every little helps. **Aragorn**.

A hunted man sometimes wearies of distrust and longs for friendship. **Aragorn**.

Fire is our friend in the wilderness. **Aragorn**.

All blades perish that pierce [that] dreadful King. **Aragorn**.

The heirs of Elendil do not forget. **Aragorn**.

What roads would any dare to tread... if the Dunedain were asleep? **Aragorn**.

If simple folk are free from care and fear, simple they will be. **Aragorn**.

If man must needs walk in sight of the Black Gate, or tread the deadly flowers of Morgul Vale, then perils he will have. **Aragorn**.

If you pass the doors of Moria, beware! **Aragorn**.

Where the warg howls, there also the orc prowls. **Aragorn**.

Surer of finding the way home in a blind night than the cats of Queen Beruthiel. **Aragorn**.

Let the guide go first while you have one. **Aragorn**.

Endure the East Wind, but... do not ask it for tidings. **Aragorn**.

Not idly do the leaves of Lorien fall. **Aragorn**.

Where sight fails the earth may bring us rumour. **Aragorn**.

Keen are the eyes of the Elves. **Aragorn**.

Not we but those who come after will make the legends of our time. **Aragorn**.

When the great fall, the less must lead. **Aragorn**.

Good and ill have not changed since yesteryear; nor are they one thing among Elves and Dwarves and another among Men. **Aragorn**.

There are some things that it is better to begin than to refuse, even though the end may be dark. **Aragorn**.

It is perilous to cut bough or twig from a living tree in Fangorn. **Aragorn**.

Seldom does thief ride home to the stable. **Aragorn**.

Every man has something too dear to trust to another. **Aragorn**.

Dawn is ever the hope of men. **Aragorn**.

None knows what the new day shall bring him. **Aragorn**.

Do not judge the counsel of Gandalf until all is over. **Aragorn**,

One who cannot cast away a treasure at needs is in fetters. **Aragorn**.

It is difficult with evil folk to know when they are in league, and when they are cheating one another. **Aragorn**.

Deeds will not be less valiant because they are unpraised. **Aragorn**.

The hasty stroke goes oft astray. **Aragorn**.

To waver is to fall. **Aragorn**.

Men are better than gates. **Aragorn**.

The tree grows best in the land of its sires. **Aragorn**.

We are not bound for ever to the circles of the world, and beyond them is more than memory. **Aragorn**.
In dangerous days men hide their chief treasure. **Aragorn**.

Others/Unattributed

Elvish singing is not a thing to miss, in June under the stars. **Narrator**.
Near the edge of Mirkwood... take the word of no one that you [do] not know as well as your brother or better. **Beorn**.
Mirkwood is dark, dangerous, & difficult. **Beorn**.
Depend on your luck and your courage. **Beorn**.
If you come in peace lay down your arms. **Captain of the Guard**.
There is no knowing what a dwarf will not dare and do for revenge. **Narrator**.
Dwarves are not heroes. **Narrator**.
It does not do to leave a live dragon out of your calculations. **Narrator**.
Lucky numbers don't always come off. **Smaug**.
Don't have more to do with dwarves than you can help. **Smaug**.
Up the Bowman, and down with Moneybags! **People of Laketown**.
The wealthy may have pity beyond right on the needy that befriended them when they were in want. **Bard**.
Gather your wisdom. **Bard**.
Your own wisdom must decide your course. **Roac**.
A fool deserves to starve. **Bard**.
Goblins are the foes of all, and at their coming all other quarrels are forgotten. **Narrator**.
All things come to an end. **Narrator**.
Dwarves make light of burdens. **Narrator**.
Stone-hard are the Dwarves in labour or journey. **Narrator**.
Rest while you can. **Orc Guard**.
Little people should not meddle in affairs that are too big for them. **Grishnákh**.
More haste less speed. **Gollum**.
Men can only come to morning through the shadows. **Narrator**.
Where there's a whip there's a will. **Durthang Orc**.
Pain and delight flow together and tears are the very wine of blessedness. **Narrator**.
Precious stones are pebbles in Gondor for children to play with. '**Lesser Men.**'
Great kings take what is their right. **Sauron**.

BIBLIOGRAPHY

J. R. R. Tolkien:

The Hobbit (Harper Collins, 2006)

The Lord of the Rings (Harper Collins, 1991)

The Peoples of Middle-earth, Christopher Tolkien, Editor (Houghton Mifflin, 1996)

The Silmarillion (Houghton Mifflin, 2001)

The War of the Jewels, Christopher Tolkien, Editor (Houghton Mifflin, 1994)

Tales from The Perilous Realm (Harper Collins, 2002)

Tree and Leaf (Unwin Hyman, 1964)

Unfinished Tales of Númenor and Middle-earth (Houghton Mifflin, 1980)

Other:

Piers Benn, *Ethics*, (UCL Press, 1998).

Laurence BonJour, *Epistemology: Classic Problems and Contemporary Responses* (Rowman & Littlefield, 2009).

Kurt Bruner & Jim Ware, *Finding God In The Lord of the Rings*, (Tyndale House, 2001)

Humphrey Carpenter, *Tolkien: A Biography* (Houghton Mifflin, 1977).

Humphrey Carpenter, *The Letters of J.R.R. Tolkien* (Houghton Mifflin, 1981).

Humphrey Carpenter, *The Inklings* (Harper Collins, 1997)

Tolkien the Medievalist, Jane Chance, Editor (London, New York: Routledge, 2003).

John Garth, *Tolkien and the Great War* (Houghton Mifflin, 2003)

Peter Gilliver, Jeremy Marshall, & Edmund Weiner, *The Ring of Words* (Oxford University Press, 2006).

Meditations on Middle-earth, Karen Haber, Editor (Byron Press, 2001)

Alastair Hannay, *Kierkegaard: A Biography* (Cambridge University Press, 2001)

Jeremy Harwood, *Philosophy: A Beginner's Guide to the Ideas of 100 Great Thinkers* (Quercus Publishing, 2012).

Tree of Tales: Tolkien, Literature, and Theology, Trevor Hart and Ivan Khovacs, Editors (Baylor University Press, 2007)

Peter Kreeft, *The Philosophy of Tolkien* (Ignatius Press, 2005).

C.S. Lewis, *The Screwtape Letters* (Zondervan, 1996)

C.S. Lewis, 'The Problem of Pain,' from *The Complete C. S. Lewis Signature Classics*, (HarperCollins, 2002).

Friedrich Nietzsche, *Beyond Good and Evil*, translated by Helen Zimmern (MacMillan: New York, 1907).

Bertrand Russell, *The History of Western Philosophy* (Psychology Press, 2004)

Tom Shippey, *The Road to Middle-earth* (Houghton Mifflin, 2003).

Tom Shippey, *Roots and Branches* (Walking Tree, 2007)

Michael Stanton, '"Advice Is A Dangerous Gift," (Pseudo)Proverbs In The Lord Of The Rings,' *Proverbium 13* (University of Vermont, 1996).

Olga Trokhimenko, 'The Function of Proverbs in J.R.R. Tolkien's Hobbit,' *Proverbium 20* (University of Vermont, 2003).

Jonathan Witt & Jay W. Richards, *The Hobbit Party* (Ignatius Press, 2014)

Ralph C. Wood, *The Gospel According to Tolkien* (Westminster John Knox Press, 2003)

Holy Bible, New International Version (Hodder & Stoughton, 1984).

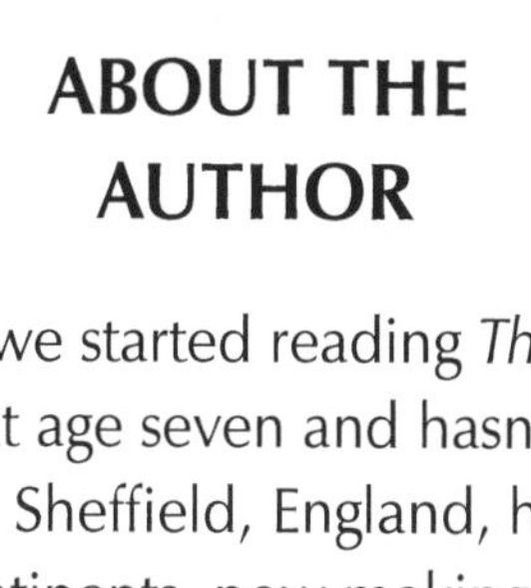

ABOUT THE AUTHOR

David Rowe started reading *The Lord of the Rings* at age seven and hasn't stopped yet. Born in Sheffield, England, he has lived in four continents, now making his home in Charleston, South Carolina, where he works for an Anglican church and teaches people how to make tea properly.

Made in the USA
Middletown, DE
22 February 2019